What's to Eat?

What's to Eat?

ENTRÉES IN CANADIAN FOOD HISTORY

Edited by Nathalie Cooke

McGill-Queen's University Press
Montreal & Kingston · London · Ithaca

© McGill-Queen's University Press 2009
ISBN 978-0-7735-3570-1 (cloth)
ISBN 978-0-7735-3571-8 (paper)

Legal deposit third quarter 2009
Bibliothèque nationale du Québec

Printed in Canada on acid-free paper that is 100% ancient forest free (100% post-consumer recycled), processed chlorine free

This book has been published with the help of a grant from the Canadian Federation for the Humanities and Social Sciences, through the Aid to Scholarly Publications Programme, using funds provided by the Social Sciences and Humanities Research Council of Canada.

McGill-Queen's University Press acknowledges the support of the Canada Council for the Arts for our publishing program. We also acknowledge the financial support of the Government of Canada through the Book Publishing Industry Development Program (BPIDP) for our publishing activities.

LIBRARY AND ARCHIVES CANADA
CATALOGUING IN PUBLICATION

What's to eat? : entrées in Canadian food history / edited by Nathalie Cooke.

Includes bibliographical references and index.
ISBN 978-0-7735-3570-1 (bnd)
ISBN 978-0-7735-3571-8 (pbk)

1. Food habits – Canada – History.   2. Cookery, Canadian – History.   3. Canada – Social life and customs.
I. Cooke, Nathalie

TX360.C3W48 2009   641.300971   C2009-901631-1

Set in 10/13 Warnock Pro with Chaparral Pro display.
Book design & typesetting by Garet Markvoort, zijn digital

CONTENTS

ACKNOWLEDGMENTS

The following chapters were written by a group of individuals engaged in an ongoing series of conversations about Canadian food culture and culinary history. One such conversation took place in Montreal, in November 2005, at the conference on "The Daily Meal in Canada" held at the McCord Museum, of which Victoria Dickenson, the museum's director, and I were co-organizers. But there have been many other conversations as well – over the telephone, by e-mail, in person – including a wonderful week in Toronto in November 2007, when a group of twelve people, led by Barbara Ketcham Wheaton, gathered for a workshop on cookbooks. Without these encounters and the insights emerging from them, this book could never have taken shape.

To Victoria Dickenson, I owe my first debt of thanks. In addition to co-organizing the 2005 conference, she was also a key member of the organizational team for the "What Are We Eating?" conference on Canadian food policy and the shaping of Canadian food tastes, which was hosted by the McGill Institute for the Study of Canada in February 2006. Victoria's expertise, range of knowledge, astute observations, and infectious enthusiasm propelled this book project into reality.

Our research team co-investigators helped this initiative in many ways as well. Marie Marquis, from Université de Montréal's Department of Nutrition, brought a new voice to the conversation, as did Jordan LeBel, from Concordia's Molson School of Business and Cornell University's School of Hotel Management. Another research team member, Rhona Richman Kenneally of Concordia's Department of Design and Computation Arts, provided constructive feedback and posed two particularly thought-provoking questions upon reading an early draft of the introduction. My thanks to all three.

One of the rare privileges of participating in an emerging field of study is the opportunity to work with individuals from different fields of experience. Readers of early drafts of the introduction and of various chapters include journalist Julian Armstrong and contributors Elizabeth Driver and Margery Fee, for example. I take full responsibility for any errors in the introduction; there are far fewer errors, and fewer paragraphs of laboured and plodding prose, thanks to Julian, Liz, and Margery. Lois Manton proved herself to be a real friend, as well as a superlative close reader, when she volunteered to help with the copy-editing of the entire manuscript. For information about Canadian Thanksgiving practice, we spoke with Mary Williamson. She, together with Fiona Lucas, a fellow member of the Culinary Historians of Ontario, had prepared a paper on Canadian Thanksgiving in 2007. Mary Williamson and English professor Gary Draper also kindly contributed some of their prized postcards as illustrations for this book.

Special thanks are also due to Lorna Hutchison, formerly a postdoctoral fellow at McGill University and now a teacher in the English department at the University of Winnipeg, and to Michele Rackham, a McGill doctoral student, who worked as editorial assistants on the first and second versions of this manuscript respectively. Without their tireless efforts, this project would have been impossible. Thanks, too, to Kendall Wallis of McGill Libraries, copy editor Judith Turnbull, Sarah Kaderabek, Chelsea Fairbank Haynes, Alastair Morrison, Pauline Morel, Christine Mervart, and Ariel Buckley for their assistance. Kathleen Holden's fine eye for graphic design and editing, not to mention her *Oxford Dictionary of Canadian English*, was much appreciated.

The Social Sciences and Humanities Research Council of Canada provided funding support for the conference in the form of a conference grant to the McCord Museum, as well as generous funding for our research team in the form of a Standard Research Grant. I gratefully acknowledge the significant contribution of the anonymous reviewers, who provided thoughtful and constructive feedback that helped me in organizing the book's chapters and shaping its introduction. Indeed, the phrasing of the book's two central questions derives from one reviewer's helpful suggestion.

I save my final note of thanks for McGill-Queen's University Press, and especially for Jonathan Crago, whose skill, diligence, and fine judgment helped me shape a conversation into a book.

What's to Eat?

INTRODUCTION

This book aims to identify the distinctive elements of Canadian domestic foodways, initiate a discussion of these traditions and practices, and signal fruitful avenues for future investigation. Its chapters articulate a tenacious hope that through a close examination of our shared past, through taking notice of something that so often goes unnoticed, we can better understand our own food practices and direct them not only towards a sustainable and healthy future but also towards a renewed sense of the pleasures afforded by the daily meal in Canada.

Although individual chapters do mention dishes and food items that have gained iconic status in Canada, the book generally does not attempt to define Canadian domestic food culture through a catalogue of foods. Instead, it approaches its central topic – the shaping of culinary taste in Canada – from different points of entry. These points of entry, or peepholes, into Canada's social and cultural history include histories of particular dishes or food items as well as analyses of narratives or rituals centred on food. The chapters in this particular study look at Canadian social history from the variety of disciplinary perspectives represented by the contributors – the university, the museum, media journalism, and gastronomy – and through the explicit lens of a particular food item, text, or practice. Despite such diversity, all of the contributors inevitably examine the question of how culinary taste has been shaped in Canada from the shared perspective of the current moment, when Canadians have come to expect both variety and diversity in the foods available to them. Today, after all, it is hard for us to imagine store shelves in Canadian urban centres that do not offer some of our favourite ingredients, such as nori, the spices for garam masala, corn tortillas, rice noodles, tofu, and coconut milk. Part of the story of the daily meal in Canada, then, involves novelty and innovation. But the story of the daily meal is about both the very dailiness of it – its importance for physical and spiritual survival – and its infinite variety. This book focuses specifically on the Canadian variants of the daily meal and those variants over time, on the meal that predominantly involves home cooking in the private sphere rather than ceremonial fare consumed in a public space.

By way of providing a context for this book and the focus for its chapters, let me suggest that Canadian culinary history, as perceived through the lens of Canadian cookbooks (the first of which were published in the mid-nineteenth century), can be divided into five periods: contact and settlement, consolidation, affiliation, articulation, and differentiation.

1. Contact and settlement: In the mid-nineteenth century, the first Canadian cookbooks emerged as guidebooks for newly arrived Canadians, the best known being Catharine Parr Traill's *Female Emigrant's Guide* (1854) and A.B. of Grimsby's *Frugal Housewife's Manual* (1840), as well as *La cuisinière canadienne* (May 1840) and *La nouvelle cuisinière canadienne* (1850).

2. Consolidation: During the last decades of the nineteenth century, cookbooks served to consolidate knowledge gleaned from various sources for Canadian home cooks. The best known of these included *The Home Cook Book* (1877), *Canadian Housewife's Manual of Cookery* (1861), *Mrs. Clarke's Cookery Book* (1883),[1] and *Directions diverses données par la Rev. Mère Caron* (1878). The consolidation of culinary knowledge in this period was intended to serve the Canadian cook in her kitchen. But it was also the first step in a larger program of consolidation that would both give rise to a sense of a distinctly Canadian cuisine and position cookbooks as useful vehicles for the articulation of Canadian tastes and values. In some ways, then, the period of consolidation might be seen to extend to the latter half of the twentieth century, reaching a crescendo in 1967.

3. Affiliation: At the turn of the twentieth century, many of the cookbooks that emerged were affiliated with institutions rather than

individuals. Such corporate cookbooks as *The Five Roses Cook Book /
La cuisinière Five Roses* (1913), as well as those of the Purity and Ogilvie flour companies, became valued resources in Canadian homes, rather in the way that the Edmonds Company cookbook became ubiquitous in New Zealand homes. Further, single-author cookbooks gained credibility from their association with educational institutions. Nellie Lyle Pattinson, for example, developed the trusted *Canadian Cook Book* (1923) as a textbook for the cooking school of which she was director; similarly, in Quebec the popular *Manuel de cuisine raisonnée* (1919) was used in homes and classrooms.

4. Articulation: Home economics was professionalized in Canada in 1939, and as home economists took up positions not only as teachers and dieticians, but also as corporate and public spokespeople, cookbooks – alongside radio and, later, television shows – served as a conduit for the articulation of identity. Cookbooks by Kate Aitken (fondly known as "Mrs A" to her audiences), such as *Kate Aitken's Canadian Cook Book* (1945), and by Jehane Benoît (or Mme B), such as *L'encyclopédie de la cuisine canadienne* (1963) and *The Canadiana Cook Book* (1970), gave people the opportunity to articulate, even to construct, an emerging sense of shared identity.

5. Differentiation: During a time of increasing normalization of foodways traditions internationally, the distinctive food traditions of French-speaking Canadians served as a reminder of points of divergence between Canada and other countries, most obviously, its neighbour to the south. Indeed, Canada's centenary celebrations ushered in an era of cultural branding north of the forty-ninth parallel. The explicit use of the word "Canadian" in the titles of cookbooks published during Canada's centenary may have underlined a shared sense of identity, but the sixties paradoxically ushered in an era of increasing differentiation, evident in cookbooks that focused on regional and cultural variations in foodways practices. These competing drives – towards identification and differentiation – are always at play to some degree in the shaping of foodways, but their co-existence was most acutely visible in cookbooks of the 1960s and

1970s in Canada. Expo 67, in particular, can be seen as a moment in which Canada not only invited the world to its doors but also into its kitchens.

Expo 67 launched what might at first glance be misconstrued as the sixth and subsequent stage of culinary history: a period of intense introspection (which continues to our own day) in which Canadians began to review and revise their culinary practices past and present – to reconceive food (sometimes retrospectively) as symbol of self, community and nation; to bestow upon humble food items (such as Red Fife wheat, the doughnut, tourtière, the butter tart, and, most recently, poutine) the burden of iconicity; and to reconfigure perishable food products into historical artifacts. I would argue, however, that this period of introspection is not so much a new stage of Canadian culinary history as it is a period of culinary scholarship. As such, it is different in kind as well as degree, for in this period of introspection cookbooks have found a place on bedside tables and desks as well as on kitchen counters and have gained currency as signifiers of societal change, no longer simply being practical prescriptions for culinary practice.

Despite such interest, however, the study of domestic foodways in Canada has not yet received sustained scrutiny from social and cultural historians and commentators. Analysis of the sort undertaken on American foodways by Warren Belasco (1990), Sherrie Inness (2001a, 2001b, 2001c, 2006), Laura Shapiro (1986, 2004), Barbara Haber (2002), Harvey Levenstein (1988, 1993), or Donna Gabaccia (1998) is still largely missing in Canada. Such food scholarship, as Barbara Haber and Arlene Voski Avakian astutely observe (2005), is influenced both by the academics writing about food (and here they point to the work of anthropologists and political, economic, and cultural historians working beyond the focus on American foodways) and by something more broadly described as "[g]ood writing" about food that requires "something of a sensual response to food and knowledge that comes from cooking it."[2] In Canada, there is an abundance of the latter, for the period of culinary introspection gave rise to a bounty of books that showcased regional fare by serving up the best recipes, often within the context of regional history. A sample of these might include Beulah (Bunny) Barss (1980) on Prairie cooking, Christina Bates (1978) on Ontario fare, Marie Nightingale (1971) offering a glimpse of Nova Scotian kitchens, Desloges and LaFrance (1989) on Quebec gastronomy, and, more recently, Julian Armstrong (1990) introducing readers to the best and bounty of Quebec's home and restaurant cuisine. Some of Canada's most popular cookbooks use recipes as vehicles for conveying the wealth of Canada's ethnic communities; of these, perhaps Edna Staebler's popular Mennonite cookbooks are the best known. First published in 1968, and not coincidentally, I would argue, just after Canada's centenary celebrations, Staebler's *Food That Really Schmecks* became an instant classic.

When cookbook authors survey Canadian fare more generally, they tend to quilt together regional offerings and histories to create a mosaic in celebration of Canadian cuisine. The sheer exuberance of these Canadian writers, indeed their advocacy for Canadian foodways, emerges in the titles of their books – as in Beulah Barss's *Oh Canada! A Celebration of Great Canadian Cuisine* (1987) or *Northern Bounty: A Celebration of Canadian Cuisine* (1995) by Cuisine Canada founder Anita Stewart and Jo Marie Powers. Popular food writer Anita Stewart engages readers through anecdotes, insights, lavish photographs, and recipes that spare no calories for the sake of quality (2000, 2008).

The field of foodways scholarship in Canada has largely been pioneered, to date, by researchers from the worlds of museums and historical kitchens and by writers who have learned to cook on hearths as well as stoves and whose interest in Canadian historical food culture is always a vocation and only sometimes a paying career. Neither of the two touchstone texts that address twentieth-century Canadian foodways specifically – *Culinary Landmarks* (2008) by Elizabeth Driver, a comprehensive and annotated bibliography of Canadian cookbooks published before 1950, organized by geographical region; and *A Century of Canadian Home Cooking* by home economists Carol Ferguson and Margaret Fraser (1992),[3] organized by decade – includes detailed analysis. Rather, as pioneering works in the field, they seek to provide an accurate overview of material and invite further exploration and scholarship. Elizabeth Driver has also authored a number of introductions for Whitecap's series of reprints of Canadian cookbooks, an initiative intended to bring research resources to scholars and thereby launch further studies in the field. Of books that survey historical foodways in Canada, Patricia Beeson's *Macdonald Was Late for Dinner* (1993) engages readers with visual gems drawn from Canada's historical photo archives and evocative thumbnail descriptions – not to mention its terrific title. Fiona Lucas's illustrated book on hearth cooking (2006) uses contemporary photographs of historical kitchens. Historical commentary often appears in cookbooks focused on a province or region. Christina Bates writes of Ontario (1978), for example; Kathleen Walker of Ottawa (1995); and Marielle Boudreau and Melvin Gallant of Acadia (1987). Dorothy Duncan's most recent book, *Canadians at Table* (2006), moves beyond her home province of Ontario to scan Canadian foodways from coast to coast to coast and from its beginnings. Her insights into the role of pemmican in changing the course of Canadian history signal a fruitful avenue for further investigation, one with enormous potential for Canadian political and economic historians interested in scrutinizing colonial and post-colonial relations in Canada through the lens of food. Just as Sydney Mintz focused on the role of sugar in modern history in his watershed study *Sweetness and Power* (1985), other historians might scrutinize how shifts in the fishing industry, hunting practices, or imports of coffee, vegetables, or rice could affect Canadian society. Steve Penfold's book on the iconic "donut" and the industry behind it (2008) is an example of this kind of research, although his focus moves beyond Canadian national boundaries; Catherine Macpherson's chapter on cocoa in this collection is another example.

Socio-cultural analysis of the kind associated with Donna Gabaccia's work in the United States is another avenue of investigation with enormous potential for Canadian scholars. *You Eat What You Are* (1979) by dietitian and professional educator Thelma Barer-Stein is a pioneering work in this field in Canada. The Ontario Historical Society was responsible for a number of publications on specific ethnic and cultural communities in Canada. Jo Marie Powers is the author of two of these, *Buon Appetito! Italian Foodways in Ontario* (2000) and *From Cathay to Canada: Chinese Cuisine in Transition* (1998). Social and gender historian Franca Iacovetta's book on the Italian Canadian community (1993) and Marlene Epp's work on Mennonite communities (2004) extend this line of critical analysis in Canada.

Topical and popular culture analyses and histories, such as the exposés by American scholars Sherrie Inness (*Dinner Roles*, 2001) and Janet Theophano (2002) of prescriptions for gender in US cookbooks, are fruitful and relatively unexplored avenues of investigation for Canadian food scholars. My own research largely focuses on the culinary historical period of affiliation and specifically on the trade spokes-characters in Canada – fictional women who, like Betty Crocker, were constructed to put a human face and persona on a corporate brand. Like Doris Witt's book on Aunt Jemima (2004) and Susan Marks's (2005) and Karal Ann Marling's (1996) respective works on Betty Crocker, my own investigations focus on the identity politics of the corporate spokes-characters in Canada, most of whom were women and, like Betty, were portrayed as middle-aged and middle class, despite the cultural heterogeneity of Canada and its outspoken pride in cultural pluralism.

Interest in Aboriginal foodways has risen in recent years. Typically, this subject is approached through anthropology (Abonyi 2001; Daly 2005; Mills 1994), ethnobotany (Deur 2005; Turner 1995), and nutrition and health research (Kuhnlein 1993). Many traditionally Aboriginal foods are available commercially. Some have become commonplace (maple syrup, blueberries), while others are still considered specialty items (wild rice, dried fish, buffalo meat), frequently at prohibitive cost. Other traditional foods, including berries, bark, roots, shellfish, and seaweed, are largely left unharvested because of the breakdown in knowledge transmission during the residential school period, when children lost their language and their connection to the teaching elders, or because of pollution, lack of access (Harris 2001), shifts in hunting practices (Morantz 1978), new work patterns and economic imperatives (Ostry 2006), or overuse of resources. Shifts in diet and exercise resulting from the unavailability of traditional foods has led to spiking rates of type 2 diabetes (see Young 1987; Kuhnlein, et al. 2004; Fee 2006). The recuperation of traditional foodways has been recommended as a way to combat the rise of obesity and diabetes (Nabhan 2002), but this is easier said than done because of the close connections between traditional foodways and access to undeveloped land and unpolluted water. Aboriginal perspectives on these connections can be found in their testimony at public hearings (e.g., Canada 1996), in fictional and autobiographical accounts (as Margery Fee argues in her chapter in this collection), in a few community compilations, and in community newspapers (e.g., *Wawatay News Online*) as well as in interview material in academic accounts (e.g., Abonyi 2001). According to Skutnabb-Kangas et al. (2003) and Jeannette C. Armstrong (1994), the recuperation of traditional foods and food practices can be situated in a context of overall revitalization of language and culture.[4]

Despite these introductory comments on cultural food studies in Canada and my suggestion of an analytical framework involving five periods of Canadian culinary history, a comprehensive commentary on each of the five periods will be the task of future publications, not this one. This book will start that discussion by focusing first on the settlement and pre-settlement period and then on the post-1967 period of culinary introspection and mythologizing. Part 1 ("Eating Canadian: What Do and Did We Eat?") focuses on food items and choices; its six chapters are largely devoted to the foods eaten by Canada's First Nations and the early settlers, with the last two chapters of this section exploring the ways in which the foods enjoyed by early Canadians have found their way back onto Canadian tables in the twentieth and twenty-first centuries. Part 2 ("What Do Our Food Stories Tell Us about Who We Are or Were?") explores the expressive potential of food practices and food texts; each of its six chapters can be understood in relation to the current moment of culinary introspection, when cookbooks are perceived as valuable conveyors of social and historical information and hence are recognized as books to be read as well as to be used in the kitchen.

What does it mean for our sense of shared Canadian foodways, Elizabeth Driver asks in her chapter, that the same recipe appears across Canada but under different titles? Actually, the significance of naming (or renaming, translating, even transliterating) food and food practices is key to all the book's chapters. If in Part 2 Driver explores the implications of variations in the titles of recipes for the same dish, Rhona Richman Kenneally looks to the various notions of "Canadian cuisine," Sneja Gunew examines the meaning of "Eating Chinese," and Marie Marquis considers "favourite" cookbooks, for example, then the chapters in Part 1 tend to explore the inverse – the rationale for maintaining a dish's name but varying the ingredients and preparation methods (often a function of the practical circumstances during the pre- and settlement periods). Dividing the book into two sections in this way signals the manner in which competing drives of identification and differentiation have operated in Canadian foodways. Taken together, the chapters begin to shed light on what we, as Canadians, ate and now eat, as well as on what our food choices tell us about who we, as Canadians, were and are. They begin to explain why and how we have come to adopt new foods and food customs while preserving others.

The chapters in Part 1 focus on food items by way of responding to this question: What do and did we eat? Organized in a loosely chronological fashion, these chapters explore continuity in historical and contemporary food practices, arguing that if we, in the twenty-first century, were to revisit the past, we would not only discover the roots of current food practice, but might also come to better understand how previous generations protected the quality of the food supply and the land supporting it. In other words, the chapters argue that contemporary audiences should not only trace, but also forge lines of continuity and identification between themselves and Canada's First Nations and the early settlers.

In chapter 1, Victoria Dickenson suggests that explorers coming to what are now Canadian shores incorporated the exotic fruits of the "New World" into the food lexicon they knew and used in their homes in Europe. In turn, they understood unfamiliar fruits of the New World in terms of those already familiar to them. While Dickenson notes that the European explorers preferred to preserve their own food traditions (she describes how in the winter of 1542, for example, Sieur de Roberval and his colonists attempted to eat in New France much as they had at home), she also signals that the Europeans readily adopted in their diet particular food items, such as elk, prepared in pies, and cranberries, in preserves. Admittedly, their willingness to sample certain Aboriginal preparations sometimes came grudgingly; it was not until they were close to death in that dreadfully long winter of 1535 that Cartier's men, suffering from the ravages of scurvy, agreed to try a local herbal remedy and discovered what seemed to them to be a miracle cure.

Margery Fee, in chapter 2, further explores the interaction between European and Aboriginal foodways, but her focus is on the Europeans' inability to appreciate the food traditions of the First Nations peoples and the wisdom of their sophisticated food systems (designed to maintain the health and sustainability of the food supply), as well as on their failure to recognize the damage inflicted on the land and its inhabitants in the name of civilization. Fee reveals that the Aboriginal peoples survived by respecting what we now call the ecosystem, by embracing values that resonate with us in the twenty-first century, when, fearful of vulnerability in food chain, we begin to scrutinize the provenance of the food we put on the table and consume in our daily meals.

Catherine Macpherson, in chapter 3, traces the appearance of chocolate on Canadian shores and its transformation from a substance taken in liquid form in the eighteenth century to one more generally sweetened and taken in solid form, as we do today, and from a very expensive commodity to which only a few had access to its more general availability in the wake of industrialization. Macpherson's illustrated chapter reveals some of the methods of preparing chocolate in Canada, and her archival research provides us with evidence about the extent to which Canadians over the years have prized this substance for its medicinal properties as well as for its pleasurable taste.

Two subsequent chapters in Part 1 scrutinize ceremonial meals, tracing the evolution not so much of a food item but of a food tradition and, like other chapters in Part 1, underscoring lines of continuity in addition to shifts in food practices. In chapter 4, Quebec gastronomist Jean-Pierre Lemasson defends contemporary pride in the regional dish known as *tourtière* by tracing its complex lineage. He reveals that the humble meat pie so near and dear to the hearts of Quebecers, which takes pride of place as a distinctively regional dish (although there continues to be fierce debates over which of Quebec's regions it rightly belongs to, Lac-St-Jean and St-Jean-sur-Richelieu being the most vocal contenders), actually derived from an ancient recipe originating not in Quebec but in Mesopotamia. Lemasson's discussion invokes subtleties not apparent in the anecdotal understanding of tourtière as a pie that was commonly made with the *tourterelle* (turtledove) or the now-extinct carrier pigeon – an explanation for the dish's title both provided and debunked by Yvon Desloges and Marc Lafrance.[5] In chapter 5, American Andrew Smith partners with Saskatchewan scholar Shelley Boyd to look at the iconic Thanksgiving turkey, the main course that has evolved over time both north and south of the border. In these two chapters, one on tourtière and the other on turkey, as well as between the lines of these chapters, readers will glimpse the ways in which food choices can be driven by subtle yet timeless personal, regional, cultural, and culinary preferences as well as by pragmatism.

While Lemasson, Boyd, and Smith write about food traditions that have enjoyed relatively consistent practice, food columnist Sarah Musgrave, in chapter 6, discusses a heritage grain that is currently regaining favour after a period of neglect. Musgrave traces the story of Red Fife wheat by way of exploring issues of provenance. Like Fee, Musgrave asserts the value of heritage foodways and introduces us to Canadians who are actively engaged in challenging assumptions about the innate benefits of novelty and progress. Starting from a twenty-first-century perspective and recognizing that the current explosion of interest in Canada's culinary heritage is an extension both of explorations begun in the late twentieth century and of food fears of the twenty-first century, Musgrave looks to England and especially to France for comparison. In those countries, she realizes, there was a similar desire to identify the emergence of a distinctive national cuisine, but in the nineteenth century. Provocatively, Musgrave muses that Canada might be "a hundred years behind in codifying its culinary consciousness."

If the chapters in Part 1 invite readers to identify with earlier food practices and to recognize lines of continuity, then the chapters in Part 2, while also acknowledging certain continuities, examine the ways in which individuals and groups differentiate themselves through distinct food practices. Whereas Part 1 focuses on identification and continuities, Part 2 focuses on differentiation. As well, while the chapters in Part 1 explore the connotations of food choices, those in Part 2 turn to meals as depicted in recipes, cookbooks, and even poetry and literature in order to explore the range of stories and scripts the meals evoke and the extent and nature of the emotional investment in their significance.

The chapters in Part 2 address this broad question: What do our food stories tell us about who we are or were? Although focused on stories told about and through the daily meal in Canada and concerned principally with narrativity – of food, food choices, and the daily meal – Part 2 is not devoted to literary analysis. While there is certainly an interesting book yet to be written on the subject of Canadian literary meals,[6] a number of engaging discussions are already in print. Canadian Diane McGee in *Writing the Meal* (2002) and Margaret Atwood in *The CanLit Foodbook* (1987), as well as Anna Shapiro in *A Feast of Words* (1996), explore the pivotal role of meals within the Canadian literary works. But the objective of such discussions differs significantly from the objective of the present study. While McGee, Atwood, and Shapiro discuss the impact of the literary meal on the shape and reception of the work in which it appears, my own chapter and those of Rhona Richman Kenneally, Elizabeth Driver, Marie Marquis, Sneja Gunew, and Gary Draper explore what the work or text can reveal about the cultural context of its textual production and reception, the world in which the text was first conceived and written and the world into which it was received. In other words, while literary criticism looks at the way in which meal scenes influence a reader's sense of the book, the chapters in Part 2 look at narratives to better understand the daily meal in Canada, the choices Canadians make about what food to eat and how to eat it, and the connotations of these choices.

Anne LeCroy, in an essay exploring the range of food writing (1989), makes a distinction between kinds of food writing. She suggests that literary works[7] differ largely in degree rather than in kind from non-fictional food narratives.[8] However, LeCroy's distinction differs from the one implicit here. In this study, cookbooks, recipes, images, and discursive texts are vehicles for understanding – or lenses through which we, in the twenty-first century and in what I call here the culinary historical period of introspection, can glimpse – Canada's culinary past in order to better understand the present moment. LeCroy is most interested in establishing an informal taxonomy of food texts. This book, in contrast, attempts to read between the lines of these texts, through their pages and perhaps beyond them, to gain an understanding of their socio-historical and cultural context. Thus, the food narratives in Part 2 are variously understood (1) as souvenirs, whose primary function, as Susan Stewart explains is "to generate narrative";[9] (2) as scripts for the production of particular dishes or even, as Draper argues, of a happier future; and (3) as articulations of communal, regional, or national differentiation (Driver, Richman Kenneally).

In itself, of course, this notion of the symbolic potential of food and food rituals is nothing new. It has been voiced by such well-known scholars as Claude Lévi-Strauss (1964), Roland Barthes (1972), and Margaret Visser (1989). It was also clearly understood by the early inhabitants of Port Royal during the dark winter of 1606–07 when Marc Lescarbot organized the now famous Order of Good Cheer, a series of ceremonial meals to lift morale. This study brings together a number of explorations into the nature of that symbolic potential as it has been understood and articulated over the long twentieth century.

Part 2 opens with an essay by Rhona Richman Kenneally (chapter 7), who identifies the centennial celebrations of 1967 as a galvanizing moment in Canada's history, one that prompted a self-conscious outpouring of nationalistic narratives at a time when Canada was also recognizing the cultural wealth afforded by multiculturalism, by a heritage of group differentiation on multiple levels. Richman Kenneally argues that the cookbooks of the centenary evoke distinctiveness on a national level through their references to shared food traditions as well as through their reliance on specific ingredients of particularly high quality, such as salmon and maple syrup.

In chapter 8, cookbook bibliographer Elizabeth Driver argues that considerable energy and emotional investment have been exercised in articulating a distinctively Canadian culinary tradition over the years. She finds in cookbooks evidence of a lack of regional differences, whether defined by ingredients or ethnic backgrounds, in varying degrees over time. What recipes and cookbooks have in common, however, only emerges for Driver after close scrutiny. More and most obviously, as Driver acknowledges, the story of group differentiation is told by community cookbooks that boast specificity of place on their cover and in their recipe titles and that identify individual recipes with the very individuals who take pride in cooking them. Taken together, then, the chapters by Richman Kenneally and Driver identify tensions between forces of convergence and divergence, group identification and differentiation, in Canada's culinary heritage.

Chapters 9 (Marquis) and 10 (Cooke) scrutinize food texts for what they reveal about individual food preferences; these chapters work to expose some of the distinctions between the food choices made by individuals and those made by groups. Both are attempts to open the door a crack and shed some light on one of the aspects of Canadian foodways that is most difficult to document – descriptive food practice. By "descriptive practice," I am referring to what Canadians actually choose to prepare and eat in their own homes, as opposed to prescriptive practice, which is what they are instructed to choose and prepare in such "prescriptive" texts as cookbooks or advertisements. Marie Marquis, working from the results of a reader survey conducted by the Montreal daily newspaper *La Presse*, examines the appeal of particular cookbooks. What makes a Quebecer prefer one cookbook to another? What makes a particular cookbook rise above the rest? The answers provide a revealing glimpse into Quebec kitchens – the preferred dishes, recipes, and cookbooks. While Marquis' study attempts to move beyond the surface characteristics of cookbooks – for example, the tendency to use the imperative voice to tell cooks what to do – in order to find out which cookbooks Quebecers really use in their kitchens and why, my own chapter attempts to look beyond our present-day angst over the demise of the family dinner ritual to see whether this angst differs significantly in nature or scale from similar Canadian concerns in other decades of the long twentieth century. To my pleasant surprise, I found that it does not. Yet, while I conclude that angst over the demise of the dinner ritual is a constant through the last century despite a certain ebb and flow of its intensity, I also find that the term "dinner" has enormous expressive potential and that the act of having dinner has been practised in very different ways by Canadians of different decades and regions.

Chapters 11 and 12, the final two chapters, look at the ways in which we turn food into metaphor and story. Sneja Gunew argues that the acts of serving and selecting food have an inherent narrativity and speak to an evolving and subtle identity politics. Gunew's chapter looks specifically at the Chinese Canadian experience; it invites readers to explore the connotations of eating differently, innovatively, or "otherwise" in Canada more broadly. Gary Draper explores the narrative and expressive potential of a recipe ubiquitous in Canadian cookbooks, one he hopes is infrequently reproduced in practice in some of its variations. (In the interest of narrative suspense, I resist providing the recipe's title and main ingredients here.) Through the lens of one particular recipe, Draper focuses on the expressive potential of the recipe genre more generally, for recipe is a powerful genre that has received very little literary scrutiny to date. While Draper's is the last chapter in this collection, it is not, nor is it intended to be, a definitive conclusion for the book and the study it represents; rather, it explores the versatility of recipes – as prescriptive, descriptive, and imaginative texts – and illustrates the ways in which these miniature formulae for transformation are themselves shared and transformed. This chapter's position at the book's end is highly appropriate, since it, like the book itself, aims to open avenues of further discussion rather than provide definitive closure.

NOTES

1 Anne Clarke's *Mrs. Clarke's Cookery Book* was published under various titles.
2 Haber and Avakian, "Feminist Food Studies," 4.
3 Ferguson and Fraser's *A Century of Canadian Home Cooking* is now out of print.

4 I am indebted to Margery Fee for the insights in and phrasing of this paragraph, which is used with her permission.

5 Desloges and Lafrance, *A Taste of History,* 16.

6 In a 1956 article in *Maclean's* ("Our Most Neglected Treasure"), for example, the author invites a discussion of the central role of food in French Canadian literature and poetry, mentioning Jean Narrashe's poetry; the folk song "Le festin de la campagne," which describes "a full meal in verse"; and Philippe Aubert de Gaspé's novel *Les anciens canadiens. Maclean's,* 29 September 1956, 16.

7 By "literary works" she means "fiction with recipes in the text and use of food woven well into the fictive material, whether to show character, develop plot, or establish setting and atmosphere." Lecroy, "Cookery Literature," 8.

8 Non-fictional works include general histories of human cuisine, essays, and recipes with short introductory essays or anecdotes. LeCroy, "Cookery Literature," 8.

9 Stewart, *On Longing,* 147.

Part One

Eating Canadian:
What Do and
Did We Eat?

1

Curiosity into Edibility: The Taste of New France

VICTORIA DICKENSON

INTRODUCTION

Much has been written of the Columbian exchange, the transfer between New World and Old of people, pathogens, flora, and fauna. The biota of two hemispheres, once seemingly irredeemably separated, were interpenetrated, both through accident and human agency.[1] Europeans began to learn about a whole new flora, a fragrant cornucopia of strange fruits and flowers, succulent roots and tubers, and sweet and oily seeds and nuts. Some they tasted only vicariously, through the descriptions of explorers, but others they imported, first as potential drugs and curatives for the apothecaries' shelves or as curiosities for the botanical gardens, and then – sooner in some cases, later in others – as new and exotic foods. The process of translation from curiosity to edibility reveals much about the way in which people in early modern Europe regarded the New World, about diet and taste, and about the ways in which cuisine responds to novelty.

From our vantage point at the beginning of the twenty-first century, the impact of the Columbian exchange on European cuisine is evident. By the eighteenth century, potatoes had become a famous (and infamous) staple of the European diet, particularly for the Irish. Tomatoes transformed the Italian diet and made spaghetti with tomato sauce a truly cross-cultural dish.[2] Chocolate, the cacao of the New World,[3] is now a specialty perhaps most associated with the Swiss and Belgians, while by the 1980s the Italian *zucchini* or French *courgette* was one of the top-ten vegetable crops worldwide.[4] Not every New World food plant, however, found ready acceptance on European tables. Novelty in itself is not a recommendation. A new food may smell, look, and taste good, but that does not mean that people will necessarily eat it.[5] Those foods that people in the sixteenth and early seventeenth centuries did adopt benefited from a combination of factors that made their taste and appearance acceptable, their transport or propagation simple, and their preparation easily understood. This chapter will examine the translation into European food culture of a number of New World plants following the voyages to North America by Jacques Cartier (1491–1557) between 1534 and 1541, and the explorations and settlements undertaken by Samuel de Champlain (1580?–1635) from 1603 to his death at Quebec in 1635. The "fruits" of the northern explorations appeared to Europeans at the time less significant and certainly less spectacular than the products of Columbus's discoveries in tropical seas. The appearance at court of a scarlet South American macaw or the presentation of a pineapple, however disdained by Charles V,[6] occasioned more interest than the gift of a salted codfish or a cedar tree, though in the end these were to prove in many ways more valuable. More important to the northern explorers and their patrons was the sense that, through their journeys across the cold North Atlantic, they were coming closer to the strange and spicy treasures of the east, the original Indies, and to the lands of Cipango and Cathay, or at least to the riches associated with the mines of Cuzco and the temples of Mexico. What the voyageurs chose to describe and to transport back to court was evidence that the new northern lands were somehow linked to the east or were themselves at least as rich, if not as wonderful, as those the Spanish had found in the south.

According to the dedication to the King of France in the account of his second voyage, Jacques Cartier sailed in 1535 to explore the "fertility and rich-

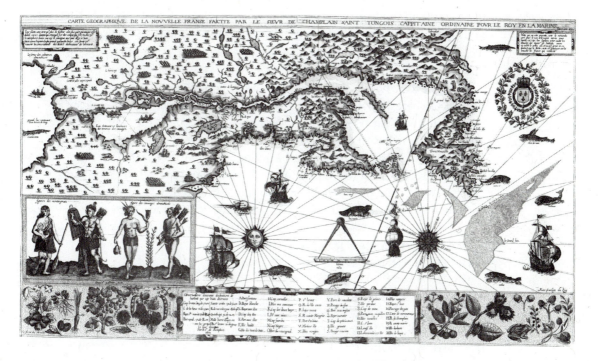

Carte geographique de la Nouvelle France ..., by Samuel de Champlain, 1612. Engraved by David Pelletier. Source: Bibliothèque et Archives nationales du Québec, 2663709.

ness" of "lands in the west formerly unknown to you and to us, lying in the same climates and parallels as your territories and kingdom,"[7] and presumably within the sphere of influence of France. He returned with a relatively factual account of a northern land of warm summers and harsh winters, and also with tales of the mythical kingdom of Saguenay, where, according to his informant, Donnaconna, "there are immense quantities of gold, rubies, and other rich things."[8] After Cartier's third voyage in 1541, his nephew recounted that Cartier had left a map with two inscriptions: "Here is the land of Saguenay, which is rich and wealthy in precious stone," and "Here in this Country are Cinnamon and Cloves."[9] Cartier himself had not visited this mysterious kingdom, but he had brought back to the king a sample of gold, "ten or twelve stones shaped like small goose quills" and "a good store of stones, which we esteemed to be Diamants."[10] Sixty years later, Samuel de Champlain sailed in the hope, not of finding rubies and spices in the north, but of discovering a route to the east through the New World, a "passage to China without the inconvenience of the northern icebergs, or the heat of the torrid zone."[11] Neither explorer succeeded in returning with the treasures of the east, though the lure of the "sweetwater seas" (the Great Lakes) and the Northwest Passage continued to haunt the European imagination throughout the period. In lieu of gold, gems, and rare and costly spices, what did Cartier and Champlain introduce to France and Europe? What were the vegetable novelties that survived the ocean crossing and found favour or utility in the gardens of Paris and London?

CURATIVE TEAS AND NEW WORLD WINE: CARTIER IN NEW FRANCE

When Cartier sailed west, he was not blazing new trails through the western sea; rather, he was following routes well known to those engaged in the New-foundland fishery. The transatlantic fishery had been established two genera-tions earlier following the discoveries of the Italian Giovanni Caboto (John Cabot), sailing for the English. Like his countryman Columbus, Caboto was looking for the east, and in particular the island of Cipango (Japan),[12] when he discovered the "New-Found-Land" (Newfoundland) and the piscatorial riches of its Grand Banks. Within five years of his 1497 voyage, a Bristol merchant working with an Azorean captain landed the first cargo of North Ameri-can cod in Europe.[13] The fishery was soon dominated, however, by Norman, Breton, and Basque ships, and by the mid-sixteenth century, the Newfound-land fleet that each year made its way to the Banks and returned with salt fish and occasionally furs outnumbered the Spanish fleet sailing to the Caribbean and Mexico by two to one.[14] It is certain that the fishers of the Grand Banks and the Basque whalers knew the productions of the coasts of Newfound-land and Labrador, but they did not find them impressive. Cartier evidently concurred. Sailing from Newfoundland on his first voyage in 1534, he came upon Brion Island in the Magdalen Islands. He called it (possibly struck by the contrast with the rocky fogbound coasts he had left behind), "the best land we have ever seen; for two acres of it are worth more than the whole of Newfoundland. We found it to be covered with fine trees and meadows, fields of wild oats, and of pease in flower, as thick and fine as ever I saw in Brittany ... There are numerous gooseberry bushes, strawberry vines, Provins roses, as well as parsley and useful strong-smelling herbs."[15] Prince Edward Island was equally appealing, covered in trees both familiar and strange ("cedars, yew-trees, pines, white elms, ash trees, willows, and others, many of them unknown to us and all trees without fruit"). As on Brion Island, the soil "where there are no trees is also very rich and covered with pease, white and red goose-berry bushes, strawberries, raspberries, wild oats like rye, which one would say had been sown there and tilled."[16] In the Baie des Chaleurs he thought he had found a "country more temperate than Spain" with wild wheat, oats, white- and red-currant bushes, roses, useful herbs, plums, figs, nuts, apples, and even beans, "which they call *sahé*."[17] On his second voyage the following year, Cartier sailed up the St Lawrence River and over-wintered at what is now Quebec City. At Quebec, he ate "hazel-nuts as large as ours and better-tast-ing, though a little more bitter," and he recognized as well "magnificent trees of the same varieties as in France," including "hawthorns, bearing a fruit as large as a damson."[18] He noted that the Native people dried the plums that they called *honnesta* for the winter just as was done in France. At Hochelaga (Montreal), he found "better than all, a great quantity of grape-vines, which were so loaded with grapes that the sailors came on board with their arms full of them."[19] The French were beginning to feel at home.

Cartier had discovered a new vegetable world that resembled northern Europe closely enough that he could name many of its products and see analogies to familiar plants. Given the vegetable assemblage before him, for example, Cartier could see "fig" – a fruit not native to North America, but one that had been eaten and grown in France since Roman times – in the fruit of the serviceberry (*Amelanchier* species, also known as shadbush, or in Newfoundland, chuckley pear), which when ripe resembles a small fig in colour and shape. In the beans and squashes of New World, he could rec-ognize "melons, cucumbers, pumpkins (*courges*), pease, and beans of various colours and unlike our own."[20] Their specific differences of colour and shape were not marked enough to make him marvel. Even the true exotics seemed familiar. The French noted "large fields covered with the corn of the country, which resembles Brazil millet, and is about as large as or larger than a pea. They live on this as we do on wheat."[21] (In the diary of the third voyage, Columbus remarked that the Spanish were by 1498 growing the corn he had brought back from his first voyage.)[22] The three legs of the North American cooking pot (corn, beans, and squash) were, however, humble foodstuffs, and what Cartier sought were rare spices, strange herbs, and exotic fruits that would delight a king's palate or make a merchant's fortune. Despite what at first glance seemed to be a vegetable paradise where grapes and grains already grew in abundance, awaiting only the hand of a skilled grower to make them rival the productions of France,[23] there were few exotic novelties to be had in what came to be called New France.

The French in fact disdained the cuisine of the original inhabitants. While Cartier described the process by which they made bread from corn, and praised the quality of the game and fish, he and his men refused the Aboriginal preparations, chiefly, it would seem, because they used no salt. During the long winter of 1542, the Sieur de Roberval and his colonists ate in New France much as they ate at home – bread, beef, butter, peas, beans (*fèves*), salt pork, salt cod, and sometimes fresh fish, even porpoise (*marsouin*) supplied by their Native neighbours.[24] It was only when they became ill that the French turned to a Native remedy, a curative tea. Overwintering at Stadacona (Quebec City) during the harsh winter of 1535–36, Cartier watched as one by one his crew succumbed to the effects of a terrible malady, only to be cured at last by the administration of a tea made from the bark and leaves of a tree called by the inhabitants *anneda* (or *ameda*). The effect of the remedy was immediate and, according to Cartier, a true miracle.[25] Not only was the brew a cure for the *grosse maladie* (scorbut or scurvy), but it also seemed to be a sovereign cure for all that ailed Cartier's men, even the pox (venereal disease). At first reluctant to attempt the local cure, after a successful try by two desperate sailors, Cartier's men eagerly stripped a tree as large as a French oak, boiled it, and drank the brew. This miracle cure was the common white cedar (*Thuya occidentalis*), unknown in Europe. Cartier must have thought that he had found an exotic panacea, a herb to rival the rarities of the east and to cure the ills of Europe. He evidently collected seeds from the *anneda* and carefully transported them back to France. Pierre Belon in his work on conifers (1553) notes that what was called *Arbor vitae* or Tree of Life was grown from seed in the royal gardens at Fontainebleau as early as 1536.[26] André Thevet also mentions the Tree of Life in his account of Cartier's voyages to Canada, and notes that when the Natives suffer fever or other internal complaints, they make a restorative drink by steeping the leaves of a tree resembling the "cedars that are found around the mountain of Tarare, which is in Lyonnais."[27] The Tree of Life entered the botanical literature but soon lost its special status. Just two generations after Cartier's voyage, when Carolus Clusius (Charles de L'Écluse) described it in his *Rariorum plantarum historia*, first published in 1579 and reprinted in 1601, the significance of the original name had been forgotten. The engraved illustration in that volume shows a branch of white cedar, and Clusius speculates that the tree had been named the Tree of Life either because it was an evergreen or, perhaps, because of its strong scent.[28] *Arbor vitae* had not proved a panacea for all that ailed Europeans in the Old World or the New, and it was replaced as a cure-all by other New World exotics, such as sassafras or Meçhoacan roots (the Indian rhubarb).[29] Its scent and evergreen property recommended it, however, to gardeners, and by the seventeenth century it was common throughout Europe.

There was at least one other horticultural rarity imported into France for its special qualities in the wake of Cartier's voyages, but at this distance it is impossible to say whether this was due to its potential as a food plant or simply because of its spectacular appearance. The sugar maple (*Acer saccharum*) was grown at Fontainebleau, presumably introduced by Cartier or Roberval. Thevet writes that the sugar maple yielded a *suc,* or juice, as good as the wine of Orleans or Beaune. This natural bounty had lain undiscovered in the tree until someone cut into it and tasted the juice that poured forth. Thevet recounts that Cartier and his men gathered it in pots, but there is no mention of the Aboriginal practice of collecting maple sap.[30] Neither is there mention in the accounts of the flaming scarlet of the autumn tree, but one suspects that the tree's spectacular seasonal appearance might also have encouraged its import.[31]

CHAMPLAIN AND THE FRUITS OF NEW FRANCE

In March 1611, Samuel de Champlain left on his third voyage to New France. On his return in September, he published *Les Voyages,* which comprised a "very accurate journal of observations made in the course of discoveries in new [*sic*] France," beginning in 1604. He also drew two large maps to accompany the publication. The larger of these was a decorative map engraved on copper by a professional engraver, David Pelletier, and it included both a cartouche of four Aboriginal figures and an unusual bottom border featuring a frieze of what might be termed the fruits of the land. As a colonial administrator, Champlain not only encouraged the development of gardens in New France, but also documented the variety and quality of its native products. The decorative border of the 1613 map features plants familiar to Europeans, as well as novelties. Some of the plants are labelled with French or Aboriginal names; others have no label. While the engraving was executed by Pelletier, the original drawings or watercolours were likely by Champlain himself.[32] Early on, Champlain had shown an interest in drawing the unusual plants and animals he saw, as is well demonstrated in the watercolours that accompany his "Brief Discours" (Brief Narrative), the unpublished manuscript of a voyage to the Indies that he undertook as a young man in 1599, with the intent "to make inquiries into particulars of which no Frenchmen have succeeded in obtaining cognizance, because they have no free access there, in order to make true report of them to his Majesty."[33]

The particulars that Champlain noted on his initial voyage to the New World included a wide array of tropical fruits and plants. Like many Europeans in the period, Champlain was seeking exotica, and in the islands of the Caribbean, he found sugar, ginger, cassia, and preserves of ginger,[34] as well as gold and silver. But what seemed to enchant him most was the exotic flora and fauna he encountered. In an account surprisingly reminiscent of Columbus's description of the island of San Juan,[35] Champlain on his first voyage to the fragrant south found "fine forests ... filled with the most beautiful trees that one could wish ... with an infinity of other kinds that I cannot name on account of the variety of them, which give the greatest possible satisfaction to the eyes; together with quantities of birds of divers plumage that are seen in the forests ... and the trees are never bare of fruit and are always green."[36] As he travelled from island to island, he noted and tasted the exotic fruits of the new Indies: "There are also in the said island quantities of good fruits, namely plantains, oranges, lemons of unusual size, ground gourds, which are very good, algarrobas, pappittes, and a fruit named coraçon, because it is in the form of a heart, the size of one's fist, and of a yellow and red colour; the skin is very delicate, and when one presses it, gives out a fragrant fluid; the good part of the fruit is like thickened milk, and tastes like sugared cream."[37]

En route to Mexico, he "admired the fine forests ... filled with ... palms, cedars, laurels, orange and lemon trees, cabbage palms, guavas, avocadoes, ebony, Brazil, and Campeachy wood."[38] He described the cocoa tree and the drink made from the cocoa powder: "[A] paste is made, which is steeped in hot water, in which the honey that comes from the same tree is mixed, with a little spice; then the whole being boiled together is drunk in the morning, warmed up, as our sailors take brandy, and people feel so well after having drunk of this liquid that they can dispense with eating for a whole day without becoming very hungry."[39] He saw guava, which he compared in size to an apple common in Normandy and in texture to a green fig, and he accounted the juice "very good." The avocado is eaten with salt and tastes like green walnuts, the carreau (*Passiflora incarnata*, according to Biggar) "tastes very good," and serolles plums have a "flavour like muscatel pears."[40] He ate roasted batata (*Ipomoea batatas,* or sweet potato) and found it tasted like chestnuts; he ate maize tortillas and noted that they must be eaten hot, since they are "no good cold, or after keeping."[41] In Cuba he sampled the pineapple: "They remove the skin, then cut it in half like an apple, and it has a very pleasant taste, very sweet, like sugar."[42] There were also more familiar foods – melons of extraordinary size, cucumbers, artichokes, cabbages, and pumpkins (*citrouilles*), even apples and pears.

Of the fifty-two watercolour illustrations in the *Brief discours*, twenty feature plants, primarily trees and fruits.[43] More than a decade later and many leagues north, on the map that accompanied his record of residence and travels in Acadia and New England, Champlain again chose to document a selection of the plants of *la France antarctique*. Unlike the Indies, this New France shared with Europe a northern flora. Champlain, like Cartier, could recognize at first glance much of what he saw on his first voyage in 1603. After coasting up the St Lawrence past shores cloaked in thick forest (albeit an unfamiliar sight to a seventeenth-century Frenchman), he came to the "fine and level country" between Quebec and Trois-Rivières: "In these parts are found quantities of grapes, pears, hazel-nuts, cherries, red and green currants." There was one particularly exotic find – "certain small roots, the size of a small nut, tasting like truffles, which are very good roasted or boiled."[44] But he was occasionally confused by the similar yet oddly different flora: "These rivers are very pleasing in appearance, the landscape being covered with trees resembling walnut-trees, and having the same smell: but I saw no fruit, which makes me doubtful. The savages told me they bear fruit like ours."[45] Later, when he did find nuts near Lac St-Pierre, he identified walnut trees "not very different from ours," which may have been butternut and hickory, two species also called walnut (*noyers*) by early explorers.[46] Going further up the St Lawrence past the Richelieu River, Champlain found islands "very productive of fruits, such as grapes, walnuts, hazel-nuts [*noizettes*], and a kind of fruit like chestnuts, cherries, oaks, aspens, poplars, hops, ash, maple, beech, cypress, very few pines and fir-trees ... One finds there quantities of strawberries, raspberries, red, green and blue currants, together with many small fruits which grow there in the thick grass."[47]

Ten years later, in 1613, when he drew the map to accompany his published account of the years from 1604 to 1612, he had become familiar with the country and its products. He had endured difficult winters, planted his gardens and reaped harvests, and shared the foods of the Aboriginal peoples, among whom he lived and travelled. Near Plymouth in Massachusetts, the inhabitants had sent him "little squashes as big as your fist, which we ate as a salad like cucumbers, and they were very good." They had also sent purslane, which he knew in Europe.[48] The Aboriginal communities he knew cultivated corn, as well as "Brazilian beans, many edible squashes of various sizes, tobacco, and roots which they cultivate, the latter having the taste of artichokes."[49] They prepared the corn by first pounding it in mortars, then making "cakes and biscuits of it as do the Indians of Peru."[50]

After his return to France, Champlain wrote *Les Voyages* from memory and notes, as he had sent his original journals to Henri IV.[51] The map appears to have been prepared specially to illustrate the publication, and intended not just for mariners or the king's eyes, but for general readers. Champlain may have been aware of the success of illustrated books on the New World, such as Theodor de Bry's series on America, *Les grands voyages* (volumes 1 through 9 had been published by this date); Jean de Léry's *Histoire d'un voyage fait en la terre du Bresil, autrement dite Amerique ...*, published in La Rochelle in 1578; or André Thevet's *Les singularités de la France antarctique* of 1558. In his illustrated book, Champlain offers a highly decorative map of his discoveries that includes representations of Aboriginal people and the flora and fauna of New France. The border, unusual in maps of this period, might be seen as a kind of promotion for the products of New France. Champlain wishes to encourage settlement, and he extols New France as a land of plenty, despite the harsh winters (of which he fears his readers might be aware):

> As for the country itself, it is beautiful and agreeable, and it brings all sorts of grain and seed to maturity. There are in it all the varieties of trees we have in our forests on this side of the ocean and many fruits, although they are wild for lack of cultivation: such as butternut trees [*noyers*], cherry-trees, plum-trees, vines, raspberries, strawberries, gooseberries and red currants [*groiselles verdes et rouges*], and several other small fruits, which are quite good. There are also several sorts of useful herbs and roots. Fish are plentiful in the rivers, along which are meadows and game, in vast quantity. From the month of April until the fifteenth of December the air is so healthy and good, that one feels in oneself no tendency to sickness.[52]

Champlain's careful depiction of the plants and fruits he encountered reveals something of his personal interests,[53] as well as something of what he presumes might be the interest of his readers in the "new foods" of New France.

THE "NEW FOODS" OF NEW FRANCE

Champlain's map includes a cartouche depicting the Aboriginal inhabitants, drawn in a manner reminiscent of the classicized figures of Native people that de Bry engraved after the original drawings of John White or Jacques le Moyne de Morgues to illustrate the first two volumes of his *Les grands voyages*, published in 1590 and 1591. The Almouchicois, characterized as a sedentary and agricultural people, hold the fruits associated with the Aboriginal inhabitants of America, different kinds of squash and an ear of corn.[54] To the right of the female figure is a tall single-flowered plant that could simply be an engraver's decoration but might be an attempt to represent a particular specimen of the unusual flora of New France – the Jerusalem artichoke (*Helianthus tuberosus*), one of the important "roots" in Aboriginal cuisine that Champlain describes and that in bloom resembles a small-flowered sunflower. By 1612, all three of these plants were well known in Europe. Varieties of the American cucurbit (*Cucurbita pepo*, referred to as pumpkins, squash, or gourds) were first described by Columbus, and Cartier also described the "gros melons, concombres et courges" on his 1535 voyage. By 1543, Leonhart Fuchs had depicted four varieties in his herbal *De historia stirpium*, including one very similar to that held by the Almouchicois woman.[55] The 1613 horticultural border also shows a number of squashes, with the annotation, "la forme des sitroules" (or "the shape of the pumpkins" – the French word for pumpkin is *citrouille*). *C. pepo* is extremely polymorphic, and Champlain is evidently attempting to depict the various shapes of these American cucurbits, which can vary from the appropriately named acorn squashes to the spherical pumpkins and the scalloped patty pans, the latter named after a French baking dish (*patisson*). *C. pepo* evidently took to the gardens of Europe with alacrity, as can be seen through its inclusion in many herbals between 1542 and 1700 (Fuchs, L'Obel, Theodorus, Dodoens, Gerard, Bauhin, etc.) and in gardening books (e.g., Parkinson's *Paradisi in Sole: Paradisus Terrestris* from 1629).[56] Corn (*Zea mays*) was also well known to Europeans by the early seventeenth century. Columbus saw it first in 1492, and he mentions in the diary of his third voyage that it was now much grown in Castille.[57] Cartier, as we have noted, recognized it on his first voyage as a grain "like pease, the same as in Brazil,"[58] and by the mid-sixteenth century, an ear of corn is depicted in a popular compilation, Giovanni Battista Ramusio's *Navigationi et Viaggi* (1556), which also includes an account of Cartier's voyages. Herbalists like Rembert Dodoens (1554) also provided excellent naturalistic renderings of the plant. Like the *Arbor vitae*, however, corn too underwent a transformation, losing its New World origins and becoming an exotic product of the equally exotic east. In his *Cruijdeboeck*, Dodoens calls it "Milium Indicum" or "Turkie corne" and describes it as a "marvellous strange plant, nothing resembling any other kind of grayne: for it bringeth forth his seede cleane contrairie from the place whereas the Floures grow." Its origin is ascribed to "Turkie," where it is eaten in times of dearth.[59] Finally, if the flower depicted is a Jerusalem artichoke, Champlain himself was the first to describe it in 1605. He wrote that the Native people of Nauset Harbour in Massachusetts cultivated roots that had "the taste of artichoke."[60] The following year he returned to the same area and again saw the cultivated roots "with a flavour like that of chards."[61] Marc Lescarbot, Acadia's first historian, also knew the plant, describing "a certain kind of root, as big as turnips or truffles, most excellent to eat, tasting like chards, but more pleasant, which when planted, multiplies as it were out of spite, and in such sort that it is wonderful."[62] Parkinson, writing in 1629, echoes Lescarbot, noting that the "[p]otato's of Canada by reason of their great increasing, have growne to be so common here with us at London, that even the most vulgar begin to despise them, whereas when they were first received among us, they were dainties for a Queene."[63]

What of the horticultural border? Which plants did Champlain figure here? The border is divided into two parts by the map legend. To the right are ten figures of plants plus an anomalous frog. To the left, thirteen plants are shown, of which eleven are named, three with Aboriginal names. In the left-hand section, the first plant with bulbous root is labelled "aux," which may be an Aboriginal name or may be a form of "aulx," or garlic, though the plant pictured does not resemble wild garlic. The bulbous root is attached to two four-petalled "flowers," and its representation may even be an attempt to depict the evening primrose (*Oenothera* sp.), which had been introduced into Europe by 1614 and was cultivated for its edible roots, but the description is imprecise.[64] In his journals, Champlain refers only to "roots." The "aux" is followed by "la forme des sitroules," discussed above, then by the "astemara." This may be the *asarabacca*, also known as *asaron*, or wild ginger. Champlain certainly found this plant growing in the country of the Hurons, and it is pictured and described in Jacques-Philippe Cornut's *Canadensium plantarum*, the first book to be published on Canadian plants (Paris, 1635). The "prune" is, according to Ganong, the wild yellow or red plum (likely *Prunus nigra*).[65] The "cachy" is not identified by Ganong, but it may be the calamus (*Acorus calamus*), or sweet flag, eaten for its pungent root. The "groiselle rouge" is the red currant, mentioned by both Cartier and Champlain on numerous occasions and very common.[66] Next to the currant is the "chataigne," or fruit of the American chestnut (*Castanea dentata*), once common in North America but now rare as a result of disease. Above the chestnut in the illustration we see the "pisque penay," identified by Ganong as the "chicamin," or the Indian potato or groundnut (*Apios americana*). Champlain ate them on his 1603 voyage and declared they tasted like truffles.[67] Lescarbot says that the "savages call them Chiquebi, and they grow in abundance near oak trees."[68] Cornut, the Parisian doctor and the author of *Canadensium plantarum*, shows the plant growing like a vine on a trellis with the tubers pictured underneath, as it perhaps grew in Paris at the Jardin royal, where Vespasien Robin cultivated the plant from a seedpod (*ex siliquis*) brought from America.[69] Next are pictured "raisins de 3 sortes" (bunches of grapes), grouped with a "prune" (the wild yellow or red plum, *Prunus nigra*) and "feves de bresil," or a species of the New World phaseolus bean. Below the "feves" is what appears to be a blueberry – certainly a species of *Vaccinium*. Lescarbot compares these "small blue and red fruits" to the Latin *myrtillus*, or European blueberry (bilberry, *Vaccinium myrtillus*).[70] In the top corner is yet another root, difficult to identify.

The remaining plants on the right bear no labels. Is it because Champlain assumes they would be immediately recognizable or because the engraver left them out? The first is a small flowering plant, resembling perhaps a purple-flowering raspberry (*Rubus odoratus*); the second small plant may also be an attempt to represent one of the raspberries, to which Champlain frequently refers, although this is very uncertain. Between them is what may be the beach plum (*Prunus maritima*) or the wild black cherry (*Prunus serotina*). Champlain also pictures three nuts. The first, in its shaggy casing, is the beaked hazelnut (*Corylus rostrata*), still known in Quebec as the *noisette*, as it was called by Champlain, and elsewhere as the filbert. Pictured as well is the acorn from one of the native oaks, likely the white oak (*Quercus alba*), whose fruit was much used by Aboriginal people. On the bottom corner is the hickory nut (*Carya ovata*), which resembles a small walnut, often called *noyer* by Champlain. Next to the frog is a small-berried plant that may be the *Gaultheria hispidula*, or creeping snowberry. In his account of the third voyage in 1611, Champlain describes a small fruit that is very good to eat: "Amongst others there is a very fine one with a sweetish taste, like that of the plantains (a fruits of the Indies) as white as snow, with leaves like those of the nettle, and it creeps up the trees and along the ground like ivy."[71] Snowberry is an evergreen that grows rampant along the ground in cool, wet woods. The white berries were eaten by Aboriginal people and do indeed have the texture of bananas but with a slight taste of wintergreen.[72] The last two fruits resemble two types of strawberries. The small spray of leaves is difficult to identify.

Why did Champlain choose to include these plants? Why are they so hard to identify? I have made the assumption that all these nuts and berries and roots were important food plants for Aboriginal inhabitants of New France and eastern North America. They are those that Champlain alludes to in his texts and also those that he probably ate, may have even drawn (though he makes no mention of this in his accounts), and attempted to bring back with him to France. In part, the difficulty in identifying some of these plants stems from the very nature of the illustration process. An engraver like Pelletier, when confronted with Champlain's request that he represent these unfamiliar plants of New France, would work either from drawings already prepared or from specimens. Drawings, usually watercolours, were as accurate as the material available to the artist. If the only information available was the textual description, the drawing and subsequent engraving would be based on the artist's imagination and the images evoked by the words themselves, often resulting in an inexplicable and unnatural rendering.[73] A more accurate drawing could be made "from nature," either from a living plant or a preserved specimen. It was preferable to work from a living specimen, as many of the great herbal illustrators did (Hans Weiditz, for example, who illustrated Brunfels's *Herbarium vivae eicones*, 1531–40). Working with a dried specimen, whose state of preservation was less than ideal, often resulted in mistaken interpretations of structure or form. A skilful artist could provide the engraver with an extremely accurate and naturalistic rendering, but if the engraver had access only to a poor or clumsy depiction, the engraving would reflect the imprecision of the original. In many cases, the engraver would opt to copy an existing engraving.[74] To an engraver-artist, a strawberry was a strawberry, whether it came from New France or the gardens of Paris, and copying a pre-existing illustration was the simplest and fastest way of producing an engraved image.

In the case of the plants in Champlain's map border, David Pelletier likely had access to preserved specimens, as well as to Champlain's accounts and perhaps drawings, and even to living plants. An examination of Champlain's watercolours from *Brief Discours* reveals that while he was an able illustrator, he was not a trained artist in the manner of John White or Jacques Le Moyne de Morgues, and his drawings of the exotic trees and plants of the Indies are relatively crude. It is likely, then, that the very schematic representations of plants on the map – those least naturalistic and most difficult to identify

– were engraved either from rough "field" sketches or from textual or even oral descriptions. Some, such as the "cachy," may have been illustrated from preserved specimens, dried and pressed, which would have distorted the true shape of the plant. Others, those most "life-like," were very likely engraved from renderings of either living specimens or from those so similar to European plants that a felicitous and naturalistic rendering (or even copying) was possible. The "sitroules," for example, were well known to Europeans of this period and widely grown. The nuts were easy to transport from the New World and were similar to Old World species, as were the plums, grapes, and strawberries. Champlain's horticultural border thus presented to his European readers an image of New World bounty both exotic and familiar. They could imagine their appearance, and in some cases even taste, both through Champlain's written accounts that compare new flavours to ones already known, and through comparing New World varieties of nuts and berries with those of Europe. But which of the fruits of the New World could Champlain's readers taste in reality?

EATING EXOTICA

The transatlantic trade in plants began with Columbus. Shipping viable plant material across the ocean was problematic, even though the characteristics of certain plants made their transport relatively simple. The easiest and most reliable means of transporting rarities was to carry them as seeds. Provided that the seeds were kept dry and away from pests and vermin, it was relatively simple to guarantee their good condition upon arrival in Europe.[75] Once the seeds were on the continent, it was up to the gardeners to determine the right conditions for growth. Some plants grown from seed acclimatized with ease, and these were the early success stories – corn, peppers, beans, and squash. The squashes were exceptionally easy to grow from seed, and Fuchs would have seen over two dozen forms of *C. pepo* by 1562, just seventy years after Columbus had first described them.[76] The *phaseolus* beans, equally easy to import, were first mentioned in the Old World in a Turkish document written between 1498 and 1513.[77] By 1551, William Turner had named them in English as "kidney" beans (alluding to their shape) to distinguish them from the Old World bean.[78] The groundnut was grown from seed and grew well in European gardens, as Cornut's illustration showed.

Not all plants, however, could be grown from seeds or nuts, and methods were devised to ensure safe shipment of bulbs, rootstocks, and live plants. Bulbs and rootstocks, even if carefully packed, could be desiccated by long transport or soaked in saltwater on a rough passage. Petrus Hondius planted a shrivelled tuber of Jerusalem artichoke in his garden at Terneuzen in 1613 and was amazed that it survived to reproduce.[79] Transatlantic shipment could be especially hazardous for live plants such as saplings or small shrubs. These were often planted in half barrels and required regular watering with fresh water (often in short supply at sea) and protection from exposure. Remarkable, indeed, was the arrival in France in the early 1620s of "les fraises du Canada," which must have come as delicate live plants. There is no description of the difficulties of their transport, but they were probably similar to those experienced by Amédée François Frézier, the French engineer who introduced the Chilean strawberry to France in 1714. In a letter, he describes his voyage from South America to France: "I returned in a merchant vessel from Marseilles, owned by the Bruny brothers, whereon they had placed as Supercargo, that is to say, entrusted with commerce, their nephew, M. Roux of Valbonne, who, after the captain, had the sole right to regulate the consumption of fresh water, which is very precious in a voyage of six months sailing ... through the torrid zone; so that if he had not taken it to heart to water these plants encased in a pot of soil, it would have been impossible for me to preserve them until our arrival at Marseilles, where there were five living ones."[80]

The passage from New France was shorter, but the perils were not dissimilar, and the New World strawberry plants that the royal gardeners, the Robins, had cultivated at Paris nearly one hundred years before (listed in their 1624 catalogue) must also have benefited from solicitous nursing on their Atlantic crossing. (Some fruits, such as pineapples and bananas, though shipped to Europe soon after their discovery, resisted efforts at cultivation for centuries. It was not until the 1730s, for example, that Linnaeus was able to nurture the banana into flower and fruit in George Clifford's garden at Hartekamp.)

Even once safely planted in a nurseryman's garden, the future of an exotic plant was far from secure. Gardeners would enquire of those who had seen the plant in its native habitat for advice on growing conditions, and the herbals and gardening literature are replete with notes of plants that failed to thrive in their new homes. John Gerard, in the dedication in his *Herball*, notes that he has "laboured with the soile to make it fit for plants, and with the plants that they might delight in the soile, that so they might live and prosper under our clymat, as in their native and proper countrey." Despite his best efforts, he could not make the sweet potato that he had bought at the Exchange in London come into flower.[81] Other plants took to their new environment with vigour. The squashes in fact were so prolific and so readily adaptable to European conditions that by the sixteenth century artists were including them in genre paintings of market scenes. And to underline that these were home-grown vegetables and not imports, Vincenzo Campi included a box of squash flowers plucked fresh from the vine in his 1580 painting *The Fruit Seller*.[82] Further, Parkinson notes that the Jerusalem artichoke had become commonplace, and Lescarbot complains that the groundnuts "have increased so much that to-day all the gardens are full of them."[83]

By the seventeenth century, New World exotics – especially corn, peppers, and tomatoes – were beginning to transform the diets of the peoples of the Mediterranean. In northern Europe, the transformation was much more gradual. While the French and the English were certainly aware of the new exotic plants, for the most part the plants were confined to specialist gardens or apothecary shelves. What was transforming the French and even the English diet in the sixteenth and seventeenth centuries was an increasing interest in vegetables, legumes, and fungi. Vegetables had long been considered "peasant food," since the upper class ate meat and fish. In Italy, however, salads had always formed part of the menu, and as the fashion for things Italian spread, so did the taste for vegetables. Jean-Louis Flandrin has examined cookbooks from 1300 to 1740 and quantified this change in taste. From 1300 to 1660, the percentage of dishes including vegetables quadrupled, while the number of species mentioned doubled.[84] For example, in *Le viandier de Taillevant*, written at the end of the fifteenth century, the only vegetables mentioned are peas, beans (fava), leeks, onions, and cabbages. By the mid-seventeenth century, when Nicolas de Bonnefons published *Les délices de la campagne*, he included fifty-six pages of recipes for vegetables, including such new foods as pumpkin (*citrouille*), potatoes, and haricot beans. Flandrin also points out that three families of vegetables were unusually prominent: mushrooms, artichokes, and cardoons. The fruits of the New World pictured by Champlain thus found a place within this new interest in the products of the kitchen garden, permitting Europeans to savour the flavours of the New World, though made familiar through acts of culinary transformation.

Squash

The squashes of the New World slipped easily into the European kitchen. Similar in shape and habits of growth to the melons, gourds, and cucumbers of the Old World, they were very early incorporated into European cuisine and by the beginning of the seventeenth century were familiar both to gardeners and cooks. John Gerard averred that "[t]he pulpe of the Pompion [pumpkin] is never eaten raw, but boiled ... The fruit boiled in milke and buttered, is not onely a good wholesome meate for mans bodie, but being so prepared, is also a most phisicall medicine for such as have an hot stomacke ... The flesh or pulpe of the same sliced and fried in a pan with butter, is also a good and wholesome meate: but baked with apples in an oven, it doth fil the bodie with flatuous or windie belchings, and is foode utterly unwholesome for such as live idly; but unto robustious and rusticke people nothing hurteth that filleth the belly."[85]

John Parkinson also recommended boiling pumpkins in "faire water and salt, or in powdered beefe broth, or sometimes in milke, and so eaten, or else buttered." Only the "poore of the Citie as well as the Country people" ate their pumpkins stuffed with apples, and baked, being evidently robust and rustic enough to digest the dish without grave consequence.[86] The French, according to Nicolas Bonnefons, preferred their pumpkin parboiled and then fried with onion and salted and spiced, like cucumbers. Pumpkins could also serve to "counterfeit" chestnuts or *andouillettes* of veal (a kind of sausage). Simply take cooked pumpkin, mash with fresh butter, the yolks of hard boiled eggs as well as raw eggs, chopped parsley or herbs and assorted spices; form into chestnut or sausage shapes, then place in a shallow earthenware dish (*lichefritte*) or silver basin, and cook, turning often until browned. Mushrooms added to the mix improve the taste.[87] The French may have preferred their pumpkin savoury, but according to Bonnefons, they also used cooked strained pumpkin to make rich golden bread, excellent for those in need of nourishment.[88]

Jerusalem Artichoke or Topinambours

The European, or globe, artichoke (*Cynara scolymus*) and its wild relative the cardoon (*Cynara cardunculus*) were much appreciated in the late sixteenth and the seventeenth centuries. Thus, the New World plant with an artichoke-flavoured root – discovered by Champlain and enjoyed by explorers and settlers in New France – was soon incorporated into the French kitchen. The plant was prolific in its new home and was easily prepared.[89] Lescarbot, writing in 1617, says that the tubers were eaten "in the manner spoken of by Pliny," cooked in water with a little vinegar or "roasted under the embers, or eaten raw with pepper, or with oil or salt."[90] Bonnefons suggests that the root be parboiled, peeled, and napped with a "sauce Allemagne," or cut into slices, fried with parsley or battered, like *scorsonnere* (Spanish salsify). It also bore a whiff of the exotic, being named *topinambour* after a group of Topinamboux from Brazil, who were brought to Paris by Seigneur de Razilly (later Governor of Acadia) in 1613. The group's appearance created a sensation, and street-hawkers who were attempting to sell the new vegetable thought to benefit from the rage for things Brazilian by naming their product *topinambours*.[91]

According to Parkinson, the English had grown tired of the "[p]otato's of Canada," which they boiled till tender, peeled, and then stewed in butter and wine: "[T]oo frequent use, especially being so plentifull and cheape, hath rather bred an loathing then a liking of them."[92] Gerard's 1633 *Herball* concurred: "These rootes are dressed in divers waies; some boile them in water, and after stew them with sacke and butter, adding a little Ginger: others bake them in pies, putting Marrow, Dates, Ginger, Raisons of the Sun, Sacke, &c. Others some other way, as they are led by their skill in Cookerie. But in my iudgement, which way soever they be drest and eaten they stirre and cause a filthie loathsome stinking winde within the bodie, thereby causing the belly to bee pained and tormented, and are a meat more fit for swine, than men."[93]

Parkinson notes that the English also ate the head or bud of the large sunflower (*Helianthus annus*), associating it with the European artichoke: "[S]ometimes the heads of the Sunne-Flower are dressed, and eaten as Hartichokes are, and are accounted to be of good meate, but they are too strong for my taste."[94] Gerard gives a recipe (of an aphrodisiacal cast) for the marigold of Peru: "[T]he buddes before they be flowred, boiled and eaten with butter, vineger, and pepper, after the manner of Artichoks, are exceeding pleasant meate, surpassing the Artichoke farre in procuring bodilie lust. The same buds with the stalks neere unto the top (the hairinesse being taken away) broiled upon a gridiron, and afterwarde eaten with oile, vineger, and pepper, have the like property."[95]

Beans

Madeleine de Scudéry, in *La promenade de Versailles* (1669), cites the early seventeenth-century poet Jean-François Sarasin, who wrote in praise of peas and fava beans, the two traditional green vegetables of spring in France:

> *Bisques, dindons, pois et fèves nouvelles*
> *Charment les Belles*
> *Et les Amours,*
> *Qui sont enfants, veulent manger toujours.*[96]

The New World haricot bean fitted easily into this complex. It could be eaten green in spring, with the "string" removed, then parboiled, sautéed, and seasoned like peas, or made richer with the addition of cream. If the green beans had been preserved in salt, they could be made into purées or fried like preserved cucumbers. Dried, they could be cooked in water, then fricasseed with a little onion and seasoned like peas with a bit of vinegar. In a thin soup, they were food fit for the best tables.[97] The English, at least according to Gerard, did not develop a taste for the dried bean: "The fruit and cods of Kidney Beanes boyled togither before they be ripe, and buttered, and so eaten with their cods, are exceeding delicate meate, and do not ingender winde as the other Pulses doe. They doe also gently loose the belly, provoke urine, and ingender good bloud reasonably well; but if you eate them when they be ripe, they are neither toothsome nor wholsome. Therefore they are to be taken whilest they are yet greene and tender."[98] Parkinson echoes Bonnefons in his opinion that the fava bean is a dish fit only for the poor, but the "French or Kidney beane" is esteemed a "a savory meate to many mens palates ..., a dish more oftentimes at rich mens Tables than at the poore."[99]

Strawberries

While strawberries were not new to Europeans, they were not cultivated widely until the sixteenth century. In England the bishop of Ely grew strawberries at Holborn in the late 1400s, but most were still being collected for sale from "woodes and grenes, and shadowy places."[100] The French were growing strawberries by the 1560s, and instructions for cultivation appeared in *L'agriculture, et maison rustique*, published in 1578, though the plant was praised more for its medicinal than gustatory qualities.[101] By the end of the century, however, strawberries had become popular garden fruits, much enjoyed in the summer, when they were eaten with wine and sugar.[102] This was the for the most part the woodland strawberry, *Fragaria vesca*, although other varieties were known, especially the musky-flavoured strawberry, *Fragaria moschata*, mentioned by the Robins in their 1624 catalogue. The circumstances of the introduction to Europe of the Virginian or Canada strawberry are unclear. The Robins cite a *Fragaria americana* in their 1624 catalogue, and Parkinson refers to the "Virginia strawberry," which he complains rarely bore ripe berries. He also refers to a plant that John Tradescant "brought with him from Brussels long agoe, and in seven years could never see one berry ripe on all sides."[103] If Tradescant did bring a plant back from Brussels at the time he included the "New England" strawberry (*Fragaria nova anglia nondum descripta*) in his 1616 manuscript catalogue, it may have been derived from plants in Paris. Two strawberries are depicted in Champlain's horticultural map border, and on 21 May 1626, Nicolas-Claude Fabri Peiresc wrote in a letter to his half-brother that he had at last eaten the strawberries of Canada, which he found excellent, more fragrant than the common, and almost musky in flavour – and he noted that there were two kinds.[104] Peiresc was in touch with the Robins, and it is likely he received the plants from them. Given the difficulties of transporting the live plants, the strawberries of New France may well have been brought to Paris by a number of different carriers. Cultivating them, as Parkinson notes, was no simple task, and the lapse of time between the depiction of the two strawberries on Champlain's map and Peiresc's appreciation of the berries may have been the result of the time required to produce a sufficiently robust cultivated plant that bore reliably.

CURIOSITY TO EDIBILITY

Champlain and other explorers tasted the fruits of the New World in their travels, both as prepared by Aboriginal hosts and as they themselves incorporated novel plants into their traditional diet. Many Europeans had a poor opinion of Aboriginal cuisine, primarily because, as both Champlain and Cartier said, it lacked salt, a taste to which the French, and particularly mariners who ate salted meat and fish, were habituated. They could also object to its manner of preparation. Champlain at one point refused to share his hosts' meal of meat and fish roasted or boiled and a kind of "bouillie," a salt-less mush of cornmeal, meat, and fish cooked together. He preferred to cook in his own "mode."[105] Distaste for Aboriginal cuisine, however, did not extend to the foods themselves, as Champlain, Lescarbot, and others often note. Fresh fish, shellfish, game, birds (including turkeys and geese), exotics like the Jerusalem artichoke and groundnut, plus more familiar fruits and nuts, were welcomed on the European table in the New World. Marc Lescarbot records that cranberries made an excellent jelly for dessert; Champlain made juice from local grapes;[106] and they both relished the roots introduced to them by the Aboriginal inhabitants. As many authors have observed, however, foodways are deeply embedded in a culture, and they often act as markers of that culture, particularly when one culture is confronted with another.[107] It was not unexpected that the French at Port-Royal should choose to use food as a marker of their culture during the winter of 1606–7 when Lescarbot organized the Order of Good Cheer. Strange foods were made familiar through techniques of preparation – elk in meat pies, cranberries as *cotignac*.[108]

The food plants the explorers brought back to France were those that could survive the rough handling of a sea voyage and flourish in the gardens of northern France and, later, England. It is not surprising that many New World plants were cultivated in the botanical gardens, but what is surprising is the selection of those that became popular with European cooks and eaters. What are the factors that contributed to the popularity of an exotic food in the Old World? What made pumpkins a staple and potatoes suspicious (at least for the French in the sixteenth and seventeenth centuries)? Ken Albala, in *Eating Right in the Renaissance*, maintains that the key to early adoption was whether or not "the new food was considered analogous to something already standard in the diet or could be substituted in a recipe with comparable results."[109] Their similarity to Old World melons, gourds, and cucumbers would certainly explain the swift incorporation of pumpkins and squashes into the European diet. Not only could the writers of natural histories find references to similar plants in Pliny, but traditional methods of propagation, cultivation, and preparation for the table were readily adaptable to the new "melons," with which pumpkins and squashes were grouped by both botanists and gardeners. Similarly, the kidney bean was easily grown alongside the fava, and few authors distinguished the former as an exotic, though the English did refer to it as the "French" bean. Corn, which seemed so remarkable to Dodoens for the manner in which it bore its fruit and flower, was similar enough to millet that it could be readily adopted by millet-eating cultures such as Italy, Spain, and Romania,[110] but was easily disdained by the wheaten bread–eating French, for whom a day-old tortilla or boiled cornmeal mush was not considered proper food.

Resemblance was thus important, both in appearance and taste. The pineapple – at first outlandish to European eyes, but delicious – could be likened in appearance to the thistle, and by analogy to the globe artichoke, the newly fashionable food of the sixteenth and seventeenth centuries.[111] The groundnut resembled in its subterranean growth the truffle, another fashionable food of this period, and Lescarbot relates that "chiquebi" grew well under oak trees, the truffle habitat.[112] The Jerusalem artichoke was also known as *le truffe du Canada*,[113] linking it in its underground growth habit to the fragrant fungus. Resemblance in appearance, then, could contribute to a new food's acceptance, even if the tastes were dissimilar, as in pineapples and artichokes, or truffles and topinambours. Resemblance in appearance could also be linked with similarity of taste. The flower of the Jerusalem artichoke resembles the flower of the sunflower, and that may also explain what encouraged some people to eat the flower head of the latter, ascribing to it an artichoke taste. Resemblance in taste could, however, override dissimilarity of appearance or even of the part eaten, as is the case with globe artichokes (of which the flower head is eaten) and Jerusalem artichokes (of which the tuberous root is the part consumed). It could also trump even the deadliest of appearances, as can be seen in the history of the capsicum pepper.

Tomatoes, potatoes, and eggplants, all members of the plant family Solanaceae, were recognized as being related to the poisonous nightshades, and although tomatoes and eggplants were early adopted and eaten in the Mediterranean, they did not enter the northern European diet until much later. The eggplant was called *mala insana* or *pomi disdesgnosi*, and its consumption was blamed for all manner of diseases, including leprosy, headaches, hardening of the liver and spleen, and a bad complexion.[114] The supposed leprous appearance of the potato tuber led to its being reported as banned in some areas of France.[115] The capsicum peppers, however, though members of the same family as the tomatoes and the *mala insana,* were hot to the taste and thus equated with the "pepper" of the East, long prized as a spice for its hot and dry qualities (in Galenic terms).[116] Tobacco, another Solanaceae plant, was thought of as hot and thus beneficial from a medicinal point of view to "warm the stomach," as Lescarbot notes.[117] Taste, used in this way as a fundamental classificatory characteristic, is foreign to us, conditioned as we are by the Linnaean emphasis on visual description. A pre-Linnaean botanist like Jacques-Philippe Cornut uses taste as an important descriptive characteristic for nondescripts. While we would hesitate to ingest even the berries of a familiar plant in the wild, Cornut tasted the leaves and roots and fruits of almost all the plants he describes, looking for pharmaceuticals, believing that similar tastes might indicate similar properties. The Origanum fistulosum Canadensis (*Monarda fistulosa*), or wild bergamot, tastes very acrid and burns the tongue like pepper, except for the root, which by he knows not what caprice of nature Cornut finds insipid. The Edera quinquefolia Canadensis (*Parthencissus quinquefolia*), or Virginia creeper, has a sharp, slightly acrid flavour. The Solanum triphyllum Canadensis (*Trillium erectum*), or red trillium, tastes sweet.[118] Rarely does he mention a potential alimentary purpose; only in the description of Asaron Canadense (*Asarum canadense*), or wild ginger, does he describe the use of its roots in flavouring wine.[119]

Finally, provenance could also affect the way in which a new food was perceived. Capsicum peppers were generally not imported into Europe directly from the New World; rather, they followed a circuitous trade route from Mexico through Portuguese hands to the Azores and Madeira, then to Goa and India, returning to the Mediterranean world in the cargoes of the traditional traders, the Turks.[120] The arrival of new foods from the Orient, where Europeans had for centuries sought spices and other gastronomic novelties, placed the New World foods into a framework through which they gained a more ready acceptance. This trade pattern also accounts for the descriptive terms like "Turkish" or "Indian" that were applied to New World products transhipped through the eastern Mediterranean (Dodoens's "Turkish wheat," for example). Although Salaman argues convincingly that the appellation of

"Jerusalem" for the knobbly tubers of *Helianthus tuberosus* was an English mispronunciation of the name of a Dutch village (Terneuzen), it is significant that the mispronunciation resulted in a name evocative of the exotic eastern markets.[121] Exoticism could also be a factor in a food's rise in popularity. Certainly the link to Brazil fuelled the rage for *topinambours* in France, and the appellation of "Peru" (Miracle of Peru, cornflower of Peru, Peruvian marigold) evoked rarity and foreign lands. Origin in Virginia or Canada made the newly imported North American strawberry more desirable, although the attribution to Virginia did not succeed in overcoming an initial distaste for the Virginia potato, even in England.

Familiarity, whether in appearance, taste, or origin, and ease of propagation would seem to be the principal factors in the incorporation of the new into the daily menu. Pumpkins, squash, and strawberries found ready acceptance in European gardens and kitchens. More surprising, perhaps, was the way in which flavours dictated the acceptance of truly unusual foods, varying widely in habit or appearance from the familiar. The prized artichoke flavour, shared in fact by members of the lettuce family, led to an appreciation of the tuber of a New World sunflower.[122] The newly discovered taste for the earthy truffle led the French to sample the underground roots and tubers of numerous plants, from the groundnut to the potato, seeking for that elusive perfume. Flavours also brought the truly strange and outlandish into the European culinary universe. Champlain, travelling through Central America or New France, finds gustatory analogies for the nondescripts he encounters: custard apples (*Anona reticulata*) taste like sugared cream; avocadoes are reminiscent of green walnuts; strange tubers are redolent of artichokes or truffles; sweet potatoes are like chestnuts in flavour. When he can find no analogy, he categorizes certain fruits or nuts simply as tasting good, and often that means sweet, as in the case of the pineapple. Champlain arrived in the New World with the palate of a seventeenth-century Frenchman, and even when the habit of growth or the shape or colour of a plant confounds him, his tongue leads him, nevertheless, to discover a cornucopia of new and acceptable foods. Taste, considered as that quality which distinguishes a food, can unite the dissimilar in a universe of the edible.

1 Seeds arrived accidentally in the New World via the manure of cattle imported by Spaniards or, in the case of oranges and peaches, when carelessly tossed away by fruit-loving conquistadores. Crosby, *Ecological Imperialism*, 198, 51. The mitigated success that followed the deliberate introduction of sugar cane to the West Indies has been well documented (Mintz, *Sweetness and Power*), as has the history of the migration of the once exotic but now most prosaic of foods, the New World potato (Salaman, *History and Social Influence of the Potato*).

2 Pasta was developed in the Middle East, passed through Spain via the Arabs, and settled in Italy, where, according to Matthiolus, the tomato, relished by the Spaniards, was eaten as early as the 1540s. McCue, "History and Use of the Tomato," 291.

3 According to Alan Davidson, the word "cacao" is derived from a word of Mixe-Zoquean origin from the Olmec culture, while "chocolate" is probably a Spanish blending of the Mayan word *chocol* or "hot" with the Nahautl word for water, *atl*. Davidson, *Penguin Companion to Food*, 212.

4 Paris, "History of the Cultivar-Groups," 162.

5 Rappaport, *How We Eat* 39.

6 Toussaint-Samat, *History of Food*, 677. The story may be apocryphal, but the poor condition of a pineapple after possibly months of transatlantic passage would certainly have affected its flavour, as Ovideo noted in 1535. See reference in Tomás and Terrada, *Las primeras noticias sobre plantas Americanas*, 186.

7 Cartier, "Second Voyage," in *Voyages*, 37. Ramsay Cook provides a commentary to H.P. Biggar's English translations of Cartier's voyages plus additional documents. The *Relations* of Jacques Cartier are published in an Édition critique by Michel Bideaux. I have consulted both editions, but used the English translations in Cook.

8 Ibid., 82.

9 Cartier, "Third Voyage," in *Voyages,* 106. After the second voyage, a Portuguese agent reported somewhat sceptically to his master, Joao III, "There are many mines of gold and silver in great abundance ... and that there is abundance of clove, nutmeg, and pepper" and "a river at whose mouth were oranges and pomegranates." Cartier, "Letter from Lagarto to John the Third, King of Portugal," in *Voyages*, 131.

10 Cartier, "Third Voyage," in *Voyages*, 101. Cartier's diamonds turned out to be pyrites, though the name Cap au Diamant has persisted in Quebec City. A popular expression in French is "false as the diamonds of Canada."

11 Champlain, *Les Voyages,* 1613 (1922).

12 Quinn, quoted in Allen, "From Cabot to Cartier," 507.

13 Pope, *Fish into Wine,* 11. Cabot had reported to Henry VII on the abundance of fish: "And they say that the land is excellent and [the air] temperate, and they think that Brazil wood and silks grow there; and they affirm that the sea is covered with fish which are caught not merely with nets but with baskets, a stone being attached to make the basket sink in the water, and this I heard the said Master Zoanne relate. And said Englishmen, his companions, say that they will fetch so many fish that this kingdom will have no more need of Iceland, from which country there comes a very great store of fish which are called stock-fish." Extract from "The Soncino Letters," reproduced in Biggar, ed. *The Precursors of Jacques Cartier 1497–1534,* http://www.heritage.nf.ca/exploration/soncino.html.

14 Turgeon, "French Fishers," 592.

15 Cartier, "First Voyage," in *Voyages,* 14.

16 Ibid., 17–18.

17 Ibid., 22–5.

18 Ibid., "Second Voyage," in *Voyages,* 49, 51.

19 Ibid., 57. The native grape is the fox grape, *Vitis labrusca,* unfortunately not noted for its quality as a wine grape.

20 Ibid., 69.

21 Ibid., 61.

22 Tomás and Terrada, *Las primeras noticias sobre plantas,* 145–6. Corn (*Zea mays*), though called "Turkish wheat" by botanists such as Dodoens, Boch, Fuchs, or Lobel, resembled cultivated millet (*Panicum* sp.) and was thus adopted in countries where millet was already a staple, such as Spain and Italy. According to Rebora, millet had entered Tuscany and Venice in the first half of the sixteenth century. Rebora, *Culture of the Fork,* 123–5. See also the illustration from Rembert Dodoens, *Cruijdeboeck* (1554), 506–7, http://leesmaar.nl/cruijdeboeck/lr/00497.jpg.

23 Cartier and later Champlain would comment on the seeming abundance of the natural products of the New World. Cartier marvels at the quantity of acorns and wild vines, but he also notes ruefully that while the latter were full of grapes, their flavour was not as agreeable as the flavour of grapes in France, a deficit he attributed to their lack of proper cultivation. Cartier, "Third Voyage," in *Voyages,* 100.

24 Roberval, "Voyage de Jean-François de la Rocque," 264. Champlain also refused to eat in the Native manner, again citing the lack of salt, as well as the methods of preparation.

25 "[V]ng vray & euident myracle." Cartier, *Bref récit et succincte narration,* 38, http://gallica.bnf.fr/ark:/12148/bpt6k1096855/f111.chemindefer.

26 Belon, *Petri bellonii cenomani de arboribus coniseris,* 38, http://visualiseur.bnf.fr/Visualiseur?Destination=Gallica&O=NUMM-52155.

27 Thevet, *Singularités de la France antarctique,* http://visualiseur.bnf.fr/Visualiseur?Destination=Gallica&O=NUMM-109516.

28 Clusius, *Rariorum plantarum historia,* http://caliban.mpiz-koeln.mpg.de/~stueber/ecluse/index.html. See also Rousseau, "L'annedda et l'arbre de vie."

29 Monardes, *Joyfull Newes,* http://visualiseur.bnf.fr/CadresFenetre?O=NUMM-53997.

30 Thevet, *Singularités de la France Antarctique.* Maple sugar was later imported to France and refined at Rouen, according to a report in the *Philosophical Transactions* in 1685 (171, p. 988). The sugar was used to make a syrup of "Maiden Hair" (*Adianthum capillus-veneris*), which became a popular drink, known as *Capillaire,* in the seventeenth and eighteenth centuries. "An Account of a Sort of Sugar," http://www.jstor.org/stable/102141.

31 The flaming colour of the sugar maple in the fall was still a wonder to Europeans as late as the mid-eighteenth century, when Thomas Davies issued a series of engravings of the autumns of Canada, one of which when coloured was designed to show the true colours of the autumnal Canadian woods. See discussion in Dickenson, *Drawn from Life,* 195–6.

32 See the discussion in Gagnon, "Champlain: Painter?" 302–11.

33 Champlain, *Brief Discours,* 4.

34 Ibid., 15.

35 See Columbus, letter, http://www.usm.maine.edu/~maps/columbus/translation.html. Also see Greenblatt, *Possessions,* 77–8.

36 Champlain, *Brief Discours,* 39–40.

37 Ibid., 20.

38 Ibid., 39.

39 Ibid., 45.

40 Ibid., 47–9.

41 Ibid., 52–3.

42 Ibid., 75.

43 See the online catalogue at the John Carter Brown Library: *Brief Discours,* http://www.brown.edu/Facilities/John_Carter_Brown_Library/pages/ea_hmpg.html. Search "Champlain."

44 Champlain, *Des sauvages,* 131. According to Biggar, the "pears" are shadbush or "swamp sugar pear," the green "currants," gooseberries.

45 Ibid., 134.

46 Ibid., 140. The black walnut (*Juglans nigra*) is indeed native to North America, as is the butternut (also called white walnut, *Juglans cinerea*). The fruit of the shagbark hickory (*Carya ovata*), while not a walnut, might be mistaken for a small walnut.

47 Ibid., 145. The identification of *noizette* is problematic, since hazelnuts are not native. Champlain is likely referring to the beechnut.

48 Champlain, *Les Voyages,* 1613 (1922), 341.

49 Ibid., 351.

50 Ibid., 358.

51 Ganong, "Identity of Plants and Animals," 201.

52 Champlain, *Les Voyages,* 1613 (1925), 59–61. Champlain spends considerable time discussing the causes of scurvy, which he attributes to a winter diet of too much salted food and vegetables, "which heat the blood and corrupt the inward parts," and partly to the winter, "for it checks the natural heat and causes greater corruption of the blood." Champlain, *Les Voyages,* 1613 (1925), 59–60.

53 Champlain appears to have taken pains and pleasure in his gardens. He notes that at Ile Ste-Croix he made his garden "fairly big." Champlain, *Les Voyages,* 1:301. At Montreal, he had "two gardens made" (*Les Voyages,* 2:179), while at Trois Rivières, he planted rosebushes (*Les Voyages,* 2:213). He was vexed over the poor care his gardens at Quebec had received in his absence (*Les Voyages,* 2:147). See also the article by Paul-Louis Martin, "Domestication of the Countryside and Provision of Supplies," in Litalien and Vaugeois, *Champlain,* 205–17.

54 See Gagnon, "Champlain: Painter?" 307.

55 Fuchs, "Den nieuwen Herbarius," 138–9, http://caliban.mpiz-koeln.mpg.de/~stueber/fuchs/herbarius/index.html.

56 Parkinson, *Paradisi in Sole,* http://www.abocamuseum.it/bibliothecaantiqua/Book_View.asp?Id_Book=458.

57 Columbus, "... maíz ... de que lleva allá, y ay ya mucho en Castilla," quoted in Tomás and Terrade, *Las primeras noticias sobre plantas,* 145–6.

58 Cartier, "First Voyage," in *Voyages,* 25. Cartier in 1535 referred to corn as "groz mil comme poix ainsi que au Bresil." Cartier, *Relations,* 115. According to Bideaux, corn was described in Pigafetta's account of Magellan's voyage as a Brazilian equivalent of millet. Cartier, *Relations,* 336n274.

59 Dodoens, *A new herbal,* http://visualiseur.bnf.fr/CadresFenetre?O=NUMM-98774.

60 Champlain, *Les Voyages,* 1613 (1922), 351.

61 Ibid., 397.

62 Lescarbot, *History of New France*, 254. Lescarbot actually confused the Jerusalem artichoke with the groundnut (*Apios americana*), as is explained in Salaman, "Why 'Jerusalem' Artichoke?" 342–3.

63 Parkinson, *Paradisi in paradisus terrestris,* 517, http://visualiseur.bnf.fr/CadresFenetre?O=NUMM-97995.

64 Medsger, *Edible Wild Plants,* 199. It might also refer to the Spring Beauty (*Claytonia* sp.), equally prized by the Native community. Medsger, *Edible Wild Plants*, 198. Meriweather Lewis described the Claytonia as "of an irregularly rounded form, something like the smallest of the Jarusolem artichoke, which they also resemble in every other appearance. they had become very hard by being dryed these I also boiled agreeably to the instruction of the Indians and found them very agreeable. they resemble the Jerusalem Artichoke very much in their flavor and I thought them preferable, however there is some allowance to be made for the length of time I have now been without vegitable food to which I was always much attatched. these are certainly the best root I have yet seen in uce among the Indians." Louis Meriwether, "Excerpts from the Journals of Lewis and Clark," http://www.lewis-clark.org/content/content-article.asp?ArticleID=2163.

65 Ganong, "Identity of Plants and Animals," 235.

66 Champlain says that on islands off the coast of Maine there are "so many red currants that one can hardly see anything else." Champlain, *Les Voyages,* 1613 (1922), 332.

67 Champlain, *Des Sauvages*, 131

68 Lescarbot, *History of New France*, 254.

69 Cornut, *Canadensium plantarum*, chap. 76. See also Mathieu and Daviault, *Premier Livre*, 327. Daviault translates "ex siliquis" as "à partir de gousse."

70 Lescarbot, *History of New France*, 256.

71 Champlain, *Les Voyages,* 1613 (1925), part 2, 177.

72 Author's experience.

73 See my discussion in Dickenson, *Drawn from Life*, chap. 2.

74 This practice was widespread even after Linnaeus and his followers demanded new standards of accuracy in plant illustration. The engravings of plants for de Charlevoix's 1744 *Histoire et description générale de la Nouvelle France* were copied directly from Cornut's work of 1635. See Dickenson, *Drawn from Life,* 99–102.

75 Some delicate seeds were shipped in small boxes covered in wax; others were wrapped in clay mixed with honey. Mathieu and Daviault, *Premier Livre*, 84–6.

76 Paris, "History of the Cultivar-Groups," 86.

77 Noted in Andrews, "Diffusion of Mesoamerican Food Complex," 200.

78 "Two New Beans from America," http://aggie-horticulture.tamu.edu/
plantanswers/publications/vegetabletravelers/beans.html. William Turner
published the first part of *A new Herball* in 1551.

79 Salaman, "Why 'Jerusalem' Artichoke?" 346.

80 Cited in Darrow, *Strawberry*, 32.

81 From the Epistle Dedicatorie, in Gerard, *Herball* (1597),
http://caliban.mpiz-koeln.mpg.de/~stueber/gerarde/high/IMG_0488.html.

82 Janick and Paris, "Early Evidence," http://www.hort.purdue.edu/newcrop/
Squash_flowers.pdf.

83 Lescarbot, *History of New France*, 254.

84 Flandrin, "Dietary Choices," 404–5.

85 Gerard, *Herball* (1597), 775.

86 Parkinson, *Paradisi in paradisus terrestris*, 526.

87 Bonnefons, *Délices de la campagne*, 123,
http://visualiseur.bnf.fr/CadresFenetre?O=NUMM-108861.

88 Ibid., 16.

89 It was so prolific that only a few years after its introduction to Europe, the
French were using it, in place of acorns and chestnuts, to fatten cattle and swine.
Salaman, *History and Social Influence*, 343.

90 Lescarbot, *History of New France*, 254. Pliny, of course, had not described
Jerusalem artichokes, but rather the *afrodille* (Asphodel) with which Lescarbot
confused them.

91 Salaman, *History and Social Influence*, 133.

92 Parkinson, *Paradisi in paradisus terrestris*, 518.

93 Gerard, *Herball* (1633), http://www.thousandeggs.com/
gerardp4.html#Sunflower. The Jerusalem artichoke does not, of course,
appear in the 1597 edition.

94 Quoted in Heiser, *Sunflower*, 49.

95 Gerard, *Herball* (1633).

96 de Scudéry, *La Promenade de Versailles*, 254.

97 Bonnefons, *Délices de la campagne*, 155.

98 Gerard, *Herball* (1633).

99 Parkinson, *Paradisi in paradisus terrestris*, 521.

100 Darrow, *Strawberry*, 17. Parkinson notes the medicinal values of decoctions
of strawberry leaves; he also notes that the berries are served in summer with
claret wine, cream, or milk as well as sugar, and that the water distilled from

the berries is "good for passions of the heart." Parkinson. *Paradisi in paradisus terrestris*, 528.

101 Estienne and Liébault, *L'agriculture,* 100b, http://visualiseur.bnf.fr/CadresFenetre?O=NUMM-52718.

102 Hyll, *Gardener's Labyrinth* (1593), cited in Darrow, *Strawberry*, 18.

103 Parkinson, *Paradisi in paradisus terrestris.*

104 Cited in Mathieu and Daviault, *Premier livre,* 169–70. The two varieties might be *Fragaria americana* and *Fragaria virginiana*, both introduced in the seventeenth century. See Darrow, *Strawberry,* chap. 3. Peiresc also noted the table qualities of squash and grapes from Canada.

105 Cartier, "First Voyage," in *Voyages*, 26; Champlain, *Les Voyages,* 1613 (1925), 282.

106 Lescarbot, *History of New France*, 257; Champlain, *Les Voyages,* 1613 (1922), 329.

107 See comments in Turgeon and Dickner, "Contraintes et choix alimentaires," 229.

108 Lescarbot, *History of New France*, 441. *Cotignac* is a kind of quince jam or preserve.

109 Albala, *Eating Right in the Renaissance*, 233.

110 For a discussion of the adoption of maize, beans, and pumpkins in Romaina, see Vaduva, "Introduction of Maize."

111 Albala, *Eating Right in the Renaissance*, 236.

112 Champlain, *Sauvages,* 131; Lescarbot, *History of New France,* 257. Cornut depicts the *Apios americana* growing on a trellis in the Robin garden, with the tubers revealed, which he affirmed were indeed good to eat. Mathieu and Daviault, *Premier Livre,* 327.

113 Salaman, *History and Social Influence,* 109.

114 David, "Mad, Bad, Despised and Dangerous," 189–90.

115 Salaman, *History and Social Influence*, 108–9.

116 Galen was a second-century Greek physician famous in the Renaissance. His theoretical writings on humoral physiology long dominated ideas about diet. The four humours refer to fluids in the human body: blood, choler, phlegm, and bile, and a balance of the humours is essential for health. That balance can be altered by the qualities of the foods ingested, and foods are characterized as being hot, cold, wet, or dry, or various combinations of these qualities.

117 Lescarbot, *History of New France*, 176. Cartier, too, had likened the Aboriginal powdered tobacco to ground pepper for is hotness.

118 Mathieu and Daviault, *Premier Livre,* 259, 99, 307.

119 Ibid., 263.

120 Jean Andrews argues that the Mesoamerican food complex of beans, maize, pepper, squash, and turkey moved along Portuguese trade corridors and

returned to Europe through Turkey, hence the names for maize (Turkey wheat, *blé d'Inde*), tomatoes (*pomo di Moro*), for turkey (*dinde*), etc. Andrews, "Diffusion of Mesoamerican Food."

121 Salaman, "Why 'Jerusalem' Artichoke?" 383.

122 Harold McGee notes that the Jerusalem artichoke (sunchoke), the sunflower, and the artichoke are all members of the lettuce family and share a similar flavour. McGee, *On Food and Cooking*, 328.

2

Stories of Traditional Aboriginal Food, Territory, and Health

MARGERY FEE

INTRODUCTION

The word *stories* in the title of this chapter signals both that all cultures make sense of the world through narrative and that Aboriginal voices and stories have often been missing in scholarly accounts. Elite Western narratives constrain what settlers and their descendents have been able to understand about North America and its peoples; Aboriginal stories reflect a different worldview. As the Okanagan storyteller Harry Robinson puts it, "God put the Indians in the head, in the heart for the things to know. [T]he white people, they got the paper ... [T]here is a lot of these white people ... they think that we don't know anything until the white people come."[1]

That we can now understand more of the Aboriginal worldview perhaps derives from Aboriginal peoples' increasing insistence on being heard, through telling their stories to anthropologists or collaborators, through appealing to those who govern them to do better, through resorting to political and legal action, and, finally, through learning to speak and write the colonizer's language. But we are also hearing and seeing more because of the increasingly obvious failure of Western stories to explain the world. The hole in the ozone layer, for example, and the melting ice caps have undermined our belief in Western knowledge.[2] The story of settler-Aboriginal encounters around food reveal some of the issues that require rethinking.

Tight links between food and territory are common to both European and Aboriginal cultures. The claim of the right to access, grow, or harvest particular foods is a claim to land (or fishing rights), the claim that underpinned the settlement of North America and the relegation of Aboriginal peoples to reserves or marginal land bases. Aboriginal people, construed as "savages" or hunter-gatherers, were seen as part of nature rather than as skilled agriculturalists, food processors, hunters, and fishermen. Thus, the complex economic and political systems they used in managing food resources, upheld by spiritual beliefs and ceremonial practices, were ignored, and a modernizing European agricultural, industrial, and commercial model was imposed instead. The rationale behind the early assignment of Aboriginal people to reserves and the history of land claims reveal competing ideas of what constitutes proper land and resource use.[3]

The history of colonization in North America is the history of the ongoing "nutrition transition" as more and more Aboriginal people have found themselves unable to harvest their traditional foods, either as their sole diet or to supplement a more Western one.[4] This difficulty is the result of displacement; confinement to reserves or villages; environmental pollution; restriction (usually legal) of access to game, fish, or plants; loss of cultural knowledge; and changing patterns of work and education. The nutrition transition is marked by a rapid increase in disease, such as tuberculosis and other infections that result from insufficient food; type 2 diabetes, stroke, and heart disease (sometimes called "the metabolic syndrome") that result from the wrong kind of food; or even "ecosystem illnesses," such as mercury poisoning from fish. To add insult to injury, the resulting decline in health is often attributed to supposed racial or cultural characteristics of Aboriginal people rather than to poverty or to the appropriation or contamination of land and food resources.[5] A heightened interest on the part of both researchers and the commercial sector in "traditional ecological knowledge" (TEK) – caused in some cases by hopes of accessing new foods or medicines – has met with Aboriginal resistance but has also led to productive alliances. Aboriginal communities' recent attempts to reverse the loss of traditional foodways have occurred in the context of a revitalization of the wider culture, including language and ceremony.

WESTERN AND ABORIGINAL STORIES

Repeatedly, Europeans and their descendents have not seen or heard clearly. Repeatedly, Aboriginal people have confronted the loss of their land, food, and health and have attempted to change things, usually to fail. One danger of telling the story of Aboriginal nutritional transition this way is to transform it (yet again) into a story of bad colonizers and good Aboriginals, victimized by a greedy superior power. The problem is that this binary (sometimes featuring good colonizers and bad Aboriginals) was created by the Enlightenment, the source of the Western epistemology that drove colonialism. Shepard Krech's *The Ecological Indian: Myth and History* shows that this simple opposition has real dangers; Ter Ellingson's *The Myth of the Noble Savage* offers a similar warning.[6] To accept this binary is to reaffirm the difference between "us" and "them," for one thing. It leads to simplistic arguments: for example, if Aboriginal people can be shown not to be ecologically minded, then they cannot be trusted with land and resources – a smokescreen for the fact that the dominant culture cannot be trusted either.

FOOD AND LAND

That food and territory are connected is hardly news, either to Europeans or to Aboriginal people. John Locke, in his *Second Treatise of Government* (1690), states that "as much land as a man tills, plants, improves, cultivates, and can use the product of, so much is his property. He by his labour does as it were, enclose it from the common."[7] He contrasts the industrious cultivation of the English landscape with the "the wild woods and uncultivated waste of America, left to nature."[8] Locke writes: "God gave the world to men in common ... but it cannot be supposed he meant it should always remain common and uncultivated";[9] and "[God] gave it to the use of the industrious and rational (and labour was to be his title to it)."[10] Jean-Jacques Rousseau saw private property as a great fall, a scheme of the rich, but he too saw the "savage" as

"Other": "[T]he savage man breathes only peace and freedom: he desires only to live and stay idle."[11] Thomas Hobbes argues that without a social contract and a sovereign power, "there is no place for industry, because the fruit thereof is uncertain, and consequently, [there is] no culture of the earth." This lack results in "continual fear and danger of violent death, and the life of man [is] solitary, poor, nasty, brutish and short."[12] Clearly, without a government that secured private property, there could be no order, no hard work, and no agriculture. The Indian Other was seen to lack a government, agriculture, property, and the civilized habits that derived from them.

Captain Cook was clearly familiar with these Enlightenment ideas. His journals describe "an indigenous population that was 'indolent,' 'wild & uncouth' and incapable of the most basic civilized pursuits (including agriculture), but blessed by tremendous natural wealth in the form of fish and other marine animals."[13] The first problem with this theory, of course, is that Locke's "wild woods and uncultivated waste of America" was a myth; much of the landscape was modified by various practices (like burning) intended to clear brush, promote the growth of berries and other crops, and make hunting easier.[14] This modification was invisible to European newcomers, who had never seen a natural wilderness and had arrived with the firm belief that Aboriginal people were hunter-gatherers. Peter Hulme notes that "[b]affled by the complex but effective native system of food production, the English seem to have latched on to the one (minor) facet of behaviour that they thought they recognized – mobility – and argued on that basis an absence of *proper* connection between the land and its first inhabitants."[15] The form of agriculture practised by Aboriginal nations in the eastern region of North America produced high yields, and the planting together of corn, beans, and squash meant that little weeding or watering was required.[16] That the whole community thus could leave their fields to go hunting or fishing, sometimes travelling long distances,[17] accorded better with European ideas about the wandering life of the hunter, as did the Aboriginal practice of abandoning villages to move elsewhere once the soil was exhausted. Hulme quotes the Jesuit missionary Pierre Biard writing in 1612: "[F]our thousand Indians at most roam through, rather than occupy, these vast stretches of inland territory and seashore. For they are a nomadic people."[18] Lieutenant Governor Francis Bond Head of Upper Canada summed up the prevailing attitudes in a speech to

Aboriginal nations assembled on the shores of northern Lake Huron in the summer of 1836: "In all parts of the world farmers seek for uncultivated land as eagerly as you, my red children, hunt in your forest for game. If you would cultivate your land it would then be considered your own property, in the same way your dogs are considered among yourselves to belong to those who have reared them; but uncultivated land is like wild animals, and your Great Father, who has hitherto protected you, has now great difficulty in securing it for you from the whites, who are hunting to cultivate it."[19] However, Joseph Sawyer (Kawahjegezhegwabe), chief of the Credit River Ojibway, resisted Head's plan to move his people to Manitoulin Island: "Now we raise our own corn, potatoes, wheat; we have cattle and many comforts, and conveniences. But if we go to Maneetoolin, we could not live; soon we would be extinct as a people; we could raise no potatoes, corn, pork or beef; nothing would grow by putting the seed on the smooth rock."[20] This was hardly the response of a wandering hunter. The European discourse of the Aboriginal hunter, however poorly it accorded with the facts, effectively separated the Aboriginal people from any idea of agriculture or a settled link to the land, and thus justified their removal from choice territory in favour of settlers.

The invisibility of Aboriginal management of the ecosystem to facilitate hunting and the production of food crops held true in other parts of the continent. Douglas Deur and Nancy J. Turner recount that during a fur-trading voyage in 1789, "members of John Meare's crew saw evidence of cultivated plots – probably of tobacco – within Haida villages. In his official log, Meare's assistant, William Douglas ... would assert that 'in all probability Captain Gray, in the Sloop Washington, had fallen in with this tribe, and employed his considerable friendship in forming this garden,'" although "Gray does not appear to have visited the village in question, and Meares was probably the first European to pull ashore there."[21] In fact, "the pre-contact antiquity of Haida tobacco cultivation is widely accepted."[22] Similar practices designed to enhance fish and seafood resources were also invisible.[23]

This invisibility is imbricated in Canadian laws, as is the principle that Aboriginal peoples are inferior because they do not engage in European practices. Here is Chief Justice Allan McEachern speaking on the Delgamuukw land claim in 1991 about the Aboriginal peoples' colonial exclusion from acquiring land: "I doubt if they would have long retained any land they might have obtained by pre-emption, because their culture had not prepared them for the disciplined life of a tax-paying agriculturalist."[24] Perhaps not surprisingly much of the research undertaken on Aboriginal land and resource use has been undertaken for land claims trials and other court hearings, which are a recent phenomenon. Arthur J. Ray dates much of this Aboriginal-sponsored research to the *Calder* decision of 1972, "which forced the Canadian government to address Aboriginal claims."[25]

SHARING FOOD AND FOOD TECHNOLOGIES

Ironically, many European explorers and settlers lived to tell of their experiences only because of food provided by Aboriginal peoples, often as gifts or in trade, though sometimes coerced or simply taken. Shakespeare's Caliban, referring to his first contact with Prospero and Miranda, says, "[T]hen I loved thee / And showed thee all the qualities o' th' isle, / The fresh springs, brine pits, barren place and fertile."[26] Hulme comments that "Ralph Lane's account (1586) makes clear the utter dependence of the Roanoke colony on supplies of Indian food,"[27] and this was a continuing dependence.

The fur trade relied on Aboriginal food preservation techniques that earlier had facilitated pre-contact trading. Ray notes that "Huron dried corn was an excellent travel food."[28] The Aboriginal Pacific coastal trade involved a dizzying array of foodstuffs, including dried seaweed, eulachon oil, dried and smoked shellfish, dried cod and halibut, dried seal and sea lion meat, dried berries, mountain goat fat and dried meat, and dried caribou meat. He observes that Aboriginal "[g]roups processed many resources in special ways to appeal to their trading partners. Many West Coast people ate salmon roe, but some produced roe cakes with flavourings as a gourmet delicacy."[29] This trade in traditional foodstuffs was readily adapted to new locations: "[T]he Ojibwe introduced corn and squash cultivation ... as well as sugar making using the Manitoba maple" into the territory west of Lake Superior.[30]

Settlers and traders were the beneficiaries of this large-scale Aboriginal food production. A Loyalist militia officer wrote to his father-in-law in 1793: "My cock-loft contains some of the finest maple sugar I ever beheld, 10,000 lbs. was made in an Indian village near Michellemackinac. We have 150 lb. of it."[31] In the 1790s, the Hudson's Bay Company and the North West Company

Group of Inuit eating on shore, c. 1919. Photograph by Captain George E. Mack. Courtesy of McCord Museum, MP-0000.597.214.

required around forty-five tons a year of pemmican, a mixture of meat, berries, and fat (usually dried buffalo meat and melted fat, pounded with Saskatoon berries).[32] Aboriginal women prepared the pemmican, pouring the mixture into *parfleches* or skin containers that held 90 pounds, the equivalent of 900 pounds of raw meat, with an "extremely long shelf life."[33] Salmon was a staple of the Hudson's Bay Company on the west coast.[34]

Aboriginal people also grew the crops introduced by the newcomers for trade among themselves. By the late eighteenth century, the Nootka (Nuu-chah-nulth) were growing potatoes, beans, and cabbages, and the Haida were trading potatoes with the Europeans as well as with other groups. As Ray notes, "By the mid-1820s they were sending fleets of forty to fifty canoes to

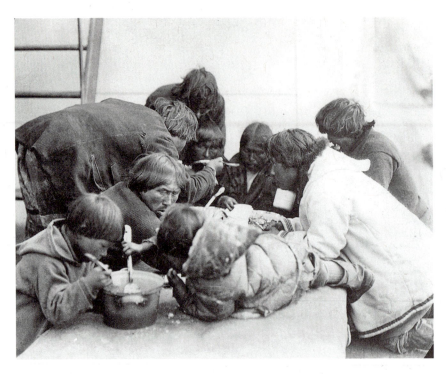

Inuit group eating from pots with large spoons, between 1910 and 1927. Photograph by Captain George E. Mack. Courtesy of McCord Museum, MP-0000.597.205.

the mainland to trade with the Nishga living on the Nass River and the Tsimshian of the lower Skeena River."[35] Other new foods were adopted by Aboriginal people during the fur trade: "The most important things to buy, in order, were ammunition, tobacco, flour, sugar and tea."[36] Trade also brought metal pots, which allowed for a more varied cuisine, including soups and stews.[37] Bannock, a Scottish food, was adopted into the Aboriginal diet very early, and now it is regarded as a traditional food. European foods, however, were supplements to the main diet of game, fish, and other wild foods; they were not the sole diet.

For the post-Enlightenment European, the point was to feed oneself and one's family. For many Aboriginal people, power came with the ability to feed the community. As Richard Daly notes, "The guiding ethic of management ... is the ability to feed others. When this ethic is implemented and reciprocated, the whole community benefits."[38] Hulme poses a key question: "What was the fundamental difference between Algonquian and English cultures? Inasmuch as a large and single answer to this question can be risked, it could be claimed that the Native American cultures under discussion here acted according to norms of *reciprocity*; and that the European cultures did not."[39] Bruce G. Trigger tells the story of Jacques Cartier's return to Canada in 1535: "When the French were stricken by a severe outbreak of scurvy, Cartier tried to conceal it because he feared that knowledge of their weakened condition would invite an attack. Yet, upon learning of their illness, the Indians showed them how to cure scurvy with a drink rich in vitamin C made from the fronds of white cedar."[40] He continues, "Despite bad relations, at various times the St Lawrence Iroquoians exchanged fish, eels and fresh meat for knives, awls and beads."[41] Ray suggests that Aboriginal peoples took easily to credit trading with the Hudson's Bay Company because the practice of reciprocal obligation was traditional.[42] Beth Brant, a Mohawk writer, in a story called "Food and Spirits," tells of an old man sharing traditional food – fry bread and whitefish – with a young couple he has befriended, saying to them, "Here, have another piece of bread. When you bite into somethin' like this, you know how good life is."[43] Food was to be shared, but as Hulme says, "settlement was always a different matter."[44] This became clear when the long-standing practices of alliance building and trade gave way to what those of European descent called settlement and the Aboriginal peoples called invasion.

The most renowned and elaborate feasts were held in what is now British Columbia and Yukon. This practice of feasting, known as the potlatch, entailed the disciplined collection and redistribution of food and other resources, and constituted a vehicle of government, as a Delgamuukw chief explains: "With the wealth that comes from respectful use of the territory, the House feeds the name of the Chief in the Feast Hall. In this way, the law, the Chief, the territory, and the Feast become one. The unity of the Chief's authority and his House's ownership of its territory are witnessed and thus affirmed by the other Chiefs at the Feast. By following the law, the power flows from the land to the people through the Chief; by using the wealth of the territory, the House feasts its Chief so he can properly fulfill the law. This cycle has been repeated on my land for thousands of years."[45] The potlatch was banned by the government between 1884 and 1951; such feasting was misrecognized as uneconomic, because it took Aboriginal people away from waged labour (and was thought to lead to whole set of other vices as well).[46] In a tradition witnessed by traders as far back as 1811, the feasts affirmed the connection between food and land: "During traditional feasts in this same territory, those bringing a contribution of game hold it up and 'specify each mountain or its territory where it comes from. Each creek is mentioned. So in our rule and laws we say that if you eat and digest the words, it's within your very soul.'"[47]

In the 1972 court case brought by the Cree to stop the James Bay hydro-electric project from flooding their traplines, Job Bearskin of Chisasibi (Fort George), Quebec, was asked how much money would compensate for their loss. He responded: "It can never be that there can be enough money to help pay for what I get from trapping. I do not think in terms of money. I think more often of the land because the land is something you will have for a long time. That is why we call our traplines, our land, our garden."[48] Here, the court case centred on food, with the lawyer trying to shake an Aboriginal witness's testimony that his people depended on geese, beaver, ptarmigan, moose, caribou, and fish for 90 percent of their food,[49] hoping to make the point that the dam would cause them no harm. But for Bearskin, land, food, and the future of his people were inextricably linked.

THE NUTRITION TRANSITION

Colonization has imposed and is still imposing, either gradually or suddenly, a change in the diet of Aboriginal peoples, from one that is harvested locally and seasonally to one that permits long-term storage and long-distance transport.[50] High carbohydrate grains – like wheat and corn – that could be stored for a long time were needed to support urbanization. The onset of the nutrition transition has varied, but occurred most recently in the North. This transition period is usually remembered as a time of hunger, even starvation. It usually began when access to traditional resources was strictly controlled but no provision was made for any alternative. The fur trade started the transition by introducing European foods and attaching hunters to trading posts, but people were still free to hunt for meat and forage for their own food. Maureen Lux's book *Medicine That Walks: Disease, Medicine, and Canadian Plains Native People, 1880–1940* is the story of what happened when the bison were nearly extinct on the prairies: "[T]reaties with the new Canadian government would soon be understood as failing to provide for ... basic human needs."[51] Starvation certainly underlay the rebellion of 1885.[52] Louis Riel made that point in his final statement to the jury in that year: "When I came into the North West in July, the first of July 1884, I found the Indians suffering. I found the half-breeds eating the rotten pork of the Hudson Bay Company and getting sick and weak every day."[53]

The consequences of treaties that blocked access to traditional foods were not always clear to Aboriginal people at the time of signing. Sometimes treaties were made when there was no other real choice; sometimes the written documents were contextualized with oral promises that were remembered by only one side.[54] After the Indian Act came into force in 1876, decisions were made about Aboriginal lands and access to food resources without any notice or consultation. *The Report of the Royal Commission on Aboriginal Peoples* (1996) recounts these stories of misunderstanding and conveniently forgotten promises, noting that "[b]y the turn of the nineteenth century, Aboriginal people in southwestern Ontario were complaining that farmers were setting their dogs on them if they tried to cross an open field to get to a hunting or fishing site."[55] Susanna Moodie, writing of the 1830s, comments on the frequent visits to her property by a group of Mississauga Indians. Part of her land had "originally been an Indian sugar bush. Although the favourite spot had now passed into the hands of strangers, they still frequented the place, to make canoes and baskets, to fish and shoot, and occasionally to follow their old occupation."[56] She welcomed them to *her* property, not realizing that they may have been promised the right to hunt, fish, and make sugar there. In 1993, Paul Day explained to the Royal Commission on Aboriginal People that "[i]n our area, Aboriginal people are denied access to most Crown lands because we have to cross private property to get to the land. As an example there is one person in our area who owns almost 1,000 acres and he has signs posted saying private property on his own property but he retains a hunt camp on Crown land. In order for us to get to that Crown land we have to cross his property but we can't cross it. On one piece of land where I hunted and fished for years, MNR [Ministry of Natural Resources] changed it to a designated park and we were charged that fall for hunting there."[57]

In her autobiography, *Halfbreed*, Maria Campbell, a Metis, describes how the Mounties bribed her with a chocolate bar to get her to reveal where her father had hidden the meat from animals he was hunting illegally; he went to jail for six months, leaving the family to survive as best it could: "It was a hard six months for all of us. We had no money and no meat. I had to set rabbit snares every day, and Mom and I would take the .22 and shoot partridges, ducks and whatever we could get. Mom was a terrible hunter."[58] Nora Marks Dauenhauer, a well-known scholar of Tlingit traditions who grew up in an Alaskan fishing family, notes that the salmon runs were depleted by the early 1950s because "canneries built barge-sized fish traps that were anchored along the migration routes intercepting thousands of salmon on their way to spawn. Entire salmon runs were depleted by fish traps and logging practices that ruined their habitat."[59] The controversy over who has the right to fish a depleted resource continues.

SCHOOLING

The residential schools for Aboriginal children that were run in Canada from 1879 to 1986 imposed a new diet on their students. Edward Dewdney, former Indian commissioner and the lieutenant-governor of the Northwest Territories, stated in 1883 that each student was to receive daily "1 pound of flour, 1/2 pound of bacon, 1 pound of beef, 1/8 ounce of tea, 2 ounces of sugar, 1/2 ounce of rice, 1 ounce of dried apples, 3 ounces of oatmeal, 1/2 ounce of pepper," in addition to "3 gallons of syrup a month."[60] Unfortunately, this standard and many others were honoured more in the breach than in the observance. Because of underfunding, many schools used the labour of the children to grow their own food on the school farm. Their produce included cash crops, such as "dairy products, milk, cream and butter ... [which] meant in many cases, however, that the children were denied these important foods" because they were sold to maintain the school.[61] Frequent reports that undernourished, improperly clothed, and overworked children were contracting tuberculosis and other infectious diseases in crowded and unsanitary schools were ignored.[62] As John Milloy remarks, "[T]he final irony in this was that in all areas of the country, except the high plains after the disappearance of the buffalo, children on entering the schools likely left behind a better diet, provided by communities that were living on the land, than that which was provided to them by school authorities."[63] Many children died from sickness as result of poor nutrition and poor care, while others committed suicide or died during attempts to run away.[64]

Mary John, a Carrier woman born in 1913, remembers the food at the Oblate-run school in Fort St James, British Columbia: "I was always hungry. I missed the roast moose, the fish fresh from a frying pan, the warm bread and bannock and berries. Oh how I missed the food I used to have in my own home. At school, it was porridge, porridge, porridge, and if it wasn't that, it was boiled barley or beans, and thick slices of bread spread with lard. Weeks went by without a taste of meat or fish. Such things as sugar or butter or jam only appeared on our tables on feast days and sometimes not even then."[65]

Alice French remembers a more substantial diet from her seven years (1939–46) at All Saints Residential School in Aklavik in the Northwest Territories: "Breakfast usually was porridge, sweetened with molasses, and bread and jam, and tea to drink with sugar and milk. It never varied except on holidays ... lunch, soup, bread and powdered milk ... Supper was the big meal of the day with fish, meat, potatoes, dessert, bread and tea."[66] They were also allowed one candy a day and were given cod-liver oil: "I guess that was why we were so healthy. But by the time the five-gallon can was empty it was so rancid you could smell it a mile away."[67] Dauenhauer recalls her father telling of his days in the Chemawa Indian school in Salem, Oregon, founded in 1880: "He said the most terrible was when they remembered their Indian foods back at home as they passed from bunk to bunk raw potatoes they swiped to eat after lights out. Someone would make the sounds of salmon boiling with seal oil and water cooking on a beach or elsewhere out of doors. They could almost smell the broth."[68] Even if the European diet had been adequate in quantity and quality, which it was not, the students still suffered the disadvantage of not learning how to access and prepare traditional food. More disturbingly, they were forbidden to speak their own language, so that when they did return to the community, they could not learn from those who would have taught them about the traditional diet.

Maria Campbell attended a public day school in Spring River, Saskatchewan. She remembers the difference between her diet and that of her white schoolmates just after World War II: "They had white or brown bread, boiled eggs, apples, cakes, cookies, and jars of milk. We were lucky to have these even at Christmas. We took bannock for lunch, spread with lard and filled with wild meat, and if there was no meat we had cold potatoes and salt and pepper or else whole roasted gophers with sage dressing. No apples or fruit, but if we were lucky, there was a jam sandwich for dessert."[69] One day, after being teased mercilessly as a gopher-eater, she went home and shouted at her parents that she hated them and "all of you no-good Halfbreeds."[70] This story illustrates another way that Aboriginal children may lose interest in traditional foods.

RELOCATION

Overhunting in the North in the 1950s led to starvation among the Ihalmiut, something that author Farley Mowat, in his books *People of the Deer* and *The Desperate People*, made known not only to Canadians but to the world.[71] Inuit and northern Aboriginal peoples were relocated more than once to move them closer to resources sought by the Hudson's Bay Company, to prevent "dependency," or to address concerns about sovereignty.[72] Uprooted from their traditional territories and traditional food resources, the people suffered: "The very sad part of the people at Whale Cove is that most of the population is made up of inlanders and these people are not partial to seal meat but would rather have caribou which has been their main staple diet inland. In talking to some of these people they mention that they get enough flour and grain products to eat but are hungry. When questioning them as to what they are hungry for their reply is caribou meat."[73]

Martha Flaherty writes of her community's move to Grise Fiord from Inukjuaq. Her father told her that "there's more wildlife up there. I was told we won't be hungry anymore."[74] She discovered the reality to be different: "I kept thinking, 'where are all those *qallunaat* [white people] who are supposed to be so helpful.'"[75] She continues, "The only people who might have some food were the RCMP. But you had to have some skins to buy food. For the first few years, there were hardly any skins to sell, especially in winter. I remember one particular time with my mother carrying a baby on her back. She and I fetched food from the RCMP's garbage a few miles away because we had no food."[76] Her childhood was very hard: "I had to hunt with my father for food, in very cold weather, with absolutely no daylight ... because I was the oldest. Sometimes I used to cry, knowing how cold it was going to be, but then my father would just say 'Do you want us to starve?'"[77]

COST OF NON-TRADITIONAL FOOD

Traditional food gathering was hard work, but now that these foods are unavailable, a healthy diet is also often unavailable. Meat and fresh fruit and vegetables are expensive even in major cities; they can be prohibitively so in isolated reserves and northern areas: "[E]ven with a subsidy, market foods are often much more expensive than they would be in southern urban centres. In some communities, virtually all after-shelter social assistance income is required to purchase the basic amount of food required to feed a family."[78] In the 1980s, Agnes Alfred, who was born around 1894 and grew up in Alert Bay, British Columbia, remembered: "Food was not as expensive then; it costs so much today. The pilot biscuits used to cost only two dollars a box when they first came out ... The period we are living in is so hard. At one time we had money for everything."[79] The novel *Monkey Beach* by Eden Robinson is set on a Haisla reserve near Kitimat in northern British Columbia. The main character, Lisa, because of her close ties with her traditional grandmother, knows some of the language and learns about special foods: "Winter in Kitamaat meant a whole season of flaccid, expensive vegetables from town. *Q°alh'm* was the first taste of spring. The skin of the shoots had a texture similar to kiwi skin, prickly soft. Once you peeled them, the shoots were translucent green, had a light crunch and a taste close to fresh snow peas. *Q°alh'm* picking lasts a few weeks at best."[80] *Q°alh'm* is likely thimbleberry sprouts.[81] Harriet V. Kuhnlein maps the declining use of a similar resource, cow parsnip shoots, among the Nuxalk: "The elders still remember it, but younger women often do not even recognize the plant or know how to prepare it."[82]

Projects that interfere with waterways affect the ecosystem and impact Aboriginal peoples' traditional resources.[83] Pollution came early: "In 1806, the ... Mississauga people were protesting to Deputy Superintendent General William Claus that the waters of the Credit River at its entrance into Lake Ontario 'are so filthy and disturbed by washing with soap and other dirt that the fish refuse coming into the River as usual, by which our families are in great distress for want of food.'"[84] They asked that the settlers be moved away from the river.[85] Anishnabe were relocated to Grassy Narrows and ate fish polluted by the 10 tonnes of mercury that was dumped into the English-Wabigoon River by the Reed pulp and paper company between 1962 and 1970.[86] The St Lawrence Seaway was completed in 1959, and the Mohawk, dependent on wild resources, particularly whitefish, eels, and sturgeon, began to worry about "the dangerously high levels of heavy metals and organochlorine compounds being found in the St. Lawrence River."[87] Health studies confirmed their fears: "Fishing is no longer a way of life, and fish are no longer the primary source of protein for the community. The former high-protein diet of the Mohawk people has changed to a high-carbohydrate diet, with a resulting dramatic rise in diabetes. Today, 75% of the population over the age of 35 suffers from some type of abnormal glucose tolerance: this in a community where there was no diabetes before 1945."[88] The James Bay project of Hydro-Quebec put 4,400 square miles of territory under water in 1983, primarily in order to sell power to the United States. The Cree who hunted in this area not only lost access to the territory, but also began to show symptoms of serious mercury poisoning from eating fish.[89]

The problem has not stopped, as a report from 2004 reveals: "[T]he cities with the lowest levels of treatment and that discharge the highest volumes of raw or minimally-treated sewage are Victoria, Montréal, St. John (New Brunswick), Halifax, Charlottetown and St. John's (Newfoundland). Each of these cities is located on the coast or on a major waterway such as the St. Lawrence River."[90] The sewage outfall from the University of British Columbia campus goes right through the Musqueam Indian Reserve, leading into the Iona plant: "Sewage contains toxic chemicals, including PCBs, POPs and PBDEs (fire retardants) ... With the largest sewage treatment plant in BC

– the Iona plant in Vancouver – only providing primary sewage treatment, these toxic chemicals are contaminating our coastal waters and harming the animals that live there, like the endangered southern resident killer whales and harbour seals."[91] Needless to say, it has been many years since the Musqueam people have harvested seaweed, mussels, or other foods from the rocks near their reserve – as they once did.[92]

DIET AND DISEASE

It is hard – except in times of famine – to disentangle those instances when illness can be ascribed to lacking immunity to an introduced disease from those when illness comes from a weakened immune system caused by a poor diet.[93] Even so, explanations for why Aboriginal people became ill often appear to favour the colonizers: "As the diseases of poverty rushed in, those who administered [the] lives [of the Plains Indians] would frame their disease as a function of their race and their supposed 'stage of civilization.'"[94] As for the children who died in residential school, "[e]xplanations for the atrocious death rates ... were looked for elsewhere – for example in the 'hereditary taint' of tuberculosis among Native people.[95] Before the 1940s, few Aboriginal people suffered from type 2 diabetes, but indeed, many were dying from tuberculosis. Kuhnlein notes, "Obesity and diabetes, the cardiovascular diseases, cancer, infant morbidity and mortality in higher frequencies, alcoholism, loss of teeth and clear eyesight, and rampant infections are all part of this diet picture that has emerged for Aboriginal people in the past 100 years."[96] Now, despite its recent occurrence among Aboriginal people and the explosion of obesity and diabetes in the wider population, diabetes is being construed as a genetic disease among Aboriginal people; this is one of many racializing discourses that overlooks the poverty of Aboriginal people.[97]

The Sandy Lake Oji-Cree suffer one of the highest diabetes rates in the North. Their diet has been assessed by nutritionists as inadequate and high in carbohydrates and saturated fats.[98] Similarly, for forty years, the Pima of Arizona have been cited as having the highest rates of diabetes in the world, and research teams have tried and failed to find a clear genetic cause.[99] The Pima (who call themselves the Akimel O'odham) once practised a highly sophisticated form of agriculture in the desert, but this practice was interrupted when settlers diverted water from the Gila River at the end of the 1900s and was conclusively stopped when the Coolidge Dam was built in 1928. The Akimel O'odham then had to survive on "commodity foods" (flour, pinto beans, coffee, sugar, and salt).[100]

ECOSYSTEMS AND LANGUAGE

Traditional ecological knowledge is starting to be recognized as a powerful form of scientific knowledge. Traditional foods and foodways are closely connected to language as well as to territory. Here a passage from *Monkey Beach* illustrates how important language is to an understanding of traditional foods. Lisa's grandmother shows her a berry bush and says the word *pipxs'm*:

> "Is that what you call blueberries in Haisla?" "No, no, just these blueberries. See they have white stuff on them. *Pipxs'm* means 'berries with mould on them.'" "Mmm. tasty." "They are." … I tried one, and it was so sweet it was almost piercing. I had never noticed that there were different types of blueberry bushes. If it was blue and on a bush, you picked it. Ma-ma-oo pointed out the contrast in the leaves and stems, but it was easier to see the distinctions in the berries themselves. We found the other kind, *sya'kᵒnalh*, 'the real blueberry,' shiny bluish-black berries, prettier, but not as sweet as *pipxs'm*. We drove around, going higher up the mountains until we found the third type, pear-shaped and plump and sweet. Their Haisla name is *mimayus,* which, loosely translated, means 'pain in the ass,' because although they taste wonderful, they're hard to find and to pick.[101]

Traditional indigenous lands in Africa, Asia, and South America contain the majority of diverse species on earth, many still to be identified by Western science.[102] Luisa Maffi argues that the maintenance of biodiversity requires the survival of Aboriginal cultures and languages.[103] Daniel Nettles and Suzanne Romaine note that even though their agriculture might be seen as "primitive," the Hanunoo people who live on the island of Mindoro in the Philippines (they number about twelve thousand) can "distinguish more than 450 types of animals and 1,500 plants. Their categories for the plants in the area exceed those of Western science by around 400."[104] This kind of knowledge is not exceptional in those who survive on traditional food. Any attempt to preserve the ecosystem in which the Hanunoo live would depend on the language and ecological knowledge of the Hanunoo, and the same is true of other indigenous territories.

Losing a traditional language, particularly one that includes words for traditional food sources, would be much the same thing as a skilled Western botanist – or rather, the discipline of botany itself – losing all memory or record of the Latin names of plants. In their book *Traditional Plant Foods of Indigenous Peoples,* Harriet V. Kuhnlein and Nancy J. Turner remark, "We would have liked to present a table of indigenous language names used for species, with English names and botanical nomenclature, but published literature is very sparse in this area."[105] Yet eating traditional food cannot be undertaken lightly without this knowledge. In an appendix to her *Food Plants of Coastal First Peoples,* Turner lists poisonous plants, some of which routinely kill cattle and could doubtless kill any human ignorant enough to eat them.[106]

REVITALIZING ABORIGINAL TRADITIONAL FOOD PRACTICES

As Gary Nabhan points out in *Coming Home to Eat*, O'odham activists recently "have quietly improvised a way to let village feasting tradition express a message of hope. It is a message about diabetes prevention through the revitalization of native foods, ones rich in soluble fiber, fructose, tannins, and other blood sugar-lowering substances. Just as the honour dance raises the level of respect for all elders, serving native food at feasts raises their cultural value among young members of the community. As one Pima friend of mine once said, 'To be Indian, you gotta eat Indian.'"[107] Still, access to traditional foods is hard to restore because these foods depend not only on language and the knowledge of elders, but also on a whole ecosystem, which is often under a patchwork of jurisdictions. Salmon or eulachon streams have been covered over or their banks have been clear cut.[108] Controlled burning is no longer permitted in clearing brush. New species have invaded. The restoration of the ecosystem is required if traditional harvesting practices are to be revitalized.

Various initiatives – based on very different principles – have been launched in response to the problem. For example, the Centre for Indigenous Peoples' Nutrition and Environment (CINE), based at McGill University in Montreal, is devoted to the study and preservation of indigenous food systems. CINE uses "participatory research" to address concerns about food in particular communities and develops courses to communicate the results of that research. Not everyone agrees, however, with the idea that restoring Aboriginal knowledge, control, and husbandry over the fragile ecosystems in which their cultures developed over thousands of years is the answer to species loss or the "diseases of civilization." Scientists in the global North are archiving the DNA of diverse organisms in gene banks (for example, the American Type Culture Collection [ATCC]) on the assumption that this sort of "salvage genetics" is enough to ensure that if a species is required in the future, it can be accessed.[109] The Indigenous Peoples Council on Biocolonialism[110] is an international association formed to fight the appropriation of traditional knowledge about food, medicinal plants, and the patenting of the DNA of the related organisms – all endeavours of the ATCC.[111]

Aboriginal peoples' struggle to return to their traditional foodways is part of a larger struggle that involves their regaining their cultural sovereignty and resolving their land claims. As Nora Dauenhauer says of her people's staple food, "The importance of salmon goes beyond the question of calories. It is part of our identity. We need salmon to continue as physically, mentally, and spiritually healthy people."[112]

NOTES

1 Robinson, quoted in Wickwire, "Stories from the Margins," 129.
2 See Latour, *We Have Never Been Modern.*
3 See Harris, *Making Native Space.*
4 Kuhnlein, "Global Nutrition." The nutrition transition also occurred in Europe, and an oral culture recorded this process. See Berger, *Pig Earth,* on peasant stories in France (8–9), and Neeson, *Commoners,* on British enclosures.
5 Paul Farmer has noted how the anthropological focus on "culture" has obscured "biosocial" realities (5–7): "Common indeed are the ethnographies in which poverty and inequality, the end result of a long process of impoverishment, are

reduced to a form of cultural difference." Farmer, *Infections and Inequalities*, 7. See Deur and Turner, *Keeping It Living* (25), on Franz Boas's lack of interest in the physical environment of his informants because of his antagonism to theories of environmental determinism.

6 Krech, *Ecological Indian*; Ellingson, *Myth of the Noble Savage.*

7 Locke, *Second Treatise of Government*, 14.

8 Ibid., 17.

9 Ibid., 15.

10 Ibid.

11 Rousseau, *Discourse on Inequality*, 136.

12 Hobbes, *Leviathan*, 76.

13 Deur and Turner, *Keeping It Living*, 4.

14 Krech, *Ecological Indian*, 106–7.

15 Hulme, *Colonial Encounters*, 157.

16 See Weatherford, "Indian Agricultural Technology," 83–4.

17 Ray, *I Have Lived Here*, 7.

18 Hulme, *Colonial Encounters*, 157.

19 Head, *Indian Treaties and Surrenders from 1680 to 1890*, 112. Quoted in Canada, Royal Commission on Aboriginal Peoples, *Report*, vol. 2, pt 2, chap. 4, 61.

20 Sawyer, quoted in Ray, *I Have Lived Here*, 159.

21 Deur and Turner, *Keeping It Living*, 4.

22 Ibid.

23 See Williams, *Clam Gardens.*

24 Quoted in Culhane, *Pleasure of the Crown*, 307–8. The *Delgamuukw* decision produced by Chief Justice McEachern was appealed to the Supreme Court of Canada, which granted a new trial, mainly on the ground of McEachern's refusal to consider evidence based on the oral tradition. The Supreme Court recognized "unextinguished Aboriginal title to all of British Columbia" and the duty of the Crown to consult with Aboriginal peoples about development on their lands (which they have taken to mean not only reserve land, but lands to which they have a potential claim).

25 Ray, *I Have Lived Here*, xvi.

26 Shakespeare, *Tempest*, 1.2.336–8.

27 Hulme, *Colonial Encounters*, 302; Trigger, *Natives and Newcomers*, 142.

28 Ray, *I Have Lived Here*, 22.

29 Ibid., 24.

30 Ibid., 99.

31 Duncan, *Canadians at Table*, 78.

32 See "Cultural Treasures," http://www.pc.gc.ca/lhnnhs/ab/rockymountain/natcul/natcul09_e.asp; Ray, *I Have Lived Here*, 168.

33 Ray, *I Have Lived Here*, 14.

34 Harris, *Fish, Law and Colonialism*, 36.

35 Ray, *I Have Lived Here*, 118.

36 Nancy Wachowich et al., *Saqiyuq*, 123; Kuhnlein, "Global Nutrition," 255; Trigger, *Natives and Newcomers*, 138.

37 Ray, *I Have Lived Here*, 76.

38 Daly, *Our Box Was Full*, 281.

39 Hulme, *Colonial Encounters*, 147.

40 Trigger, *Natives and Newcomers*, 130–1.

41 Ibid., 131.

42 Ray, *I Have Lived Here*, 88.

43 Brant, "Food and Spirits," 83.

44 Hulme, *Colonial Encounters*, 149.

45 Gisday Wa and Delgam Uukw, *The Spirit in the Land*, 7–8.

46 Cole and Chaikin, *An Iron Hand*, 15.

47 Daly, *Our Box Was Full*, 281.

48 Richardson, *Strangers Devour the Land* (Post Mills, VT: Chelsea Green, 1991), 121.

49 Ibid., 35.

50 This process, of course, affects everyone, not just Aboriginal peoples; the Slow Food movement and the local foods movement (see Nabhan, *Coming Home to Eat*) are responses to it.

51 Lux, *Medicine That Walks*, 19.

52 Ibid., 20–70.

53 Morton, ed., *Queen vs. Louis Riel*, 30.

54 See, for example, Cardinal and Hildebrand, *Treaty Elders of Saskatchewan*.

55 Canada, Royal Commission on Aboriginal Peoples, *Report*, n57.

56 Moodie, *Roughing It in the Bush*, 280–1.

57 Day, "How Losses Occurred," 58.

58 Campbell, *Halfbreed*, 55.

59 Dauenhauer, *Life Woven with Song*, 5.

60 Milloy, *A National Crime*, 116.

61 Ibid., 120.

62 Ibid.; Lux, *Medicine That Walks*, 109–10.

63 Milloy, *National Crime*, 121.

64 Ibid., 121–7, 154, 287–8.

65 Moran, *Stoney Creek Woman*, 53.
66 French, "My Name Is Masak," 206.
67 Ibid., 209.
68 Dauenhauer, *Life Woven with Song*, 29.
69 Campbell, *Halfbreed*, 46.
70 Ibid., 47.
71 According to Clarence Karr, "Mowat was the country's most successful non-fiction writer, selling more than four million copies in twenty-two languages other than English by the early 1980s." Karr, "Writers and the Market," 141.
72 Tester and Kulchyski, *Tammarniit (Mistakes)*, 41, 113.
73 Ibid., 359.
74 Flaherty, "I Fought to Keep My Hair," 274.
75 Ibid., 276.
76 Ibid.
77 Ibid., 277.
78 Doran, "Voices from the Field," 1; see also Kuhnlein, "Global Nutrition."
79 Alfred, *Paddling to Where I Stand*, 172.
80 Robinson, *Monkey Beach*, 73.
81 I thank Nancy J. Turner for this identification. e-mail correspondence, 6 February 2008.
82 Kuhnlein, "Global Nutrition," 252.
83 See Waldram, *As Long as the Rivers Run*.
84 Quinepenon, Speech of Chief Quinepenon, 58.
85 Ibid.
86 See "Mission to Grassy Narrows," http://www.amnesty.ca/grassy_narrows/; Shkilnyk, *Poison Stronger Than Love*.
87 "The State of Canada's Environment, 1995," http://www.ec.gc.ca/soer-ree/ English/soer/1996 Report/Doc/1-6-6-5-5-3-1.cfm.
88 Ibid.; Kuhnlein, "Global Nutrition," 256–8.
89 Richardson, *Strangers Devour the Land*, x–xi. "Methane from decomposing plants and trees, which have been drowned in the flooding, converts the inorganic mercury already present in the soil into organic methyl mercury, a lethal poison" (x).
90 "Canada: Sewage Treatment Lacking," http://www.vanaqua.org/aquanew/ fullnews.php?id=1629.
91 Ibid.
92 Larry Grant, Musqueam First Nation elder and University of British Columbia adjunct professor, personal communication.

93 Crosby, *Ecological Imperialism*. Crosby discusses lack of immunity in North America generally, but on the East Coast, where contact lasted centuries before settlement, some argue that poor diet resulting from contact was the reason for the high death rates in the settlement period. Trigger, *Natives and Newcomers*, 238–9.

94 Lux, *Medicine That Walks*, 19.

95 Ibid., 109–10.

96 Kuhnlein, "Global Nutrition," 259.

97 See Fee, "Racializing Narratives," 2988–97.

98 See Joel Gittelsohn et al., "Developing Diabetes Interventions," http://www.phac-aspc.gc.ca/publicat/cdic-mcc/16-4/e_e.html. See also Harriet V. Kuhnlein et al., "Arctic Indigenous Peoples," for a similar study of Inuit, Dene/Metis, and Yukon First Nations.

99 See Fee, "Racializing Narratives," 2988–97.

100 See Nabhan, *Desert Smells Like Rain*; Nabhan, *Coming Home to Eat*.

101 Robinson, *Monkey Beach*, 159–60. English and Latin names, courtesy of Nancy J. Turner (e-mail correspondence, 6 February 2008), are *Vaccinium ovalifolium* (*pipxs'm* or oval-leafed blueberry), *Vaccinium alaskaense* (*sya'konalh* or Alaska blueberry), and *Vaccinium membranaceum* (*mimayus* or black huckleberry).

102 McFarlane, "Eating in the 'Hot Box,'" 158.

103 Maffi, *On Biocultural Diversity*.

104 Nettles and Romaine, *Vanishing Voices*, 166–7. This comment is based on the work of anthropologist Harold Conklin.

105 Kuhnlein and Turner, *Traditional Plant Foods*, 3.

106 Turner, *Food Plants of Coastal First Peoples*, 138–45.

107 Nabhan, *Desert Smells Like Rain*, 247.

108 Knudsen and Macdonald, *Sustainable Fisheries Management*.

109 McFarlane, "Eating in the 'Hot Box,'" 159; see also Brown, "Ethnobotany Blues," 273n.

110 Indigenous People's Council on Biocolonialism, http://www.ipcb.org.

111 See Marks, "Human Gene Museum?" 198–218.

112 Dauenhauer, *Life Woven with Song*, 6. See Roche and McHutchison, *First Fish, First People*.

3

A Cargo of Cocoa: Chocolate's Early History in Canada

CATHERINE MACPHERSON

INTRODUCTION

As part of a larger international research effort to document the history of chocolate in North America, the McCord Museum in Montreal has undertaken the sweet, yet sweeping, task of researching the history of chocolate in Canada, from the colonial era through the twentieth century.[1] Very little has been written on the subject before this venture. Dorothy Duncan, for example, in her book *Canadians at Table: Food, Fellowship and Folklore – A Culinary History of Canada*, devotes considerable attention to tea but less to coffee and chocolate – the "other" beverages.[2] Chocolate was consumed as a beverage for nine-tenths of its history and was prized by early settlers in Canada, especially inhabitants of New France, and by early explorers and fur traders. High taxation on tea together with the accessibility of the British cacao holdings in Jamaica often made chocolate a more attractive option than tea as a warming brew in the early colonies.

While the role of chocolate as a popular confection is a relatively recent phenomenon, many of the home-grown chocolate companies familiar to Canadians – such as Ganong, Moir's, Laura Secord, Purdy's, and Roger's – have been around for generations, some since the early twentieth century and others from the late 1800s. It might seem logical to begin the exploration of chocolate's development in Canada by tracing the history of these companies, but certain questions should first be asked about chocolate's historical "life" among Canadians of the past. For example, what daily role, if any, did chocolate play in the social or cultural lives of earlier Canadians? Was chocolate an important part of the Canadian diet in the nineteenth, eighteenth, or even seventeenth centuries? Was it always a popular sweet or did it play another alimentary role? How easy or even desirable was it to obtain chocolate and was there any sort of indigenous manufacture?

In order to answer these questions, we need to understand chocolate's earliest history, its life in Mesoamerica, and its subsequent introduction to Europe.[3]

EARLY HISTORY

The cacao tree is temperamental and does not grow in regions that are more than 20 degrees north or south of the equator. It requires warm, consistent temperatures, constant irrigation, and adequate shade cover. It grows best when planted among taller species, such as the banana tree.[4] *Theobroma cacao,* as named by Linnaeus in 1753[5] and translated to "food of the gods," was held in high esteem by its earliest consumers, the ancient tribes of Central and South America.[6] Chocolate is derived from the seeds of the cacao pod. A complex process of fermenting, drying, roasting, grinding, and pressing eventually yields two end products: cocoa powder and cocoa butter. The two substances are then recombined, sugar is sometimes added, and the product begins to resemble what most of us know as "chocolate."

The documented history of chocolate goes back thousands of years. The early Olmec and later the Mayan and Aztec civilizations consumed a beverage made from ground cacao beans. Cacao was so prized among early Mesoamerican civilizations that the seeds or beans were used as currency. The Spanish conquistadores encountered chocolate as early as 1502; historians speculate that Hernan Cortes may have brought chocolate back to Spain in the second quarter of the sixteenth century.[7] Cortes observed the Aztecs preparing chocolate: they mixed ground cacao beans with spices and water, then poured the mixture from vessel to vessel to create a froth, and drank it cold.[8] Colonial Mexico produced the *molinillo*, or "chocolate mill," which was essentially a wooden swizzle stick or whisk that was used to blend the chocolate drink and provide a more effective means of achieving the much-desired froth on the beverage.

The Spanish court soon became fond of chocolate, and by the seventeenth century, the court was renowned for its prepared chocolate beverages. Chocolate was slowly introduced to the rest of Europe, often with an emphasis on its perceived medicinal virtues. The Italians were among the first to use chocolate in cookery, and the French alternately praised and demonized the side effects of its consumption. In 1659, David Chaliou was granted a twenty-nine-year monopoly to sell chocolate throughout France.[9] In the eighteenth century, the French added chocolate to biscuits and sweetmeats.

Chocolate was first sold in London in 1657, at the first of many coffee and chocolate houses to come – among them, White's Chocolate House and the Cocoa Tree Chocolate House. England's supply of cacao came from the Jamaican plantations that the British had captured from Spain in 1655. By the end of the seventeenth century, chocolate was available in New England and was offered as a beverage in public houses as early as 1670.

CHOCOLATE ON ÎLE ROYALE AND IN NEW FRANCE

The Fortress of Louisbourg on Cape Breton, which was called Île Royale during the eighteenth-century French occupation, is a true treasure trove for contemporary archaeologists. In 1713, the French first came to Louisbourg, and by 1719, construction had begun on the fortified town. The French town was captured by the British on two separate occasions, the British razing the fortress walls after the second capture in 1758. With almost no subsequent inhabitation of the site, much that remains of the colonial town of Louisbourg sits preserved just below the surface. Among the various ceramics unearthed, there is a preponderance of brown faience ware, similar to ceramics found at excavations of early towns in Quebec. While certain jugs have been identified

left: Wooden chocolate mill and metal pot. Reproductions of original mill and pot. Photograph by Ruby Fougère. Courtesy of Fortress of Louisbourg National Historic Site of Canada.

right: Metal pot with hot chocolate. Reproduction of original pot. Photograph by Ruby Fougère. Courtesy of Fortress of Louisbourg National Historic Site of Canada.

as chocolate pots, they may also have held milk, water, or other liquids. The same could be said for a two-handled ceramic glazed cup unearthed at Louisbourg and frequently labelled as a "chocolate cup."[10]

More definite proof of chocolate use at Louisbourg can be found in the metal vessels discovered at the site. The lids and partial lids of these vessels have holes pierced through the middle of them, which allowed a chocolate mill to pass through. The lid could remain closed while the mill was twirled between the palms of the hands to mix grated chocolate with hot water, milk, or cream, and create a pleasing froth. There is a small swivel lip that covers the hole, presumably to keep the beverage hot when the mill was not in place.

Metal swivel lid unearthed at Louisbourg, now part of the archaeology collection at the Fortress of Louisbourg. Photograph by Ruby Fougère. Courtesy of Fortress of Louisbourg National Historic Site of Canada.

What constituted chocolate at the time? According to various inventories from Louisbourg, solid chocolate was sold as balls or sticks of varying weights. Chocolate came either "prepared," meaning that it had already been ground down into a paste of cocoa solids and fats, mixed with sugar and aromatics (usually cinnamon and vanilla, and sometimes anise, orange flower water, or ambergris – flavourings preferred by the French),[11] then allowed to harden, or "unprepared," consisting of a hardened paste of plain chocolate. In the latter instance, spices and sweeteners would be added after the grated chocolate ball or stick was mixed with hot liquid.

Louisbourg was a bustling trade town with chocolate arriving from France, the West Indies, and New England. According to an account written during the first siege of Louisbourg, a French ship, the *Notre Dame de la Deliverance*, taken by the English off Scatarie (a Cape Breton port just southwest of Louisbourg), had a very valuable cargo of "over 300,000 pounds sterling, in gold and silver, from Peru and a cargo of cocoa, Peruvian wool, and Jesuits' bark."[12]

Chocolate was a luxury, and not everyone would have consumed it. The upper classes, senior officers, and the governor would have had chocolate. The governor of Louisbourg in 1744, Dusquenel, had quite a lot of chocolate in his personal inventory. Listed among the items found in his dressing room at the time of his death were "2 *livres* [pounds] of ginseng; almost 30 *livres* of chocolate, 10 of it from Manilla; 44 *livres* of prepared chocolate, and fifteen from the 'isles' not yet prepared; 7 different boxes of tea; 3 'quarter pounds' of rhubarb."[13] The "isles" refer to French territories in the West Indies; cacao was harvested extensively on Martinique. Dusquenel stored the chocolate in his bedroom wardrobe with other valuables and health remedies – confirming that chocolate both was very dear and was thought to have medicinal properties.

Are there traces or records of chocolate in Canada that precede those found at Louisbourg? It is doubtful that the Acadians had chocolate, but similar chocolate consumption patterns existed in New France. The earliest mention of chocolate in Quebec is found in the inventory of M. Charles Aubert de la Chesnaye, dated 1702.[14] Aubert de la Chesnaye was possibly the most important merchant in seventeenth-century New France. Chocolate was often given to the ill or frail as a healthful drink. In October 1745, an extract drawn from the correspondence of Pierre Guy states, "[W]hen they heard that Mme Guy was ill, they sent the 'best chocolate' that they could find."[15] Chocolate was preferred over coffee or tea as a tonic for the sick.

In general terms, chocolate's earliest connection to Canada can be found in the journals of Samuel de Champlain. Before his exploration of Port Royal, New France, and the founding of Quebec City in 1608, Champlain travelled to Mexico and the West Indies. There, he supposedly made extensive notes on the local flora and fauna, documenting these in rather exquisitely illustrated journals. The journal of 1602 contains an illustration labelled "arbre appelle cacou," which is accompanied by a lengthy description of the tree and its uses. Curiously, the description conflates the attributes of the cacao tree with those of the agave plant. The text reads: "There is [a] tree, which is called cacao, the fruit of which is very good and useful for many things, and even serves for money among the Indians ... When this fruit is desired to be made use of, it is reduced to powder, then a paste is made, which is steeped in hot water, in which honey, which comes from the same tree, is mixed, and a little spice; then the whole being boiled together, it is drunk in the morning, warm ... and they find themselves so well after having drunk of it, that they can pass a whole day without eating or having great appetite."[16] Whether or not Champlain had first-hand knowledge of the plant is a subject of some debate. His confusing description feeds some historical concerns about the authenticity of this text, which has been generally accepted as the work of Champlain. Champlain would have been familiar with cacao and chocolate, but it is unclear whether he brought any with him on his travels to North America.

Another historic figure, Pierre Le Moyne D'Iberville, renowned son of New France and hero in defending French interests in Hudson Bay, purchased a lucrative cocoa plantation in Saint-Domingue in 1701, but this was after his time of service in Canada. It is unlikely that he possessed cocoa or chocolate whilst in Canada, although its value would have been recognized at the time. Chocolate had only recently been introduced to the French upper classes and was hardly a common commodity among Europeans at this point. With the French holdings in the West Indies, however, its popularity and use would continue to grow.[17]

An additional point of interest about chocolate in Quebec concerns a silver chocolate pot crafted by Quebec silversmith Laurent Amiot. Born in Quebec in 1764, Amiot briefly apprenticed in France from 1782 to 1786 and then returned to Quebec, where he became known as a premier craftsman of ecclesiastical silverware. The silver vessel in question is most likely from the late eighteenth or early nineteenth century and is housed in the Archbishop's Palace in Quebec City.[18] The clergy frequently consumed chocolate, especially during the Lenten fast. After much debate, the Catholic Church decreed that the consumption of chocolate did not violate the abstinence that was called for during the fast. Therefore, chocolate was a much-welcomed source of energy and calories.

EARLY ENGLISH SETTLEMENT IN CANADA

What chocolate consumption patterns did English Canadians exhibit during the eighteenth century? Records and trade statistics from the British Admiralty and the Colonial Office fonds reveal that the Canadian colonies received very little in the way of British unprocessed cacao shipments from territories in the Caribbean, as most of these shipments went directly to England. Prepared chocolate products, however, made their way from England to the colonies via trade and the military. In *The Winslow Papers*, a collection of

Mather Byles' Letter Books #4 (c. 1785), pp. 16–17. In the middle of the page on the left-hand side, Byles describes an instance of chocolate smuggling by someone known to him: "Waddington had been detected running brandy and chocolate and was under prosecution for it at the time of the election which is the foundation of all the squibs upon him." Source: Winslow Papers, University of New Brunswick.

Loyalist-era journals and letter books, there is an account of soldiers drawing on the military for chocolate.[19] By the middle of the nineteenth century, approximately half of all of the raw cocoa shipped to Britain was destined for use by the Royal Navy.[20]

The domestic manufacture of chocolate would not establish itself in Canada until the early nineteenth century, even though chocolate was a fairly readily available commodity. The earliest advertisement for chocolate found in Canada comes from the 30 March 1752 issue of the *Halifax Gazette* (the second issue of the paper).[21] The *Halifax Gazette* is considered to be the first newspaper published in Canada. The merchant John Codman advertises "Bohea Tea, Loaf and Brown Sugar, Chocolate, Coffee, Starch, Mustard, Chandlery Ware ... ," among numerous other sundry items for sale. It is exciting to see chocolate represented so early on in Canada's publishing history. The advertisement is typical for its time with respect to the type and variety of goods sold by one merchant. Codman placed a number of subsequent advertisements, identical to this one, in later editions of the paper. An advertisement for wooden chocolate mills (presumably the wooden mills or whisks used for frothing chocolate) appeared in the *Halifax Gazette* in 1785. A dozen chocolate pots were listed for auction in a St John's, Newfoundland, paper, the *Royal Gazette and Newfoundland Advertiser*, in 1815.[22]

Simeon Perkins, eighteenth-century businessman, politician, and diarist of Liverpool, Nova Scotia, occasionally mentions chocolate and cocoa in his journals. Perkins was keenly interested in matters of trade. On 6 December 1786, he notes the "Prices Current" of sundry items listed in the *New York Morning Post* of 2 November of that same year; chocolate is among the items noted. Perkins was also involved in privateering, particularly during times of warfare. On 10 September 1797, he writes of a Spanish prize brigantine, the *Nuestro Senior de la Carmen*, taken by the privateer ship *Charles Mary Wentworth* on 4 September. The ship, which was loaded with cocoa and cotton, was sailing from Havana bound for Spain.[23]

Smuggling also played a role in the consumption of chocolate in British North America. Mather Byles' Letter Books, also part of *The Winslow Papers* collection, offer an interesting account of smuggling chocolate. Byles writes: "Waddington had been detected running brandy and chocolate and was under prosecution for it at the time of the election which is the foundation of all the squibs upon him."[24] Both chocolate and brandy were prized goods; in fact, the English often took their hot chocolate with a little brandy.

THE FUR TRADE AND ARCTIC EXPLORATION

Traces of chocolate's early use were also found further west, in the inventories of fur forts. While it was not a regular staple among fur traders, chocolate was nonetheless prized as a food that kept well, travelled well, and provided energy. Early accounts of Canadian exploration contain inventories that list chocolate as a supply item, but it was most likely a foodstuff that only certain classes, ranks, or wealthier individuals would have possessed.[25] There is no evidence to suggest that chocolate was an item of trade between early European arrivals and northeastern North American Aboriginal peoples. A recipe for *biscuits au chocolat* (dated to 1750) is cited in a possible menu for a winter's meal at a Canadian fur fort, around 1799, although it may only have been included in the hypothetical menu because the recipe was traditional for the time and chocolate was considered a desirable ingredient among traders and explorers.[26] Chocolate and flour would have been transported to interior posts by canoe; the eggs called for in the recipe could have been produced on site.

In his journal of 1749, Pehr Kalm, who travelled around what is now Canada, remarks on the daily meals of the inhabitants and describes a typical breakfast of bread accompanied by either spirits or a cup of chocolate: "[L]es hommes prennent souvent un morceau de pain, qu'ils mangent après l'avoir trempé dans de l'eau-de-vie; ou bien ils boivent une gorgée de cet alcool et mangent ensuite un morceau de pain; ou prennent également aussi souvent du chocolat."[27] Kalm notes that men, and especially women, consumed coffee but rarely drank tea. He attributes this to the fact that coffee and cocoa (chocolate) would be readily available from French territories in the West Indies, while tea would have to be imported from China.

There are numerous accounts of chocolate as a staple in the caches of arctic explorers. Since it kept well and was a valuable source of energy, chocolate was a common provision for arctic expeditions. Foremost among the explorers was Sir John Franklin, who brought chocolate from England to the Canadian Arctic and frequently made note of its excellent restorative and keeping properties. On 15 July 1820, upon surveying the stores for an excursion, he writes: "Our stock of provision unfortunately did not amount to more than sufficient for one day's consumption, exclusive of two barrels of flour, three cases of preserved meats, some chocolate, arrowroot, and portable soup, which we had brought from England, and intended to reserve for our journey to the coast next season."[28] Franklin writes of eating chocolate for breakfast and, on occasion, administering chocolate to help stave off hypothermia: "Our friend Augustus was seized with a shivering fit ... [and] was put between blankets and provided with warm chocolate, and the only inconvenience that he felt the next morning was pain in his limbs."[29]

CHOCOLATE IN DAILY LIFE

The nineteenth century brought major developments to the processing and manufacture of chocolate; these innovations not only made chocolate a more affordable and plentiful commodity, but also turned it into a much more refined product, akin to the chocolate we are familiar with today. Chocolate continued to be consumed as a beverage, but also it evolved as both a confectionery and a baking ingredient.

In Halifax, circa 1809, John F. Ferguson established what is possibly Canada's earliest chocolate mill and factory. By 1833, the Nova Scotia House of Assembly reported on a petition on behalf of Ferguson, who was seeking a bounty on the manufacture of chocolate as well as a tax on imported chocolate. The final report on John Ferguson's petition was issued in 1839 and reads in part as follows: "That the petitioner has carried on the manufacture of Chocolate in Halifax for upward of thirty years; and last year manufactured about 100,000 lbs, weight, yielding upwards of £2000. A large proportion of this quantity was exported by the petitioner, to Canada, NB, Newfoundland, and the West Indies; and the cheaper of the two sorts manufactured by him, which he can afford to sell at 7d. a pound, is used extensively by the Fishermen of our own Province." The document goes on to highlight the importance of taking protectionist measures: "If he is obliged to pay the duty of 5s. Sterling on Cocoa, besides the Imperial Duties on Lard and Flour, which are largely used in his manufacture, and cannot be protected either by a drawback or bounty, he is exposed to a most unequal competition with the American Manufacturer, who gets all the Raw Material he uses, free of duty; and the consequence will be the surrender of the Newfoundland, West India, New Brunswick and Canada market, to the Foreign supplier and the destruction of our own Manufacture and Export."[30]

In the end, Ferguson won his petition and was granted a bounty on chocolate, paid quarterly by the province. It is interesting to note the possible use of flour and lard in Ferguson's chocolate manufacture. Perhaps this yielded a cheaper product, affordable and beneficial to local fishermen as a portable energy supplement. Carbohydrates were sometimes added to chocolate elsewhere as well; the Mesoamericans had added ground maize to their cacao preparations. Was Ferguson's use of flour designed to stretch the product for the caloric benefit of the fishermen or for the monetary benefit of Ferguson himself? Or was Ferguson involved in the biscuit trade as well – a not uncommon occurrence among those manufacturers equipped with a mill? As the domestic manufacture of chocolate and other products grew throughout Canada and Nova Scotia, so too did concerns over adulteration. Parliamentary papers from the mid-nineteenth century detail the introduction of regular food inspections for chocolate and cocoa among other comestibles, such as coffee, milk, alcohol, spices, and breads.

EARLY BREAKTHROUGHS IN COCOA PROCESSING

In 1828, a Dutchman named Conrad van Houten invented a screw press for processing the ground cocoa beans and nibs (the nibs are the broken pieces of bean that remain after the cacao beans are roasted, cracked, and dehulled). It effectively removed about two-thirds of the cacao butter from the chocolate paste, leaving behind the powder that became known as cocoa. Cocoa's solubility in water and improved digestibility (compared with full-fat chocolate) led to a whole industry of cocoa manufacturing; in fact, powdered cocoa would eventually take over from grated chocolate pastes as the preferred way of preparing "drinking chocolate."

The year 1880 heralded another major development in chocolate processing. Rodolphe Lindt developed the process of "conching." The creation of a palatable eating chocolate always involved adding some of the extracted cocoa butter back to the ground cocoa, but Lindt increased the amount of cocoa butter added back to the chocolate mass, and via a slow, steady process of heating and mixing, he was able to create a smoother product that felt pleasant in the mouth. Lindt's innovation paved the way for chocolate's transition from restorative beverage to popular confection. This breakthrough, in combination with falling prices of the raw commodity and an increase in the disposable income of the middle class, served to usher in the modern era of chocolate.

Powdered cocoa was heavily marketed from the middle of the nineteenth century onwards. Billed as a healthy drink that was beneficial to the sick and frail, easily digested by the old and young, and healthier than the fatty chocolate pastes of the previous era, cocoa was twinned with such adjectives as "hygienic," "soluble," "homeopathic," and "absolutely pure."[31] An advertisement for Baker's cocoa that appeared in the *Canadian Grocer* towards the end of the century states: "W. Baker & Co.'s Breakfast Cocoa, from which the excess of oil has been removed, is absolutely pure and it is soluble. No chemicals are used in its preparation. It has more than three times the strength of cocoa mixed with starch, arrowroot or sugar, and is therefore far more economical, costing less than one cent a cup. It is delicious, nourishing, strengthening, easily digested, and admirably adapted for invalids as well as for persons in health."[32]

Started in 1780, Baker's had one of the earliest chocolate and cocoa mills in the United States (Baker's chocolate is to this day one of the more popular baking brands). In the middle of the nineteenth century, Canada saw manufacturers of commercial domestic cocoa and chocolate open shop. John P. Mott started Mott's Spice & Cocoa Company in Dartmouth, Nova Scotia, circa 1853.[33] He advertised heavily in Maritime newspapers during the 1850s, extolling the virtues of his cocoa. One such advertisement reads as follows: "Motts Broma is one of the most innocent and nutritious beverages that can be obtained from the cocoa nut – it imparts tranquillity to the nerves and gives strength to the whole system; Mott's soluble cocoa is instantly soluble and a cup of boiling water added results in hot chocolate; cocoa is highly nutritious and agreeable; from the facility with which it may be prepared, it is particularly convenient for travellers and is sold for 6d/package."[34] By the end of the nineteenth century, Mott's company was producing upward of fifteen different types of cocoa and chocolate products, ranging from "homeopathic" cocoa powder, broma, and breakfast chocolate, to cocoa nibs and shells, various sorts of cooking chocolate, and chocolate liquors.[35]

Evidence suggests that Mott profited handsomely from cocoa and chocolate manufacture. A William Notman photograph of Mott in a carriage, in front of

"Cowan's Dainty Recipes"

Cover of *Cowan's Dainty Recipes*. First published by the Cowan Company of Toronto in 1915.

what is most likely Niagara Falls, suggests that Mott had the leisure time and the means to travel.[36] Investing in a professional photograph of oneself was a rather expensive proposition at the time, generally reserved for members of high society. Furthermore, Hazelhurst, Mott's residence in Dartmouth, was a lavish estate.[37]

Mott makes an appearance in the legal fonds of another prominent Nova Scotian in the chocolate business – James Moir. In 1873 James Moir received permission from his father, William Church Moir, to shift the emphasis of the Moir Steam Bakery and Flour Mill from biscuits to chocolate. Court summons suggest that Mr Moir was occasionally lax in paying his invoices to Mr Mott.[38] Presumably, Mott was selling some form of cocoa or raw chocolate to James Moir.

The Cowan Company of Toronto was another Canadian cocoa manufacturer that started up in business in the nineteenth century. Like Mott, John Warren Cowan was an adept self-promoter. At the turn of the twentieth century, trade cookbooks were becoming a popular marketing tool for manufacturers, and the Cowan Company followed this trend, publishing a number of cookbooks that promoted its brand and provided ideas for cocoa's culinary use. Similarly, Walter Baker & Company put out a number of cookbooks with covers that featured their distinctive emblem, "La Belle Chocolatière."[39]

Cowan's Dainty Recipes was first published in 1915, and it enjoyed many subsequent editions. The cookbook gives tips on how to measure and melt chocolate, and lists many recipes for hot and cold chocolate beverages. The dessert recipes range from custards, puddings, and ice creams to sauces, cakes, cookies, and candies. Cowan was among a growing number of manufacturers producing a range of diverse cocoa and chocolate products at the turn of the century. Mott, Cowan, Walter Baker, and another Canadian company, Todhunter, Mitchell & Company, were all selling cocoas and chocolates for baking or eating to the Canadian market. The prices current section of the 2 January 1891 edition of *Canadian Grocer* lists roughly twenty items in Cowan's repertoire.

THE CHOCOLATE MAKERS

"Eating chocolate" (chocolate for eating rather than for drinking) ushered in the age of chocolate candy companies. Many of the Canadian chocolate makers mentioned above launched their businesses in the last quarter of the nineteenth century or in the first quarter of the twentieth. Both Moir and Ganong started up their companies in 1873, but their immediate focus was not chocolate confectionery. Ganong began as a general merchant, while Moir was in the biscuit business. However, chocolate soon proved to be a viable venture for both of these families.

Ganong Brothers Ltd., based in St Stephen, New Brunswick, and still family owned and operated, lays claim to many of the innovations in the Canadian chocolate candy business. In 1910, Arthur Ganong invented and introduced the first five-cent chocolate nut bar in North America. The company was also the first Canadian confectioner to use cellophane packaging. In 1887, Ganong

Brothers installed the first lozenge-making machine in Canada. Still in use today, it is possibly be the oldest operating candy-making machine in the world. The Ganongs also introduced the heart-shaped box to the Canadian marketplace, originally issuing it at Christmastime.[40]

The early twentieth century saw competition grow as the Walter M. Lowney Company, William Neilson Ltd., and Willard's Chocolates Ltd. established factories in Canada. The first Laura Secord shop (or "studio," as these shops were originally called) opened in Toronto in 1913. It is interesting that both Ganong Brothers and Laura Secord chose to use Canadian heroines as the face for their chocolates. In 1904, the Ganongs introduced the figure of Evangeline on their chocolate boxes, the romantic heroine of Acadia who was immortalized by Henry Wadsworth Longfellow in his poem "A Tale of Acadie." She embodied the qualities of purity, excellence, constancy, romance, sentiment, and sweetness – in short, all of the qualities that Ganongs wished to associate with their chocolates. Evangeline was a constant with Ganong Brothers until 1978. As the masthead for the chocolatier, meanwhile, Laura Secord has undergone various beauty treatments in her time, morphing from dour doyenne to the rosy-cheeked lass who adorned chocolate boxes at the end of the twentieth century.

CHOCOLATE TODAY

In the contemporary story of chocolate, some interesting developments are afoot. More and more scientific investigations into the chemical compounds of *theobroma cacao* are being conducted in an effort to conclusively link cocoa's flavonols with such medical benefits as lowered blood pressure, improvement in the processing of blood sugar, and promotion of heart health. Yoga classes in which participants nibble on raw chocolate between poses are gaining in popularity, the idea being to heighten the supposed euphoria that stems from both the yoga and the chocolate. Furthermore, the modern food-savvy public increasingly demands not only improved products, but also more global conscientiousness from food manufacturers in terms of health, fair trade, and environmental responsibility. Fair trade cocoa and chocolates and artisanal chocolates from single-estate cocoa plantations currently share shelf space with the industrial chocolate brands. Boutique chocolatiers combine chocolate with spices, such as chilli, lavender, pepper, cinnamon, and other exotics that recall the earliest chocolate recipes. A rich, unctuous "drinking chocolate" is making an appearance on the menus of cafes and restaurants. While these trends are only the tip of the iceberg, it would seem that the culture of chocolate as experienced by Canadians, past and present, has come full circle. The renewed reverence placed on the bean and its by-products evokes the life of chocolate among the early Mesoamericans, when it earned its title as "food of the gods."

NOTES

1 Portions of this chapter appear in *Chocolate: History, Culture, and Heritage*, ed. Louis E. Grivetti and Howard-Yana Shapiro, chap. 24, "Chocolate's Early History in Canada" (Hoboken, NJ: John Wiley & Sons, Inc., 2009), 301, and are reprinted with the permission of John Wiley & Sons, Inc. The research presented in this chapter forms part of a greater body of work carried out by an international team of scholars and historians who are recording the unabridged history of chocolate's life in North America. The project has been funded by Mars Incorporated and administered in part by the University of California, Davis. The McCord Museum was charged with the task of documenting the Canadian portion of that history. Using the McCord's resources, researchers attempted to record a summarized, overarching history of chocolate in Canada. The research strives to document a portrait of chocolate's "life" such as it was in Canada from the colonial era up until the early twentieth century.

2 We are grateful to an anonymous manuscript reviewer for pointing out that Duncan mentions chocolate in two menus on page 116 and makes reference to chocolate bars on page 118 and to chocolate on pages 165 and 194.

3 For a more overarching examination of chocolate's history, particularly its early history, see Coe and Coe, *True History of Chocolate*. See also entries on chocolate, cocoa, and cacao in Davidson, *Oxford Companion to Food*; and Kiple and Ornelas, *Cambridge World History of Food*.

4 Coe, *True History of Chocolate*, 19–21.

5 Ibid., 17–18.

6 Ibid., chaps 2–3.

7 See discussion of this in Coe and Coe, *True History of Chocolate*, 129–30.

8 West, "Brief History and Botany of Cacao," 105.

9 Coe and Coe, *True History of Chocolate,* 157.

10 Fougère, personal communication.

11 D'Alembert and Diderot, *Encyclopedie, ou, Dictionnaire Raisonné,* 360. Courtesy of Fortress Louisbourg.

12 Chapin, "New England Vessels," http://fortress.uccb.ns.ca/search/Chapin.html. Jesuit's Bark, also referred to as Peruvian Bark, is the dried bark of several species of trees or shrubs of the genus *Cinchona.* First described and introduced by Jesuit priests in Peru, the bark yields such medicinal alkaloids as quinine and quinidine and was used to treat malaria.

13 Adams, "Construction and Occupation of the Barracks," http://fortress.uccb.ns.ca/search/ha13_24.htm.

14 Charles Aubert de la Chesnaye's probate inventory is taken from the files of notary Florent Lacetière, dated 27 October 1702. Archives nationales du Québec à Québec. Thanks to Yvon Desloges, Parks Canada, for this reference.

15 Library and Archives Canada, Collection Baby, 1629–1907: Correspondence, 2, Havy and Lefebvre to Pierre Guy, Quebec, 29 October 1745, 742, cited in Young, "Merchant Women in New France," 405. Thanks to Anne Marie Lane Jonah, Fortress Louisbourg, for this reference.

16 Champlain, *Narrative of a Voyage,* 26–7, http://www.canadiana.org/ECO/ PageView/33073/0156?id=0fb85d17d4b1c51e. The honey substance referenced by Champlain is mentioned twice in this description; it is pressed from the pith at the heart of the tree. He also describes a sort of thread from this tree, used by the Indians: "This tree bears numbers of thorns, which are very pointed; and when they are torn off, a thread comes from the bark of the said tree, which they spin as fine as they please; and with this thorn, and the thread which is attached to it, they can sew as well as with a needle and other thread. The Indians make very good, fine and delicate thread of it." These latter traits, as well as the honey substance, do not apply to *Theobroma cacao*; however, they do describe the maguey plant, or *Agave americana*. In the illustration that accompanies the description, the two trees are combined: we see the distinct pods of the cacao tree suspended directly from the trunk. Yet the bark is incredibly spiny and a figure – a Native American – is pictured beneath the tree, sewing with thorn and thread. What might explain these inaccuracies? The description is taken from the above-cited volume under the section titled *Brief discours des choses plus remarquables que Samuel Champlain de Brouage a reconnues aux Indes occidentals*. While it is often attributed to him, Champlain never published this particular text. He may have written the text later in life, or someone to whom

WHAT DO AND DID WE EAT?

Champlain recounted the details might have written it. This could account for the confused description. The illustrations are generally credited to and accepted as the work of Champlain; they are originals, whereas the text is a copy. Because the illustration listed as "cacou" reflects the combined physical attributes of the cacao and agave plants, it is unclear whether Champlain was basing the drawing on the confused description in the text, on information drawn from multiple external sources, or on his own memory, muddied by time. For further discussion of the authenticity of this text, see Claude de Bonnault, "Encore le Brief discours: Champlain a-t-il été à Blavet en 1598?" *Bulletin des recherches historiques* 60 (1954): 59–69; Jean Bruchési, "Champlain a-t-il menti?" *Cahiers des Dix* 15 (1950): 39–53; Marcel Delafosse, "L'oncle de Champlain," *Revue d'histoire de l'Amérique française* 12 (1958–59): 208–16; Jacques Rousseau, "Samuel de Champlain, botaniste mexican et antillais," *Cahiers des Dix* 16 (1951): 39–61; L.-A. Vigneras, "Le voyage de Samuel Champlain aux Indes occidentales," *Revue d'histoire de l'Amérique française* 11 (1957–58): 163–200; Vigneras, "Encore le capitaine provençal," ibid., 13 (1959–60): 544–9; and Marcel Trudel's entry in the *Dictionary of Canadian Biography Online*, http://www.biographi.ca/EN/ShowBio.asp?BioId=34237&query=Samuel%20AND%20de%20AND%20Champlain (accessed 3 February 2009).

17 Pothier, "Le Moyne D'Iberville," http://www.biographi.ca/EN/ShowBio.asp?BioId=35062&query=Pierre%20AND%20Le%20AND%20Moyne%20AND%20D'Ibervill.

18 Langdon, *Canadian Silversmiths*, pl. 29.

19 Miller, *Miller's Letter Books, #1*, 5, http://www.lib.unb.ca/winslow/winslowunb.html.

20 West, "Brief History and Botany of Cacao," 113–14.

21 *Halifax Gazette*, 30 March 1752, sec. 2, 2.

22 *Royal Gazette and Newfoundland Advertiser*, 26 October 1815, http://daryl.chin.gc.ca:8000/BASIS/acns/user/www/sf.

23 Perkins, *Diary of Simeon Perkins*, 120.

24 Byles, *Byles' Letter Books #4*, 16, http://www.lib.unb.ca/winslow/winslowunb.html.

25 Gottfred, "Compendium of Material Culture," http://www.northwestjournal.ca/X2.htm.

26 Gottfred, "Fur Fort Food," http://www.northwestjournal.ca/II4.htm.

27 Béthune and Rousseau, *Voyage de Pehr Kalm*, 297. Translation: "The men often take a piece of bread, which they eat after having dipped it in spirits; or they may

take a sip of the alcohol and then eat the piece of bread; or they take chocolate just as frequently." Thanks to Anne Marie Lane Jonah, Fortress Louisbourg, for this reference.

28 Franklin, *Thirty Years in the Arctic Regions*, 95.

29 Ibid., 463.

30 *Journal and Proceedings of the House of Assembly of the Province of Nova Scotia* (Halifax, 1839), app. 53, x–xi.

31 Atlantic Canada Newspaper Survey, cocoa advertisements from numerous newspapers throughout Newfoundland, Nova Scotia, Prince Edward Island, and New Brunswick, accessed at Canadian Heritage online reference library: http://daryl.chin.gc.ca:8000/BASIS/acns/user/www/sf.

32 Advertisement for Baker's cocoa, *Canadian Grocer,* 6 March 1891, 16.

33 Lawson, *History of the Townships.* 97.

34 *Islander,* 14 December 1855, http://daryl.chin.gc.ca:8000/BASIS/acns/user/www/sf.

35 *Maritime Merchant – Maritime Grocer and Commercial Review,* 12 January 1893, n.p.

36 Nova Scotia Archives and Records Management, Notman Studio Collection, reference no. 1983-310/ 91250. William Notman operated the largest photographic enterprise in North America, with seven studios throughout Canada and nineteen in the northeastern United States, including seasonal studios. The superior quality of the Notman photographs found in collections in archives across Canada makes them not only valuable from a research perspective, but also valuable as photographic records of Canadian social history.

37 Nova Scotia Archives and Records Management, Notman Studio Collection, reference no. 1983-310/ 5367.

38 Moirs Limited Fonds, 1–91, 1–71.

39 *Choice Recipes by Miss Maria Parloa.* "La Belle Chocolatière" was painted by Swiss artist Jean-Etienne Liotard, circa 1743, and became the emblem for Walter Baker & Company Ltd. See West, "Brief History and Botany of Cacao," 115.

40 Folster, *Ganong,* 52–70.

4

The Long History of the *Tourtière* of Quebec's Lac-St-Jean

JEAN-PIERRE LEMASSON

INTRODUCTION

Among the traditional dishes of Quebec's cuisine there is one that stands in a class of its own. It is known as the *tourtière*, and more precisely, the tourtière from Lac-St-Jean. Particularly since the beginning of the 1970s, this dish has become a genuinely national and iconic dish, one that is consumed during the winter holiday season. Each family in the region of Saguenay–Lac-St-Jean has its own particular version of the recipe, passed down through the generations and ritualistically prepared to celebrate the year's end. At summer community gatherings in Roberval for the last fifty years or so, each family brings its own tourtière to share with neighbours at table. Certainly at these events no one would have the audacity to suggest that the tourtière –so obviously belonging to the culinary patrimony of the *Saguenéens* (residents of the region of Saguenay, Quebec) and, by extension, to all Quebecers – in fact belongs first and foremost to those who first made the dish. This "authentic" Québécois dish is actually, as culinary history has shown so many others to be, a borrowed dish. Thus, it would seem that the Quebec tourtière, whose multiple linguistic and physical metamorphoses this chapter will trace, is the last avatar of a dish with a very long history.

THE FIRST KNOWN RECIPES

The Babylonian collection at Yale University houses clay tablets dating from 1600 BC from several archaeological sites in the Babylonian area. Written in Akkadian and Sumerian, these tablets were only – relatively speaking – recently deciphered by Jean Bottéro,[1] the French anthropologist who, in doing so, "discovered" the very first recipes known to humanity.

Most of the recipes, thirty-five in number, were for soups. However, several of them were in fact for what we would consider today as pies. Of these, many were only fragments of recipes or were barely legible because of the deteriorated state of the tablets, but the most complete recipe was henceforth baptized by Jean Bottéro himself as "little birds pie." The preparation is as follows:[2]

> To prepare one ... of ... the little birds, you remove the head, neck and legs; you open the stomach, and you take out the gizzard and viscera. After having slit the gizzard you peel it. You then wash the bird and you mince the viscera. Then, having scoured the cauldron, you put in the birds. Gizzards and intestines. Once you have taken the cauldron off the fire, you clean the contents with a good quantity of cold water.
>
> In a pot, you pour in water and milk and you put it on the fire ...[3] You then wipe birds, gizzards, intestines [each] properly, and sprinkle them with salt, and you put everything together in the pot. You put in a piece of fat, from which you have removed the strands. And you also put in a sufficient amount of "aromatic wood" in the same quantity as the leaves you've picked from the rue plant.
>
> When it boils, you add a little onion and samidu, leek and garlic which you crush with the onion. And you add, likewise, a small quantity of clear water. You then clean the sasku-semolina, soak it in milk and, once moist, you knead it with the brine-siqqu and you add, while leaving it supple, samidu, leek, garlic, milk and fat-from-the-pot.

While kneading it, watch it closely. Divide this dough into two equal halves. Leave one to rise, stored in a pot; and cook the other, in the oven, in little sebetu-breads of 2 (?) grams each, which you remove (from the bottom surface) once cooked.[4]

You again knead the sasku-semolina that is soaked and moist with milk while adding oil (?), leek, garlic and samidu. Then, you take a dish whose surface can hold the birds from the cooking and this dough, you dip it, while letting its other end resurface four fingers higher than the edge of the dish.

You will then seek the large vase (in which you were storing half of the first quantity of dough) and this dough you place in and spread out in a dish, which you will have likewise chosen for its being big enough to cover the surface taken up by the birds. You sprinkle the dish with mint and, to make a cover, you spread the dough that you had first put aside. You then set aside the high-part that seals the oven and which you replace with two (plates?) on which you set the two dishes garnished with pastry. Once everything is cooked, you remove the thin pastry from the serving dish that will serve as the "covering" and you spread oil on it. While waiting for the meal, you store this thin layer of pastry in its dish. Once the birds and broths are cooked, you crush together, in order to add them to the other ingredients, leek, garlic and andashu.

Just before the meal, you take the presentation display-dish garnished with the spread-out pastry and arrange on it with care the cooked birds; over it you strew the cut viscera and gizzards, which were in the pot with the little sebetu-breads that had cooked in the oven.

The fatty broth that covers the meat in the pot, you set aside.

You cover the presentation-dish with its (pastry) "lid" and you serve it at the table.

As the recipe makes clear, the dish consists of a bottom pastry shell, birds and certain of their parts, small pre-baked breads, and a top layer of pastry that serves as a covering. It is essential to note that such a dish – an obvious luxury – was prepared strictly for wealthy and powerful Babylonians and was no doubt the product of a culinary tradition predating the tablets. Therefore, we may safely assume that it dates back to 2000 BC and perhaps even earlier.

It is in some later time – that is to say, about 400 AD – that we find additional evidence of the existence of tourtière of the kind produced in Quebec's Saguenay–Lac-St-Jean region. In fact, the *De Re Coquinaria*, or *Apicius* – a work whose authorship is a topic of debate – provides several recipes for "patina." The following is a daily recipe for the dish:

> Take the tripe of a cooked sow and cut into pieces the flesh of a fish and of a cooked chicken. Mince all of it carefully. Take a bronze mould, break eggs into a cooking pot and beat them. Place pepper and lovage into a mortar, pound them, moisten with garum, wine, and wine made from straw-dried grapes, and a bit of oil, pour into the pot and bring to a boil. Bind after boiling. Throw the meat that you minced into the sauce. At the bottom of the bronze mould place the pastry shell and a full ladle of meat, baste with oil and arrange in the same manner a layer of pastry. Alternate pastry layers with ladles of stuffing.
>
> For the top layer, place a layer of pastry perforated with a hollow reed. Turn it upside-down on a plate, sprinkle with pepper and serve.[5]

This recipe calls for commentary. First of all, it is important to remember that the pastry here is in all likelihood made of wheat and that the covering layer seals the pie very tightly; to prevent the crust from breaking, a straw is inserted into the patina to let the steam escape. Second, the use of a bronze pan indicates the need for a mould strong enough to resist the pressure of very rich contents. Consequently, we can assume that the cooking is not being done in an oven but rather on a fire in a damp environment. Third, this dish is made of superimposed layers ("Alternez les feuilles de pâte et les louches de farce"),[6] a feature that constitutes one of the principal variations from the original dish, testifying to its rich and festive quality. We must concede here that there is, between the patina and the Saguenéen tourtière, a troubling similarity. However, a fourth feature of the patina shows a further distinction between it and the tourtière – the patina is overturned before serving ("Renversez sens dessus dessous sur un plat").[7] We can conclude that the thickness of the pie crust or even its composition – maybe both – was distinctly different from those used today.

These first metamorphoses – from the oven-baked small birds pie to the fire-cooked multilayered one – would influence the pies to come, such that the patina would become the basis of the modern pies. However, we must remember that the Roman culinary culture emerged from the Greeks, whose cooks were renowned amateurs of bread and various pastries. Without claiming that the culinary art of the Greeks was original in the Mediterranean of that era, we must still recognize that from the Greek culinary tradition we inherited the *galette* (a round, flat cake), whether made or not from fermented wheat. Similarly, dough finds its origins in the foodways of the early Greeks – in particular, dough stuffed with meats and resembling the Latin American *empanadas*, East Indian *samosas*, and even certain Turkish *böreks* of today. This stuffed dough was called *Artocréas*, a name retained by the Romans. Although the general form of the Artocréas was similar to the patina, involving food encased by a pastry or dough envelope, the patina represented a more luxurious variation for the rich and powerful. Artocréas then appeared in Rome, towards the end of the Roman Empire, and consisted of a popular oven-baked pastry whose many variations recall a number of meat pies.[8] Patina, on the other hand, was a luxurious dish suitable for receptions and whose thick and generous stuffing was a signifier of the host's wealth.

FROM MEDIEVAL ABUNDANCE AND CREATIVITY TO THE COLONIZATION OF THE AMERICAS

In the Middle Ages, the Artocréas and patina reappeared in several countries, notably in what are today Italy, France, and England. Despite several transformations, the two basic forms of the dishes remained distinct up to that time, but they would later merge in both the French and English versions.

In Italy, the patina became the parmesan pie, in a direct culinary lineage that is well analysed by Anna Martellotti. Over some nine hundred years, the recipe had changed very little, apart from the name derived from a tradition rooted particularly in the city of Parma. Its mixture was no longer the same, but its structure was strangely similar:

[T]here is a large pasty covering, with six different layers of filling while, between one layer and the next, stoneless, stuffed dates are added. The layers are as follows:

1) first of all, pieces of chicken fried in a large quantity of onion and heavily spiced, in an egg fricassee;
2) then white and green cheese ravioli (parsley is added to obtain the green color);
3) sausages made from minced meat and ham;
4) minced pork meat with cheese and eggs;
5) sausages made from brain or marrow-bone with cheese and herbs (similar to luganica sausage);
6) ravioli made with almonds, half of which are sweetened with sugar.[9]

We recognize in this dish the medieval hallmark of associating meat with sugar within a setting of abundance and refinement – for example, the marrow-bone sausages. In an article on this impressive dish, Anna Martellotti conjures up the atmosphere of the event with a flourish: "When it is cooked 'it is brought before the Lord with great pomp' as the Latin cookery book rightly says."[10] The second half of Martellotti's article is dedicated to the resurrection of the pie, in Italy, under such diverse names as "pasticcio," "timballo" or "timpano de maccheroni." She writes: "[T]he pie is no longer a dish of lords but a speciality of popular cooking, something for the poor to gorge themselves on occasionally."[11]

Something similar occurred in France and England. In France, the recipe retained a name strangely reminiscent of the Italian version – *tourte parménienne*. Many versions existed, but the recipe from the Vatican appears to be one of the oldest versions in the French language. The recipe, brought back by Barbara Ketcham Wheaton, reads as follows:

Take the mutton, veal, or pork meat, and chop it finely; then you will need to obtain a chicken, boil it, and cut it into quarters, and you will need to cook the aforementioned chicken before it is minced, and season it with fine spices in reasonable quantities, and fry the chicken in lard fat. And after having removed the upper pastries that served as lids and that are the size of small dishes, and having garnished it with crenels, having a thicker pastry than the others but also more dense so that it can support the chicken, to which you can add pine nuts and Corinth raisins as you like and clarified sugar over top, place in each pastry three or four pieces of chicken into which to drive the banners of France and of the Lords who will be present, and brown them with saffron so that they are more presentable. If you do not wish to rely on so much chicken, be satisfied with pork ribs or roasted or boiled mutton. When the pies are filled with chicken, you will need to brown the underside.[12]

This recipe was still sweet, yet less so than the parmesan pie with its interspersed layers of dates. It was no longer cooked in a large container. Here, it had become decidedly more of an *entremets* (a side dish, or dish served between the courses, before the dessert), a moment of entertainment, as the lords of the period were inclined to appreciate. The castle-like appearance of the pie, complete with crenels and topped with the banners of the lords at the table, transformed this dish into a perfect representation of feudal power.

In the England of the 1660s, a century later, continental influences were ever more profound. It comes as no surprise, then, that among the recipes of the aristocracy's great chefs were recipes that were strangely similar. Thus, in *The Whole Body of Cookery Dissected* (1682), William Rabisha presents two "battle pies." In the first recipe, entitled "To Make a Battlery, or Bisk Pyes in the Spring," the author comments that "[y]ou may make your Coffin round, or Castle fashion" and then proceeds to give a description of pigeons, rabbits, quails, and pieces of lamb that are thrown together in a splendid heap. The second recipe, with fish as its primary ingredient, is more typically English. The recipe "To Make a Batylle of Pye of Fish" is as follows:

You must set a large Coffin, cut with Battlements and set forth round the Coffin, with as many Towers as will contain your several sorts of fish; you may set in the inside also, from one bending to another, for partitions, to lay several sorts of Fish with their Lear asunder: dry your Coffin well, and wash it over in the inside with yolks of Eggs:

flower it in the bottom to soder it: then whatever Fish you have prepared before for your Pie, must be either boiled or fryed brown; in the
middle of your Pye, you may put the head of a Salmon cut off beyond
the gills, forced and baked in the Oven: bake the heads likewise of
your other Fish that they may stand upon forced meat bottoms, then
dish up all your fish in order, every sort one opposite to another,
placed in the several partitions and having your Oysters, Cockles,
Perrywinkles and Pranes, being boyled up in Lears (as you have formerly been taught) ... and garnish on your shell-fish all over and let
the forced heads stand over the battlements.[13]

Such recipes attest to a love of dishes overflowing in abundance. These dishes
are of medieval inspiration but also integrate certain techniques – such as the
use of broth – that were typical of the cooking of the period.

During this time, however, the *tourte parménienne* had already ceased to
exist in France, where we find a proliferation of pies of all kinds, with varied
styles of mixtures. The seventeenth-century text *Le Cuisinier François* by La
Varenne,[14] presents over thirty pie recipes. They are considerably simpler
than the medieval pies, even though it was also the custom to serve them at
the royal table. But the fashion of seventeenth-century France privileged the
refinement of the mixture over the quantity of food. In this sense, the tastes of
the French royal court shared an affiliation with popular tastes of the time, as
exemplified by the popular meat pies sold on street corners.

In England, even if enormous pies in the style of "Battle Pies" were still
appreciated, we also see an increase in the popularity of more modest pies.
The mixtures that were used in these pies were varied, but their spices and
preparation techniques were still marked by medieval traditions. Meat pie
was therefore a versatile dish that appealed to both the wealthy and the poor.
As Alberto Cappatti and Massimo Montanari suggest, "Meat pie is an edible
object that seems made for the purpose of crossing the entire social stratum.
Extremely practical, easy to make and preserve, apparently within the means
of all and thus able to connote, on the whole, a gastronomic civilisation, meat
pies follow various practices (the filling can be complex or simple, costly or
cheap), and their cooking techniques may vary."[15]

From the very beginning of the eighteenth century, the paths of the meat pie
in France and England began to diverge. In France, the pie that had reigned as

Bake oven, Château de Ramezay, Montreal, QC, c. 1900. Photograph by Wm Notman & Son. Courtesy of McCord Museum, VIEW-3346.

a side dish on royal tables had disappeared by the beginning of the nineteenth century, as Antonin Carême demonstrates: "This pastry entrée is no longer considered enough of a delicacy to appear on the tables of the wealthy, for its bearing is too uncouth."[16] The dish subsequently disappeared from the list of desirable Parisian foods and only endured in France until after the Second World War, in the margins of regional cooking. In England, too, we witness the disappearance of what one might call the "aristocratic" meat pie. As Louis Eustache Ude, renowned chef of the English elite, noted in 1813: "This dish ('lark croustade') does not earn many admirers, since birds in croustade, and even raised pies, are rarely requested. The nobility of this country likes to be able to see what they are eating. With a raised pie, they are afraid that they might find parts not to their liking. The reason is simple and justifies their aversion. The so-called raised pies being, in general, inexpensive first courses, are made of the legs or other lower pieces of poultry or game meat. In general, people only appreciate the fillets."[17] But on the tables of the British gentry, who lived off the products of the land, the modest raised pie flourished. We find the meat pie in every cookbook, showing its continued popularity. Thus, Hannah Glasse's touchstone cookbook, *The Art of Cookery*, published for the first time in 1747, presents about twenty pie recipes, among which the "Cheshire Pork Pie" is of importance.[18] Here, pork meat reappears, but with the designation of a particular region in England: Cheshire. In the later American edition of 1805 (published in Alexandria in the United States),[19] a new section was added – without the knowledge of the author – that included three new pies, two of which were made with pork. One of these, "The Pork Pie," calls for closer attention. It is made with chopped meat seasoned with salt and pepper and cooked dry (that is, without sauce). This is the Quebec recipe that is sometimes called "meat pâté" (*pâté de viande*), since some refuse to grant it, as we will see further on, the status of the tourtière.

In England, the pie enjoyed an enduring success, with hardly a cookbook neglecting to mention it. Thus, it found itself in good standing in such a book as Isabella Beeton's *Household Management*. If certain pies are rather modest, others attract attention, consisting of a typically bourgeois compromise between aristocratic fine cookery and the popular tradition of the simple meat pâté. Beeton's "Warwickshire Pie," for instance, was made by alternating layers of fatty and lean pork, lending a more sophisticated air to the dish. In her "Raised Pie of Veal and Ham," we also find several alternating layers of minced veal and ham or bacon. Without actually reproducing the opulence of the past, the dish with its several layers of alternated meat nevertheless gave a strong sense of the splendour of the pies of old. As well, this last recipe is a "Raised Pie," a pie with raised sides, and as such a promise of abundance.

SEA PIE, CIPAILLE, AND TOURTIÈRE, OR THE METAMORPHOSES OF THE NEW WORLD

The *tourte* and the pie crossed the Atlantic in the minds and food practices of the French and English settlers. The tourte came in its most basic form, as a meat pâté, and was a simple restorative food for colonists. The presence of the more prestigious pie, however, can be traced through cookbooks. In this regard, the first cookbook that was considered North American, dating from 1792 and authored by Amelia Simmons, offers a sumptuous surprise in the form of a recipe entitled "Sea Pie": "Four pound of flour, one and half pound of butter rolled into paste, wet with coldwater, line the pot therewith, lay in split pigeons, turkey pies, veal, mutton or birds, with slices of pork, salt, pepper, and dust on flour, doing thus till the pot is full or your ingredients expended, add three pints water, cover tight with paste, and stew moderately two and half hours."[20]

We can draw two conclusions from this recipe: first, the sea pie is made in a cauldron (pot) and is a kind of raised pie, but one that is cooked directly in a mould lined with pastry, recalling, in this respect, Apicius's patina. We cannot clearly determine whether the pieces of meat are layered. Second, the sea pie contains only meat and no seafood ingredients whatsoever. Why then, one wonders, does it carry such a name? Although there remains some contention surrounding the exact origins of the sea pie, it seems quite plausible that this dish comes from Great Britain (the exact region is difficult to determine, but it may be Scotland) and was likely the type of food consumed by naval officers when they were at sea. This particular version of the pie's origins has the advantage of accounting for, on the one hand, the dish's popularity among sailors, who were only too happy to eat meat rather than the ubiquitous fish, and, on the other, why the recipe calls for a solid, protective mould, which would have been necessary during sea journeys. Basically, the sea pie was a raised pie and was thus easily transported in a cauldron.

The sea pie appears to be the direct forerunner of the tourtière of Lac-St-Jean, even though at first glance such a connection would seem heretical to many a Quebecer. How had such a genealogy established itself? The sea pie would have entered Quebec through the Gaspésie, where it appears to have taken on various names, several of which are based on French transliteration of the English phonetic. Thus, the sea pie became *la cipaye, la cipaille,* and *la cipare.* However, several names – such as *la six pâtes* (six pastries), *six pailles* (six straws), and *cipâte* – raise a question: could it be possible that francophones, through a kind of homophonic transformation of the English term "sea pie," had thought that the sea pie was in fact made of six layers of pastry and thus, when they themselves adopted the dish, had spontaneously added layers in its preparation?

The question is difficult to answer but must be posed, since *la cipaille* – which is the name we will use for sea pie from this point on – is a dish that is characterized by layered ingredients (meats can be superposed and also interspersed with layers of thin pastry). Is this method of layering indeed the result of an anglo-francophone linguistic performance, or is it directly inspired from other dishes? Certainly, a number of seafood dishes of the time were composed of layers – for example, the *pot en pot* of the Îles-de-la-Madeleine or even the clam bake of the First Nations. Furthermore, the name *cipaille* seems to come from New England, and in fact, commercial trading between diverse regions of the North American east coast, as Loyalists arrived in the years 1780–90, could fully explain the presence of the cipaille among us. A third explanation for why Quebec cooks adopted a layered method of raised pie preparation can be traced to successive waves of immigration. The significant proportion of anglophone immigrants from Great Britain – England, Ireland, and Scotland – might surely account for the continuity of British culinary traditions, including that of the raised pie, in the New World.[21]

Quebec's potato culture began under English rule, likely around 1770, and it is around this time that we start to find cipaille dishes in which layers are created through the use of potatoes alone or sometimes through potatoes being interspersed with thin layers of pastry to make the dish even more substantial.[22] The following is a typical recipe: "Debone the chicken, partridge, and hare, and chop all the meat (or in addition to the preceding kinds, fresh beef, veal, and pork, and venison) into cubes, except the salted lard. Mix together spices and onions. Add meat and mix well. Cover and marinate at a cool temperature for the whole night. Chop the lard into cubes and melt it in a big cauldron. Remove it from the heat and add a row of meat and onion followed by a row of potatoes. Repeat until all ingredients are used. Cover with a thick layer of pastry; make a hole in the center. Into this pour the hot broth up to the level of the pastry. Cover and place in the oven. Cook for 7 hours at 120° Celsius. Add hot broth as needed while it cooks."[23] Not only is this dish found today in all of Gaspésie, but many versions of it are especially common on the south shore of the St Lawrence River. How did this dish become the originator of the tourtière of Lac-St-Jean, a place so far removed from the river? How did this dish, which separates its meat with layers, evolve into Lac-St-Jean's tourtière, which mixes its meat contents directly?

Bake oven, Lac-St-Jean, QC, c. 1892. Photograph by Wm Notman & Son. Courtesy of McCord Museum, VIEW-2718.

Before these questions can be answered and to avoid certain misunder-standings, it is important to specify that in France *la tourtière* was the dish in which a meat pie was cooked. Through metonymic association not uncommon in culinary culture,[24] the pie (*la tourte*) became *la tourtière*. While the word *tourte* is proscribed in dictionaries in France,[25] Napoléon Caron's insistence on avoiding the colloquialism *tourtière* in 1880 suggests that the term was, by then, relatively well established. We thus speak here of tourtière with the understanding that the metamorphosis was linguistic rather than culinary.

To return to the original question, then, how did the word *cipaille* become *tourtière?* Answering this question definitively is difficult, since it requires both retracing migratory movements that we know little about and mining the elusive details of former kitchen practices. One can justifiably assume that certain Gaspesians could have settled in Quebec's Charlevoix region before moving to the Lac-St-Jean region (west of the Charlevoix). Other population movements included migration to the south shore of the St Lawrence (notably to the islet Kamouraska), where we find numerous recipes for the cipaille, and towards Lac-St-Jean. While the migratory path is unclear, however, it is certain that Lac-St-Jean's tourtière had all the characteristics of the cipaille.

The cooking reference book *Vers une nouvelle cuisine québécoise* indicates that "[i]n Canadian cooking, not a day goes by in which the recipe for the Saguenay cipaille is not reclaimed."[26] Here, one sees that the word *tourtière* was not used consistently. And to complicate things further, the name *la tourtière* was also given to a dish that retained the structure of the cipaille. Thus, in 1971, Madame Céline Roland Bouchard provided the following recipe for the Saguenay tourtière ("Tourtière saguenéenne"):

> The evening before, after having cleaned the hare and partridge, cut into pieces. Similarly, separate one pound of moose into big pieces. Cut 2 pounds of pork from the top round into ½ inch cubes. Put all the meat into a dish, add grated onion, salt, and pepper. Mix while adding a hint of cinnamon: cover with an air-tight lid and chill. The same day, peel and cut into cubes 3 to 4 pints [quarts] of potatoes. Line the bottom and sides of a thick cauldron with the pastry of your choice. Fill up with alternate layers of potatoes and meat. Add enough hot water to cover the ingredients after having added a piece of salted lard (¼ pound) in the centre of the mix. Salt and pepper and cover with a thin layer of pastry. Make an incision to allow the steam to escape. Cook in a hot oven at 450 F, for 30 minutes, then reduce the heat to 325 F; cover, and continue to cook for another 3 ½ hours. One hour before it has finished cooking, leave the lid partially open so that the pastry becomes crispy. Add water, if needed.[27]

Everything points to the possibility that the tourtière of Lac-St-Jean was a Gaspesian cipaille that at first retained its name only to lose eventually, at a later stage, its characteristic layers. Why is this so? Without hesitation, we can say that, at the turn of the twentieth century, a tradition of Gaspesian-style tourtière and another tradition from the Charlevoix cohabited and that this latter tradition was not the dominant one. Everything shifted shortly after the Quiet Revolution, and the dish – both in name and form – henceforth became the object of a regional consensus and pride.

Where did such a consensus come from and why was it not established during the first part of the twentieth century? In the first place, the 1970s was a decade of intense affirmation for French Quebec. Within a short period of time, the French language underwent significant development and transformation, and the term *la tourtière*, with its very tangible point of reference to culinary method, might well have been favoured over a term of uncertain reference and possibly English origin. In the second place, Quebec subsequently experienced a period that saw the writing and publication of numerous cookbooks. These cookbooks reclaimed the term *la tourtière* for the most part, creating the conditions for a consistent terminology while reducing the impact of the more heterogeneous oral traditions and responding to a greater formality in language among the newly well-educated young people of the 1970s. In this period, too, the will to reconstruct a typically Québécois culinary patrimony emerged. This patrimony was founded on a return to regional cooking and served to promote culinary distinctiveness at the provincial level. In this sense, the desire to create a national cuisine had the effect, ironically, of reinforcing *regional* identities and, further, encouraging an increasing homogeneity of recipes and consistency in methods of preparation at a local level. Precisely at this time, the tourtière of Lac-St-Jean, because of its richness and association with conviviality, became a genuinely iconic national dish. The 1970s were also marked by a growing exodus of young people from Lac-St-Jean to Montreal, and this trend towards urbanization in post–Quiet Revolution Quebec not only enabled the widespread diffusion of an appealing dish, but also contributed to the nostalgic connotations increasingly ascribed to it.

Since the 1970s, the tourtière of Lac-St-Jean has eclipsed in fame and popularity not only the tourtière from the Charlevoix, but also the Gaspesian cipaille, becoming the culinary emblem of a culturally rich and complex country with a fierce pride in its French cultural heritage and its promising future. The tourtière, or raised pie, has a profound symbolic resonance in today's Canada, just as its original form had in the Babylonian era, although the precise trail linking one to the other is yet to be discovered.

Author's note: I would like to thank Lorna Hutchison for translating this chapter from the original French.

1   Bottéro, *Plus vieille cuisine.*
2   The following is an English translation of Bottéro's French text. It should be noted that Bottéro uses the familiar "tu" rather than the more formal "vous" more conventionally understood in modern recipes. Further, for this recipe, he indicates the separation of lines of instruction by numbering them 1–49. The question marks appear in his transcription and are reproduced here to indicate moments of particular ambiguity or illegibility of the original.
3   In Bottéro's French transcription of the original, a note is added at this point: "NB: ce dernier passage a été embrouillé par le copiste distrait." Bottéro, *Plus vieille cuisine,* 52.
4   Ibid., 52–3.
5   Apicius, *L'art culinaire,* 37. The quotation has been translated into English.
6   Ibid.
7   Ibid..
8   The Roman Empire took some centuries to disappear. Its decline began in about AD 400, but the Artocréas most likely dates from the time of Christ. However, dating of recipes cannot be exact, since there exists significant debate about the authorship of the *Apicius,* as a number of different individuals named Apicius lived during the four centuries following the birth of Christ.
9   Anna Martellotti, "The Parmesan Pie," *Petit Propos Culinaires*, pt 1, 12.
10 Ibid., 13.
11 Ibid., 12.
12 Wheaton, *L'office et la bouche,* 296–7. This is an English translation of Wheaton's transcription of the original French Vatican version. "Crenels," or *creneau* in modern French and *créneaulx* in Wheaton's transcription, refers to an architectural detail on a medieval castle that afforded protection when the castle was under attack.
13 Rabisha, *Whole Body of Cookery Dissected,* 216. While the letters have been regularized to conform to modern English, the original spelling and capitalization are retained in this transcription.
14 La Varenne, *Cuisinier François.*
15 Cappatti and Montanari, *Cuisine Italienne,* 92–3.
16 Carême, *Pâtisser Royal Parisien,* 106.

17 Ude, *French Cook,* 252.

18 Today this pie has become "Fidget Pie" in Mason and Brown's *Traditional Food in Britain,* 194.

19 Glasse, *Art of Cookery.*

20 Simmons, *The First American Cookbook,* 23.

21 Lambert, *La Cuisine familiale au Québec,* vol. 2, 188–96.

22 Gagné, *Recettes typiques de la Gaspésie,* 23, 100.

23 Lorraine Boisvenue, *Le guide de la cuisine traditionnelle,* 166.

24 In a similar manner, the dish known today as *tajine* is a Moroccan dish whose name comes from the earthenware plate in which it was cooked in the past. The same process has occurred, for example, with the Japanese *dunburi*: the dish (rice, with foods placed over top it) took on the name of the actual earthenware plate on which the rice was served.

25 Thus, we find in Napoléon Caron's *Le petit vocabulaire à l'usage des canadiens français: Contenant les mots dont il faut répande l'usage et signalant les barbarismes qu'il faut éviter pour bien parler notre langue* (1880), the following definition of *tourte*: "Pièce de pâtisserie dans laquelle on met des viandes, du poisson etc., et qu'on sert chaude. Littré: ne pas dire tourtière!" (A pastry in which we place meats, fish etc., and which is served hot. *Littré*: do not use the term *tourtière*!)

26 Institut de tourisme et d'hôtellerie du Québec, *Vers une nouvelle cuisine québécoise,* 24–5. "En cuisine canadienne, il ne se passe pas de jour sans que soit réclamée la recette du cipaille du Saguenay."

27 Bouchard, *Le Pinereau,* 114. This is an English translation of the French original.

5

Talking Turkey: Thanksgiving in Canada and the United States

ANDREW SMITH AND SHELLEY BOYD

INTRODUCTION

European explorers and colonists have celebrated Thanksgiving since they arrived in North America during the sixteenth century. The Spanish did so in Florida (1513, 1565), Texas (1541), and New Mexico (1598), just as the French later did in Florida (1564). After a difficult crossing of the Atlantic Ocean in 1578, the English explorer Martin Frobisher made a point of celebrating Thanksgiving with a ceremonial dinner on Baffin Island. Noting that a baker travelled aboard Frobisher's vessel, Ethel Gillingham argues that communion bread was in all likelihood a part of that first Thanksgiving dinner as well as the "meager supplies remaining from their voyage, and the local wildlife and fish."[1] An archaeological dig in the early 1990s by Canadian and American researchers revealed a cache of supplies that Frobisher's crew had placed in the ground for a future return voyage; found were the remains of carbonized wheat biscuits and well-preserved green peas, the "leftovers" of one of North America's first Thanksgiving dinners.[2]

Thanksgivings were frequently observed in colonial America, particularly in New England. These Thanksgiving Days usually commemorated local events, such as the safe return of loved ones from a long trip, a military victory, a successful harvest, or providential rainfalls. These were solemn religious occasions spent in prayer, and little evidence has surfaced that would point to the inclusion of a formal meal as a part of the Thanksgiving observance. Only two records mention food, and they are both unusual. In November 1732, there was a Thanksgiving celebration in Georgia, and after the formal ceremony, the celebrants shared a "plentiful Dinner" with "8 Turkeys" and other food.[3] On 7 July 1733, the town of Savannah, also in Georgia, celebrated Thanksgiving with a "very substantial dinner."[4] What is interesting about these dinners is that those celebrating them had come directly from England and were not from the American colonies. The English influence behind these dinners suggests that the present-day American celebration of Thanksgiving dinner derived from English traditions.

NEW ENGLAND THANKSGIVING MEALS

In the United States, the Thanksgiving dinner was firmly established by the American War of Independence (1776–83). To celebrate the victory at Saratoga in 1777, the Continental Congress declared a day of thanksgiving. In his journal, Joseph Plumb Martin, a soldier, noted that for this celebration "[e]ach man was given half a gill of rice and a tablespoonful of vinegar."[4] More sumptuous fare appeared in 1779 descriptions of Thanksgiving meals. In one, a goose was served;[5] in another, venison, goose, and pigeons were served along with a plethora of side dishes and desserts.[6] Although there is a suggestion that Loyalists may have brought Thanksgiving dinner with them when they immigrated to Canada during the revolutionary war, it was not until the middle of the nineteenth century that Canadian Thanksgiving meals were first mentioned in print. Indeed, one of Canada's most renowned pioneers and writers, Catharine Parr Traill, who emigrated from England to Upper Canada in 1832, makes no explicit mention of a Canadian Thanksgiving holiday in either *The Backwoods of Canada* (1836) or the popular *Canadian Settler's Guide* (1855). Harvest celebrations do appear, however, as Traill refers to meals and dances that follow "Husking-Bees" during the fall harvesting of the corn crop.[7]

In Traill's writings, we see an early precursor to Canadian Thanksgiving, as her *Guide* includes recipes for pumpkin pie and cranberry sauce, dishes that would become staples of the traditional Thanksgiving meal. In clearing and settling the backwoods, Canadian pioneers found, however, that turkeys were not a pragmatic choice. In fact, Traill observes that turkeys "were only to be met with on old cleared farms in those days," as young turkeys were "great ramblers ... [doing] much hurt to the young grain."[8] For autumn meals, Traill notes, "[p]igeons are best for table just after wheat harvest: the young birds are then very fat."[9]

By the late eighteenth century, the dinner became a particularly significant part of the celebration of Thanksgiving in New England. Families would spend a week or more in preparation for the dinner and much of Thanksgiving Day in cooking and eating. A participant in a 1784 Thanksgiving meal in Norwich, Connecticut, proclaimed: "What a sight of pigs and geese and turkeys and fowls and sheep must be slaughtered to gratify the voraciousness of a single day."[10] In 1806, William Bentley, the pastor of the East Church in Salem, Massachusetts, reported that "[a] Thanksgiving is not complete without a turkey. It is rare to find any other dishes but such as turkeys & fowls afford before the pastry on such days & puddings are much less used than formerly."[11] Bentley's description suggests that the meal was made up of two courses: the first consisted of turkey and perhaps other meat dishes, while the second was dessert. This pattern was common during the early nineteenth century in the United States, and these traditions were maintained until the late nineteenth century.

Edward Everett Hale, an American author and Unitarian minister, confirms this pattern as he details the Thanksgiving dinners that his family celebrated in Massachusetts during the early nineteenth century. His family first ate chicken pie and roast turkey, then proceeded to several different types of pies, tarts, and puddings, and ended with dried fruit.[12] A New Hampshire Thanksgiving dinner of the same era began with a ham and a large roast turkey; these were followed by chicken, duck, celery, plum pudding, pies, fruit, and, finally, coffee and tea.[13] An 1831 dinner in Geneva, New York, included turkey, beef, duck, ham, sausage, potatoes, yams, succotash, pickles, nuts, raisins, pears, peaches, pie, tarts, creams, custards, jellies, floating islands, sweetbreads, wines, rum, brandy, eggnog, and punch.[14] In the middle of the nineteenth century, Carol King, a resident of Salem, Massachusetts, reports that the dinners were "always the same," consisting of chicken pie and boiled turkey and oyster sauce.[15] In Portsmouth, New Hampshire, Sarah Rice Goodwin recalls that "[t]he dinner began with a ham, handsomely decorated, at one end of the table and a large roast turkey at the other. Chickens and ducks followed, with celery dressed and undressed."[16] The writer Harriet Beecher Stowe remembers that her family's Thanksgiving feast in Litchfield, Connecticut, took a week to prepare and included turkey, chicken, chicken pies, plum puddings, and four types of pie.[17]

The New England Thanksgiving celebration that emerged in the early nineteenth century was in some ways a substitute for traditional English autumn holidays that were not observed by the Puritans. Guy Fawkes Day, for instance, celebrated the foiling of the Gunpowder Plot in 1605. Catholic conspirators, led by Guy Fawkes, had attempted to blow up the British Parliament, but the plot was uncovered and the plotters executed. Thereafter, 5 November was celebrated as a "public thanksgiving to Almighty God," and it is still celebrated today with bonfires and fireworks. At the time, Puritans considered it a frivolous holiday, one that frequently encouraged drunkenness and other excesses.

Another traditional British holiday was the Harvest Home Festival, which was celebrated in October or early November and dated back to the time of the Druids. In these celebrations, Harvest Home "queens," robed in white, either rode in carts or were carried on men's shoulders through the villages. The Puritans thought this was idol worship and refused to partake in the festivities.[18] Furthermore, for religious reasons, they condemned the traditional holidays celebrated by the Church of England and the Catholic Church, such as All Saints Day (1 November) and Christmas (25 December); they also denounced the gluttony, drunkenness, lewdness, and other frivolities that generally accompanied the celebration of these holidays.

Although the American Thanksgiving celebration may have been derived from traditional English holidays, it nevertheless evolved in a unique way in New England. For instance, Thanksgiving was to become a celebration in which the extended family gathered to share a grand dinner. As the importance of the family dinner at Thanksgiving emerged in the late eighteenth century, specific culinary traditions arose around the meal that were not associated with traditional English autumn feasts, such as the special role of New

World bounty – turkeys, corn, cornbread, pumpkin pies, sweet potatoes, succotash, and cranberries.

Many influences contributed to the transformation of the regional New England Thanksgiving dinner into a national holiday. One major factor was the migration of New Englanders who sought better farmland in other regions of the United States (and occasionally in Canada), since New England soil was not well suited to farming. The central valley in New York, for instance, was largely settled by New Englanders, as was much of the Midwest. Transplanted New Englanders kept the Thanksgiving dinner alive in their new homes and urged their newly adopted communities to celebrate the occasion as well.

Could it be that New Englanders immigrating to Canada in the nineteenth century brought their Thanksgiving traditions with them? Fiona Lucas notes that, in the nineteenth century, Canada's growing observance of the holiday likely stemmed both from England, where there was "a romantic revival of the British Harvest Home," and from the United States, where the popular American "invention of the Pilgrim's 'First Thanksgiving'" was being promoted in the media through the circulation of American publications in Ontario.[19]

Unlike Canadian Thanksgiving, which took longer to become established as an intrinsic part of the cultural milieu, the American celebration quickly became part of popular culture. Thanksgiving poems were common fare throughout the nineteenth century. "A Merry Ode for Thanksgiving," published in a newspaper in 1801, announced that turkeys were carved "in heaps" at Thanksgiving.[20] Perhaps the most famous Thanksgiving poem was written by Lydia Maria Child. Her poem, "The New-England Boys Song about Thanksgiving," is better known by its first line: "Over the river and thro' the wood."[21] In addition to through poetry, Thanksgiving was embedded into American culture by being made a day in which those who were well off gave food to the poor and destitute, a practice that continues today, with politicians and other prominent Americans serving food to the homeless.

While the development of a Thanksgiving observance in Canada lagged behind the American tradition, there was nonetheless a growing presence of the holiday both in Canada's popular culture and in the private writings of Canadians throughout the mid- to late 1800s. Lucas points to an article in the *Canadian Farmer* that commented in November 1865: "'Thanksgiving Day' – now established, we are glad to believe, as a national institution – has

Vegetables from D. Ross's garden, Edmonton, AB, 1902. Photograph by C.W. Mathers. Courtesy of McCord Museum, MP-0000.59.1.

been [recently] observed."[22] Similarly, in 1865, Waterloo Township resident Matilda Bowers Eby mentions Thanksgiving in her diary, her entry of 18 October reflecting on the Thanksgiving holiday as a somewhat new but welcome occurrence: "'This was Thanksgiving day and was observed as a public holiday in this place. I was surprised to see such was the case, ungodly place that it is. It seems to one it must be the most wicked spot in the world. It is heartrending.'"[23]

Although the Thanksgiving tradition seems tentative in these early texts, by 1892, the popular magazine *Saturday Night* featured an article in which the author waxes nostalgic for the grand Thanksgiving meals of his boyhood, feasts that included turkey, stuffing, and pudding.[24] By 1900, some of Canada's most prominent writers of the time address Thanksgiving traditions in their works. Sir Charles G.D. Roberts, one of the Confederation poets, depicts a Thanksgiving meal in his work of prose *By the Marshes of Minas*, which takes place in Port-Royal (in what is now the province of Nova Scotia) following the capture of this French Acadian settlement by British and New England troops in 1710. In light of the fact that Thanksgiving was only recognized by Parliament as a public holiday in 1879 and had been celebrated in Canada as such for a mere two decades by the time *By the Marshes of Minas* appeared in 1900, Roberts's retrospective vision of a Thanksgiving from a much earlier time speaks to the holiday's uncertain status as a truly *national* celebration in the minds of Canadians at the turn of the century. In his text, Roberts creates a fairly idealistic rendering of early Thanksgiving practices – the successful serving of an appetizing meal – yet his text indicates the underlying history of conflict with respect to the "adoption" of this Thanksgiving tradition. The French Acadians of Roberts's narrative feel that this tradition belongs to the invading militia, since Acadian-grown produce is appropriated for the meal by the Americans. In the story, Lieutenant Hanworthy of New England remembers his major's speech about their improvised Thanksgiving dinner: "These good people of Acadia ... do not observe our feast, but I have noted that they can supply the wherewithal for its proper observance. Their ducks and geese feed fat upon these marshes. Their gardens are instructed in the growth of sage and onions. They are not unskilled in the subtleties of apple sauce; and I have found pumpkins!"[25]

Before Lieutenant Hanworthy joins his fellow New Englanders at the Thanksgiving meal, he is diverted at one Acadian home by the bewitching Mademoiselle de Belleisle, who resides there. Recently returned from Quebec, Mademoiselle de Belleisle provides Hanworthy with a buffet dinner of his own, including Bordeaux wine and "some cakes of the country" – in effect creating a "Thanksgiving dinner, but translated into French!"[26] Clearly, while Thanksgiving became more established in Canada during the latter half of the nineteenth century, Canadians continued to appreciate its complex history, recognizing the many cultures and colonizing forces that contributed to this holiday tradition within their society.

It will be noted that none of the previously mentioned Thanksgiving proclamations, poems, or descriptions of feasts included mention of either a "first Thanksgiving" or the role of the Pilgrims. The first association between the Pilgrims and Thanksgiving appeared in 1841, when Alexander Young published a copy of a letter written by Edward Winslow to a friend in England, dated 11 December 1621. It described a three-day fall event but made no mention of the dates on which the event was celebrated. Winslow writes: "Our harvest being gotten in, our Governor sent four men on fowling, that so we might after a more special manner re[j]oice together, after we had gathered the fruit of our labours. They four in one day k[i]lled as much fowl as, with a little help besides, served the Company almost a week. At which time, amongst other recreations, we exercised our arms, many of the Indians coming amongst us, and amongst the rest their greatest king, Massasoit with some 90 men, whom for three days we entertained and feasted. And they went out and killed five deer which they brought to the plantation and bestowed on our Governor and upon the Captain and others."[27]

In a footnote to the 1841 reprint of the letter, Alexander Young claimed that the event described by Winslow "was the first thanksgiving, the harvest festival of New England. On this occasion they no doubt feasted on the wild turkey as well as venison."[28] Winslow, however, had not used the word "Thanksgiving" to describe this or any other event in the fall of 1621. Furthermore, the Puritans made no subsequent mention of this event, and neither the Pilgrims nor the Puritans celebrated Thanksgiving in later years. The feast described by Winslow makes no mention of prayer but does include many secular elements that the Puritans would not have considered to be consistent with a Thanksgiving celebration. Nevertheless, before long many people came to believe Winslow's claim that the 1621 event at Plimoth Plantation was the first Thanksgiving, and by the middle of nineteenth century, it was generally accepted in New England that the Pilgrims had invented the American Thanksgiving celebration.[29] We now know that Jamestown, which was settled in 1607, observed many days of Thanksgiving years before the Pilgrims landed at Plimoth Plantation. In fact, a plaque in Jamestown marks the purported site of the real "First Thanksgiving," but factual knowledge could not stop the dissemination of the myth that the Pilgrims were the first to celebrate Thanksgiving.

AN AMERICAN HOLIDAY

The driving force that made Thanksgiving a national holiday in the United States was Sarah Josepha Hale, the editor of *Godey's Lady's Book*. Hale commenced her campaign to create a national Thanksgiving holiday in 1846. For the next seventeen years, she wrote annually to members of Congress, prominent individuals, and the governors of every state and territory, asking each of them to proclaim a common Thanksgiving Day. In an age before word processors, typewriters, or mass media, this was surely a difficult campaign to wage.

Hale believed that a Thanksgiving holiday would unify the United States. She was nearly successful in 1859, when thirty states and three territories celebrated Thanksgiving on the third Thursday of November. During the Civil War, she was unable to communicate with many of the Southern states, so instead of continuing to write to each state, she approached President Lincoln and petitioned for Thanksgiving to be designated a national holiday. In 1863, a few months after the North's military victories at Gettysburg and Vicksburg, Hale succeeded when Lincoln declared the last Thursday in November to be the national day of Thanksgiving. Since that time, Americans have regularly celebrated the holiday.

A CANADIAN THANKSGIVING

Despite claims that Frobisher's early celebration on Baffin Island was North America's (and Canada's) first Thanksgiving, the First Nations could be recognized as having that distinction, for they had held celebrations for centuries marking the harvesting of maize and wild rice. French settlers who arrived in New France at the beginning of the seventeenth century with Samuel de Champlain also brought with them Thanksgiving feasts in keeping with both religious and harvest traditions. One of the earliest primary references to a Canadian Thanksgiving meal in Ontario dates back to an 1855 celebration. Four years later, the *Detroit Free Press* reported that the Canadian celebration in Ontario did not materially differ "from the mode adopted by the Yan-

left: Postcard with poem, "Thanksgiving Day." Courtesy of Gary Draper.

right: Postcard, "Thanksgiving Greetings." Courtesy of Mary F. Williamson.

kees."[30] An 1865 article in an agricultural publication claimed that Canadian Thanksgiving was actually a British Harvest Home celebration.[31] From the late eighteenth century, many days of Thanksgiving were celebrated in both Lower Canada and Upper Canada, marking such events as a British military victory in Europe (1799), the cessation of an epidemic (1833), an abundant harvest (1859), and instances of the mercy of God (numerous).[32]

Postcard, "Good Wishes for Thanksgiving Day." Courtesy of Mary F. Williamson.

Since many of these Thanksgiving Days celebrated English victories over France or over French forces in Canada, it comes as no surprise that Thanksgiving has a more problematic history in francophone Canada than in other parts of the country, a distinction suggested in Roberts's retelling of a Thanksgiving observance imposed on the French Acadians at Port-Royal. It is important to note, however, that Quebecers, in the Catholic tradition, celebrate "action de grâces," the French version of a religious Thanksgiving. While Quebecers rejoice in a more secular version of Thanksgiving today, the holiday has a long history of religious observance in their province. Indeed, in a published account of a sermon given by M. l'Abbé E. Roy (from the Quebec Seminary) at the L'église de Ste-Marie de la Beauce in 1888, "un ancien élève du collège" writes in a preface to the sermon: "Après la messe, monsieur le Curé accompagné de Messieurs du clergé se rendit au collège pour y présider le dîner."[33]

Verso of "Good Wishes for Thanksgiving Day." Courtesy of Mary F. Williamson.

In 1872, the Canadian Confederation observed its first Thanksgiving to commemorate the restoration of the Prince of Wales's health. This occasion did not have the same symbolic power that the myth of the first American Thanksgiving did, but it seemed to suffice, for in 1879, in order to guarantee the celebration of Thanksgiving as a statutory holiday, the Canadian Parliament declared the 6th of November to be a "national holiday." Thanksgiving was subsequently celebrated in late October or early November. Despite its official designation as a national holiday, it was still the subject of much debate, as anti-American sentiment entered into discussions about the questionable nature and mixed origins of the holiday. In a debate over holiday laws in 1893, the Canadian Senate addressed Thanksgiving Day and the Honourable Mr Almon argued that, from his perspective, Thanksgiving was a secular American holiday and an excuse for gluttony and amusement: "What did the Thanksgiving holiday originate from? Is it British, is it Catholic or Protestant?

No, it is an American institution got up by the Pilgrim Fathers to do away with love of the old country."[34] Other members of the Senate disagreed with Almon's disparaging of Thanksgiving. The Honourable Mr Kaulback stated, "I think the Hon. Gentleman from Halifax has slandered Nova Scotia when he says that Thanksgiving Day is not observed there. In Lunenburg I know it is observed as religiously and with as great zeal and earnestness as Sunday is kept."[35]

Canadian Thanksgiving continued to be the subject of debate when it shifted on the calendar in response to the creation of Armistice Day in 1918 (now known as Remembrance Day), which was to be observed on 11 November following the end of World War I. Because Thanksgiving, then celebrated on 6 November, was so close to Armistice Day, the two days were combined in 1921. While the business community had urged the change, veterans and many other Canadians disapproved of holding a day of solemn remembrance with a celebration of harvest.[36] The dual observance of Thanksgiving and Remembrance Day, however, should not be underestimated as having been a matter of mere convenience; rather, it highlighted the way Canadians perceived Thanksgiving as a truly national holiday in terms of it being *both* a statutory holiday and a day embraced by citizens. Canadian historians have long viewed World War I as the war that propelled Canada onto the international stage and forged a profound sense of identity for the young country. Thus, the aligning of Armistice Day with Thanksgiving Day suggests an increasing desire on the part of Canadians to reflect on their sacrifices and give thanks as a nation.

During the decade when the two holidays coincided, the November 1928 issue of *Chatelaine* featured an article about giving thanks for peace and wisdom. The article showcases a poem entitled "The Eleventh Hour," which addresses the paying of respect at the cenotaph to Canada's war dead.[37] In the same issue, an article entitled "Do You Decorate for Thanksgiving?" reveals the subtle influence of Canadian nationalism on the manner in which Canadians celebrate Thanksgiving. In the piece, Anne Wilson promotes the distinctiveness of Canadian Thanksgiving, its heritage, and its national significance: "[W]e in Canada have in Thanksgiving Day, a really triple significance to cater to, merged as it now is with Armistice Day. If our holiday lacks the historic background of the American Pilgrim atmosphere, it has the older richness of the British harvest-home tradition."[38] Wilson makes several suggestions for table centre-pieces that highlight not only the British roots of Canada's celebration, but also the desire for an expression of national pride. In a bevy of options, Wilson recommends a basket of autumn vegetables for "a real 'harvest home'" feeling; the use of pine boughs so that miniature turkey ornaments "have a very real and Canadian look"; the inclusion of prairie grasses for western Canadian homes; and the use of regimental colours and military-themed decorations (such as miniature canons) in order to pay respect to family members who are war veterans.[39] For just over a decade, Canada celebrated both holidays on the same day, but in 1931, the two holidays were divided as Thanksgiving was exclusively celebrated in October. In 1957, the Canadian Parliament declared the second Monday in October to be the day that Thanksgiving would be observed, and it has thereafter been celebrated on this day.

TRADITIONAL THANKSGIVING DINNER

By the turn of the twentieth century, cookery magazines and cookbooks had enshrined the Thanksgiving dinner, publishing menus for proper Thanksgiving meals and offering recipes that taught the uninitiated how to prepare the traditional dishes. Fannie Farmer, the principal of the Boston Cooking School, offered a Thanksgiving menu with twenty-three dishes in her *Boston Cooking School Cook Book* (1896). Other menus were even more elaborate. "The Thanksgiving Dinner," for instance, in *The Picayune's Creole Cook Book* (1900), a New Orleans culinary bible, features thirty-three dishes, among them "Baked Red Snapper à la Creole" and "Turkey Stuffed with Chestnuts." This book includes a menu for "A More Economical Thanksgiving Dinner" with only twenty-eight dishes. The cookbook also offers suggestions for Thanksgiving decorations that would emphasize the "wild luxuriance and freedom of growth, the spirit of American liberty which gave birth to this day."

Most American Thanksgiving dinners featured a turkey. In early nineteenth century dinners, the bird was served with other meats, such as venison and other types of game. But as the nineteenth century progressed, game largely disappeared from the American table, particularly in urban areas, and by the end of the century, it was no long on Thanksgiving menus. The domesticated

Postcard, "Hearty Thanksgiving Greetings." Courtesy of Mary F. Williamson.

goose, which had been the main course for the traditional English Christmas, was another important meat served at Thanksgiving during the nineteenth century. However, since goose were smaller and more expensive than turkeys, serving goose at Thanksgiving slowly went out of fashion. Beef was occasionally mentioned in accounts of Thanksgiving dinners (it was an important meat source in New England and generally cheaper per pound than poultry), but the chicken pie, a traditional English savoury dish, was by far the closest rival to the turkey as the centrepiece of the meal. Yet even this alternative to the turkey had disappeared from the Thanksgiving menu by the end of the nineteenth century. By the 1880s, Thanksgiving had become known euphemistically as "Turkey Day."

Turkeys were prepared in many different ways. They could be deboned and boiled, fried, baked, or roasted. The ritual of carving the turkey at the table, generally the responsibility of the senior male at the dinner, originated in the Middle Ages and was preserved in America until at least the middle of the

POST CARD.

FOR CORRESPONDENCE

OCT 21
9 AM
1909

FOR ADDRESS ONLY

Miss Gladys E. Strum
Mader's Cove,
Lunenburg Co.
N. S.

Verso of "Hearty Thanksgiving Greetings." Courtesy of Mary F. Williamson.

twentieth century. The large body cavities of a turkey presented unique opportunities for the creative cook. The recent popularity of the New Orleans turducken, a deboned chicken within a deboned duck within a deboned turkey, with stuffing placed between the layers, is in fact a Renaissance way of preparing turkeys. Most cooks stuff the cavities with a wide variety of ingredients, such as oysters, chopped liver, prunes, dried bread, cherries, berries, lard, artichokes, egg yolks, grated cheese, chestnuts, and onions seasoned variously with mint, marjoram, parsley, pepper, cloves, nutmeg, grated cheese, and garlic. A wide array of side dishes were also institutionalized. In the South, candied yams, sweet potatoes, and tangy relishes became important components, whereas in Mexican-American families *posole* stew (a stew made from corn, pork, and chili), *menudo* (a spicy soup made with tripe), and tamales were often part of the feast.

For the majority of present-day Canadians, turkey is often synonymous with Thanksgiving, but the traditional menu evolved more slowly than in the

Postcard, "Thanksgiving Day." Courtesy of Mary F. Williamson.

United States. Lucas observes that, during the first half of the nineteenth century, the Thanksgiving foods referred to in Canadian cookbooks were primarily from American sources; the first Canadian reference to a homegrown meal (one consisting of roast goose) was published in Ontario in 1855.[40] Private writings also reveal the establishment of traditional fare. In her diary, Ontarian Bessie Mabel Scott rejoices in the spirit of Thanksgiving (1 November 1890), and indicates that the day's celebrations culminated in the customary dessert: "Thanksgiving day! and a glorious fine day, makes one feel glad to be alive a day like this – Oh! So much I have to be thankful for such a year this has been … [I] retired soon after pumpkin pie … " (ellipses in original).[41]

There is clear evidence of the beginnings of a Thanksgiving dinner tradition in the popular media, private documents, and American cookbooks that circulated north of the border in the 1800s and early 1900s. Lucas notes that "Thanksgiving was slow to make an appearance in Ontario cookbooks," and the first formal menus did not appear until the 1930s, in such books as the *Wimodausis Club Cook Book* (1934) and Nellie Lyle Pattinson's *The Canadian Cook Book* (1938).[42] There are signs in 1928, however, in both the popular women's magazine *Chatelaine* and the national magazine *Maclean's* that a traditional Thanksgiving menu had been formalized by this time. The November 1928 issue of *Chatelaine* provides a Thanksgiving menu that would "meet the average demands" of most celebrations and includes grapefruit cocktail; roast turkey with chestnut or celery stuffing; cranberry jelly; giblet gravy; sweet potatoes; creamed cauliflower; apple, nut, and celery salad; pumpkin pie with whipped cream; and coffee.[43] The article stresses the importance of tradition in the Canadian Thanksgiving and in the preparation of a "characteristic" meal: "Unlike most of the festive occasions during the year, Thanksgiving celebrations do not achieve success chiefly through novel innovations. Sacred memories and hallowed traditions have given a special significance to Canadian Thanksgiving, and have created a wholesome respect for simplicity. Certain viands, such as turkey and pumpkin pie, are particularly characteristic of this Feast of Harvest Time, and around these important items may be built up a very simple and inexpensive menu or one quite as elaborate as the purse strings allow."[44]

In a similar tone, a 1928 *Maclean's* article by Ann Adam, "The Thanksgiving Dinner: Old Fashioned Good Things Are Doubly Appetizing When Served in the New-Fashioned Way," provides a menu that is in keeping with "the outstanding traditions of the Thanksgiving Feast," while also catering to the need for practicality for "the average home[,] where the mistress – if she is not actually the cook – must supervise and assist with anything in the nature of a special occasion."[45]

The 1928 menus in both *Chatelaine* and *Maclean's* emphasize nostalgia and tradition when it comes to food choices for Thanksgiving. Similarly, in 1936, Helen Campbell suggests lighter meals and refrigerator desserts as "modern" choices, but continues to respect the conventional meal, noting that "[p]umpkin pie is the traditional topper-off, and I'd hate to be the one to cast aspersions on it."[46] Campbell includes a recipe for pumpkin pie, but notes that her readers are likely using the recipe for which "grandma was famous."[47] She also acknowledges pudding as a customary dessert, albeit an adapted one for

the "modern" fall celebration. Campbell tells readers, "Leave the plum pudding until Christmas" and instead to use a "lighter variety ... if you are set on pudding." She does, in fact, include a recipe for "Fruited Indian Pudding."[48]

In her 1928 *Maclean's* article, Adam notes that baked ham can be a cost-effective alternative to "the traditional turkey" or can "share the honors with the turkey" for a particularly large Thanksgiving dinner.[49] It appears that in the early decades of the twentieth century other meats, especially ham, often made an appearance at the Thanksgiving table. In *Chatelaine*, one article from 1934 mentions that while fowl is traditional, ham or beef "would be worthy of the finest tables and may be preferred by many Canadians for the early date which we have set aside for our Thanksgiving."[50] Indeed, on the western prairies, turkeys raised on the farm before World War II were not sufficiently plump by the fall months, which meant that baked ham was often the central component of the Thanksgiving meal.[51] Since the latter half of the twentieth century, turkey has dominated Canadian Thanksgiving – even particular kinds of turkey.

facing page: "Ma and a few of her turkeys." Agnes Rutherford on a farm near Hodgeville, SK, around 1934. Courtesy of Shelley Boyd.

right: "Great prairie chickens." Mac McKay and John D. Williamson near Langford, SK, 1908. Courtesy of Mary F. Williamson.

In the 1951 *Maclean's* article "How to Tackle That Turkey," James Dugan addresses some of the differences between American and Canadian preferences. Dugan notes that while American scientists worked in the early 1940s to breed the Beltsville White (a smaller bird of less than twenty pounds but with a large portion of white meat and less bone and gristle), Canadians preferred the larger birds, such as the Bronzes.[52] Dugan states that in the United States the Beltsville White was developed to suit "the smaller family unit and the modern housewife's dislike of leftovers."[53] A 2007 article in *Harrowsmith* traces heritage breeds and notes that this smaller bird was "perfect for apartment[-]sized fridges, but far too tiny for the food industry."[54] As for Canadians, their preference for the larger Bronze turkey led to the creation of a vari-

ety known as the "Ridley Bronze"; it weighs approximately thirty-six pounds and was developed at a hatchery in Saskatoon by George Ridley.[55]

Clearly, in the decades prior to World War II, ham was a frequent option for Canadians' Thanksgiving dinner, but when Dugan wrote his 1951 *Maclean's* article, the increased production of turkeys meant that they were more readily available to consumers. Dugan mentions that turkey consumption was on the rise and that while Ontario's farmers bred most of the turkeys, "the prairie provinces do the heaviest per capita turkey eating, according to the Dominion Bureau of Statistics."[56] At that time, the Bronze and the Beltsville White were respectively the turkeys of choice for Canadian and American consumers. Today, both the Ridley Bronze and the Beltsville White are listed as "critical," meaning that less than one hundred birds survive.[57] In 2007, Bridget Wayland remarks in *Harrowsmith* that Canadians now consume a kind of "'robot turkey'" that is "top-heavy because post-war consumers wanted loads of snowy, white meat." Derived from the Broad-Breasted White, these industrialized birds cannot breed naturally, they grow at a rapid pace with low feed costs, and they have been bred to be all white to avoid unappealing dark pin-feather follicles.[58]

Just as turkey breeds and preferences have changed over the decades, the traditional turkey dinner has become open to interpretation as contemporary Canadians of diverse ethnic backgrounds create new versions of the meal through such additions as curried recipes or Italian side dishes.[59] *Harrowsmith's* 2007 fall issue includes a range of options for dealing with leftovers, including "Curried Turkey, Apple and Sweet Potato Soup," "Turkey and Ham Frittata," "Turkey and Mushroom Pot Pie," and "Stir-Fried Cantonese Turkey."

THE PILGRIMS AND THANKSGIVING

As mentioned, Sarah Josepha Hale made no mention of the Pilgrims or the "first Thanksgiving" prior to 1865; nor did the hundreds of previously published local and state Thanksgiving Day proclamations or any newspaper or magazine articles. But after the Civil War, the Pilgrims and the first Thanksgiving were frequently mentioned in newspapers and magazines, and by 1870 school textbooks had begun telling the Pilgrim-centred Thanksgiving tale.[60] Magazines, newspapers, and books propagated the story during the 1870s and

1880s.[61] By the early twentieth century, pageants celebrating the first Thanksgiving were commonly conducted in schools, and immigrant children often performed in them.[62] The association of Pilgrims and the first Thanksgiving became imbedded in American schools.[63] In 1921, many schools and communities celebrated the three hundredth anniversary of the first Thanksgiving, and the fictitious dinner was part of the celebration.[64]

The myths of the Pilgrims' dinner were also enshrined on the covers and inside pages of some of America's most popular magazines. The *Saturday Evening Post* and the *Country Gentleman* regularly featured images of Thanksgiving on their covers. For instance, J.C. Leyendecker's cover for the November 1907 *Saturday Evening Post* pictures a Pilgrim stalking a tom turkey.[65] American painters also contributed to the myth: Jennie Augusta Brownscombe's 1914 painting *The First Thanksgiving* appeared in numerous school textbooks; and Jean Louis Gerome Ferris's depiction of the first Thanksgiving shows a long table, serving dishes, and women decked out in nineteenth-century finery.[66] Artists, books, and textbooks have continued to propagate the myths ever since.[67]

The association of the Pilgrims and the first Thanksgiving was important enough by 1879 to prompt several scholars to write histories of Thanksgiving. The Reverend W. DeLoss Love systematically collected Thanksgiving proclamations and published many of them in his *The Fast and Thanksgiving Days of New England* (1895). His massive compilation proved that there was no Pilgrim first Thanksgiving,[68] but the popular press had already made the connection, and the reality did not matter.

The widespread adoption of the Pilgrim Thanksgiving myth in the United States has less to do with historical fact and more to do with the arrival of hundreds of thousands of immigrants. Earlier immigrants had come primarily from the United Kingdom, and a small number emigrated from Germany, France, and Scandinavia. In the 1880s, this immigration pattern changed as people from southern and eastern Europe flooded into the United States. The pace of immigration exploded in 1900 with nine million people settling in American cities. Since these immigrants came from many lands, the creation of a common American heritage was one of the principal tasks for the American public education systems. One curricular need was to compile an American history that could be easily understood by the public. The

Pilgrims served as an ideal symbol of American roots and values. Thus, the first Thanksgiving dinner became an origin myth that traced the roots of the United States to Plymouth and the Pilgrims. Even though Jamestown had a better historical claim than Plymouth, its reputations as being the place where American slavery originated made it unacceptable as the mythical birthplace of America. Since this origin myth did not become prominent until after the Civil War, the South was in no position to challenge the primacy of the mythical Pilgrims idealized by New England advocates for Thanksgiving. As a result, many Southerners refused to celebrate Thanksgiving long after the Civil War had ended.

Immigrant families, who had not celebrated Thanksgiving in their native lands, readily adopted the holiday and the dinner. In the process, they modified and enhanced the traditional Thanksgiving menu. James Robertson suggests that "turkey is consumed at Thanksgiving feasts because it was ... native to America, and ... a symbol of the bounteous richness of the wilderness."[69] Although some immigrant families have not retained the turkey as the central feature of the Thanksgiving dinner, historian Elizabeth Pleck holds that the turkey generally "became the symbol of the dominant culture, and the stuffing and side dishes, and desserts the immigrants' contribution."[70]

THANKSGIVING PROTESTS

Perhaps because of the national significance of Thanksgiving, many Americans and even some Canadians take advantage of the holiday to promote particular causes. In 1835, William Alcott, a physician, writes that he was opposed to the feast on moral grounds as well as for medical reasons. He calls Thanksgiving a carnival "loaded with luxuries not only on the day of the general Thanksgiving, but for several days afterward."[71] He was particularly concerned because New Englanders were also beginning to celebrate Christmas, and he claimed that the two feasts had already merged into one long period of overindulgence that caused serious health problems. Alcott had other reasons to oppose the traditional Thanksgiving dinner: in 1830, he became a vegetarian and would later be one of the founders of the American Vegetarian Society.

Few Americans paid any attention to either Alcott or the vegetarians until the late twentieth century, when the Thanksgiving concerns of animal-rights organizations, such as People for the Ethical Treatment of Animals (PETA), began to be recognized. For PETA members, Thanksgiving is not a time to eat turkeys but rather a time to convince Americans to give up eating meat. PETA has sponsored petitions and published leaflets encouraging a turkeyless Thanksgiving under the slogan "Give Turkeys Something to Be Thankful For!" To counteract Butterball's "Thanksgiving Talk Line" (a hotline that answers questions about proper cooking techniques), PETA has encouraged its members to call the hotline and tell Butterball that there is no proper way to kill and cook turkeys.

Another organization, the Farm Sanctuary, attracts media attention in an effort (or for its efforts) to encourage Americans to celebrate Thanksgiving without eating turkey. The Sanctuary also publishes "Thankful Turkey Recipes" – "delicious Thanksgiving recipes that give the turkeys something to really be thankful for."[72] It also distributes a video, *The Making of a Turkey*, with undercover footage of "inhumane factory farming practices, transportation cruelties, and slaughterhouse abuses."[73]

Variations on "Mock Turkey" recipes became a regular feature in vegetarian and other cookbooks. Even if turkey does not appear on vegetarian tables, food products that resemble a turkey frequently do. Beginning in the 1980s, vegetarians could feast on tofu turkey or Tofurkey, a soy-based product shaped like a turkey, rather than on the traditional holiday bird. Other vegetarians prefer not to eat anything resembling a turkey or any foods that are intended to taste like turkey.

Yet another protest was launched by Native Americans. Frank James, a Wampanoag leader, was invited to speak at the celebration of the three hundred and fiftieth anniversary of the Pilgrims' arrival in Massachusetts. Before he had a chance to present his Native American perspective, however, the text of his speech was leaked to the press and his invitation to speak was rescinded. On Thanksgiving Day, James, along with hundreds of other Native Americans and their supporters, gathered at Coles Hill, which overlooks Plymouth Rock, and declared a National Day of Mourning. Every year since then, the United American Indians of New England have sponsored similar days. James died in 2001, but his son has carried on the tradition.

In Canada, too, citizens and politicians have used Thanksgiving to promote certain agendas. On Thanksgiving weekend in 1961, hundreds of university students from Ontario and Quebec, many of them members of the Combined Universities Campaign for Nuclear Disarmament, descended on Parliament Hill in Ottawa to protest against the Cold War.[74] More recently, in October 2007, Foreign Affairs Minister Maxime Bernier and International Development Minister Bev Oda made a Thanksgiving weekend visit to Canadian troops stationed in Kandahar, Afghanistan. With the United Nations mission in Afghanistan becoming increasingly unpopular with Canadians, and particularly with Quebecers, Bernier and Oda chose this national holiday in order to draw attention to their visit and to the troops. The Conservative Party had been facing the uncertainty of their minority government status, and the Thanksgiving visit to Afghanistan was a clear attempt to generate support, particularly among Quebec voters (who can make or break a political party's success during a federal election). Tellingly, Bernier and Oda went as far as to bring boxes of Joe Louis chocolate cakes – "Quebec's iconic snacks" – for the Quebec-based regiment serving in Afghanistan.[75]

THANKSGIVING TODAY

Many Canadians observe a family feast at Thanksgiving in the same way that the Americans do, with dishes such as turkey, seasonal vegetables, mashed potatoes, gravy, cranberries, and pumpkin pie. Because Canadian Thanksgiving occurs in early October and is more removed from the Christmas shopping season than is the American celebration, commercialization has not infiltrated the Canadian holiday. Perhaps this lack of commercialization creates the illusion that Thanksgiving is not a significant event in Canada; for Canadians, however, Thanksgiving is an important time for family and friends, for giving thanks, and for sharing a traditional meal. It is a mostly secular holiday that marks the end of harvest and the changing of the seasons. University students travel home for the holiday, people fly across the country to visit family, and others use the time to winterize their summer cottages.[76] Some Canadians bemoan the nation's more understated version of Thanksgiving Day, claiming that the "Americans have it right."[77] But others testify to the significance of the Canadian tradition and the sense of family heritage equated with the meal: "The smell of turkey after a brisk walk through the fallen leaves takes me back to my first year away from home. Friends turned most of their tiny Toronto apartment into a dining room for more than 20 of us – all 'orphans' from Saskatchewan ... As we passed mashed potatoes, gravy, dressing, somebody's mom's pickles and another mom's precious Saskatoon pie down long tables ... , we were home again on the Prairies with its fowl suppers in church basements."[78]

In the United States, Thanksgiving is still one of the nation's most important holidays. Retailers have commercialized the day as the start of the Christmas shopping season, and football games are a major part of the entertainment. Illustrators, filmmakers, and television producers have generated new Thanksgiving images. However, the holiday continues to be celebrated with a family-style dinner whose Thanksgiving traditions have not faded.

NOTES

1 Gillingham, "First Thanksgiving," 48.
2 Boswell, "Sorry Americans," A14.
3 "From the South-Carolina Gazette ... First Colony Sent to Georgia," 2.
4 "Savannah," 2.
4 Martin, *Private Yankee Doodle*, 100.
5 A letter from Julianna Smith, dated 1779, quoted in Smith, *Colonial Days and Ways*, 291–7.
6 Thacher, *History of the Town of Plymouth*, 212.
7 Traill, *Canadian Settler's Guide*, 113.
8 Ibid., 229, 200.
9 Ibid., 158.
10 Letter from Shubael Breed, Norwich, Connecticut, to Mason Fitch Cogswell, New York, as quoted in Oliver, *Saltwater Foodways*, 242. An earlier description of Thanksgiving dinner, from 1779, appears in Smith's *Colonial Days and Ways*; it was later frequently cited. The original diary that this selection from *Colonial Days* was taken from has not been located, and several statements in the published description have led many observers to question the veracity of this account. It is more likely a late nineteenth-century fictional creation.
11 Bentley, *Diary of William Bentley*, 264.
12 Hale, *New England Boyhood*, 144–5.
13 Sarah Parker Goodwin, "Pleasant Memories," Memoirs of Sarah Parker Rice Goodwin, 1889, Goodwin Family Papers, Strawberry Banke Museum,

Portsmouth, New Hampshire, reproduced in Nylander, *Our Own Snug Fireside*, 275.

14 Hedrick, *History of Agriculture*, 217.

15 King, *When I Lived in Salem*, 112.

16 Goodwin, "Pleasant Memories," reproduced in Nylander, *Our Own Snug Fireside*, 275.

17 Stowe, *Oldtown Folks*, 347.

18 Santino, *All Around the Year*, 168.

19 Lucas, "Condition of Turkey," 6.

20 "Merry Ode," 4.

21 Child, "New-England Boys Song," 25–8.

22 Quoted in Lucas, "Condition of Turkey," 6.

23 Quoted in Hoffman and Taylor, *Much to Be Done*, 239.

24 Mack, "Thanksgiving Turkey," 7.

25 Roberts, *Marshes of Minas*, 24–5.

26 Ibid., 38–9.

27 Winslow, letter of 11 December 1621, 60–5.

28 Young, *Chronicles of the Pilgrim Fathers*, 231.

29 The spelling "Plimoth" (in "Plimoth Plantation") was one of a number of variations used during the early seventeenth century. Today, the Plimoth Plantation Museum continues to use this older variation as a way of differentiating itself from the town of Plymouth, Massachusetts.

30 *Mackenzie Message*, 21 December 1855, and *Detroit Free Press*, 3 November 1859, quoted in Lucas, "Condition of Turkey," 6.

31 *Canadian Farmer*, 1 November 1865, quoted in Lucas, "Condition of Turkey," 6.

32 "Proclamation and Observance," http://www.pch.gc.ca/pgm/ceem-cced/jfa-ha/graces-eng.cfm.

33 Roy, *Sermon prononcé*, 5. "After mass, the priest, accompanied by the clergymen, went to the college to preside over dinner."

34 *Debates of the Senate of the Dominion of Canada*, 182.

35 Ibid., 183.

36 "Armistice Day Linked with Thanksgiving," http://www.warmuseum.ca/cwm/exhibitions/remember/thanksgiving_e.shtml.

37 Wilson, "'Woman's Reason,'" 16.

38 Wilson, "Do You Decorate?" 8.

39 Ibid., 8–9.

40 Lucas, "Condition of Turkey," 7.

41 Quoted in Hoffman and Taylor, *Much to Be Done*, 239.

42 Lucas, "Condition of Turkey," 7. Pattinson's *The Canadian Cook Book* was originally published in 1928. Lucas refers in her article to a 1938 revised edition.

43 "Thanksgiving," 38.

44 Ibid.

45 Adam, "Thanksgiving Dinner," 71.

46 Campbell, "For the Thanksgiving Dinner," 50.

47 Ibid.

48 Ibid.

49 Ibid., 75, 77.

50 "For These We Offer Thanks," 54.

51 Day, personal communication.

52 Dugan, "How to Tackle That Turkey," 28.

53 Ibid., 24.

54 Wayland, "Let's Talk Turkey," 72.

55 Ibid.

56 Dugan, "How to Tackle That Turkey," 28.

57 Wayland, "Let's Talk Turkey," 72.

58 Ibid., 64.

59 Brahman's and Chianello's Thanksgiving articles (Chianello, "Turkeytime," and Bramham, "Tradition Seasons") note the inclusion of such dishes as curried turkey (made from leftovers), antipasto, *linguine al pomodoro,* and rapini.

60 Scott, *School History of the United States,* 65, 85.

61 "Thanksgiving-Day," 1084; Bliss, "Thanksgiving: 'The Day We Celebrate,'" 1; Bacon, *Genesis of the New England Churches,* 349; *Journal of Health* 22 (January 1876): 10; Coffin, *Old Times in the Colonies,* 133.

62 "Pilgrim Pageant," 8.

63 Hobsbawm and Ranger, *Invention of Tradition,* 279–80; Applebaum, *Thanksgiving,* 218; Siskind, "Invention of Thanksgiving," 182–3, 186; Pleck, "Making of the Domestic Occasion," 780–1.

64 "First Thanksgiving Day," 87.

65 Leyendecker, "Pilgrim Stalking," cover.

66 Jennie Augusta Brownscombe's *The First Thanksgiving* is in the Museum of Pilgrim Treasures in Plymouth, Massachusetts; Jean Louis Gerome Ferris's *First Thanksgiving* is owned by a private collector.

67 For instance, see the collection of first Thanksgiving stories in Schauffler, *Thanksgiving,* 1–66.

68 Love, *Fast and Thanksgiving Days.*

69 Robertson, *American Myth,* 16.

70 Pleck, "Making of the Domestic Occasion," 780–1.

71 Alcott, *Moral Reformer*, 351–3.

72 "Farm Sanctuary's Adopt-A-Turkey," http://www.adoptaturkey.org.

73 Ibid.

74 Hewitt, "Spying Goes to College," 15.

75 Fisher, "Bernier, Oda Treat Troops," A4.

76 The entry for "Holidays" in the *Canadian Encyclopedia Online* makes particular note of cottage owners using the Thanksgiving weekend to prepare for winter. http://www.thecanadianencyclopedia.com.

77 Chianello, "Turkeytime," L2.

78 Bramham, "Tradition Seasons Every Dish," B3.

6

Grain Elevated: The Fall and Rise of Red Fife Wheat

SARAH MUSGRAVE

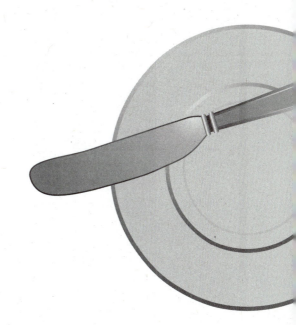

Towards the end of 2005, two Canadian wall calendars came across my desk. At first glance, they appeared to have little in common. Taken together, however, they raised questions about some of the myths and realities underlying the culture of Canada's culinary identity. Both mined the country's rural imagery for inspiration, conveying a sense of place, tradition, and continuity; yet within the month-by-month parade of photographs was a sense, too, of loss, change, and nostalgia.

Canada 2006 was a typical landscape calendar, displaying the nation's vast forests, rugged shorelines, and sweeping plains. November caught my eye; it showed a field of golden wheat stretching towards the horizon under a wide blue sky, with a battered grain elevator rising majestically in the distance. Among the "Top-Ten Canadian Scenes of All Time," this one would certainly rank high. The second calendar was less typical and arguably more titillating. A low-budget publication titled *Faces of Our Farmers,* it featured cheerful if cheeky photos of agricultural workers from Prince Edward County, Ontario, in various states of undress, with gleaming tractors, boxes of fresh produce, and farm equipment strategically placed in front of their own equipment.

Upon closer inspection, the text accompanying the images in both calendars revealed that things were not quite as they seemed, suggesting that the new year had perhaps brought with it a widening gap between an idealized past and an increasingly placeless future. *Canada 2006* noted that the traditional landmark in its prairie picture was not quite as timeless as it might appear: "Wooden elevators such as these in Mozart, Saskatchewan, are quickly disappearing and being replaced by huge concrete structures."[1] The naked farmer calendar, one of several to appear as part of a recent fundraising trend in North America and the United Kingdom in support of rural communities, also hinted at a threatened heritage: "Even if we preserve farmland from urban sprawl, without young farmers coming up through the ranks to replace the older generation, it will be all for naught."[2]

If snapshots of wheat fields and friendly farmers are still widely regarded as classic Canadiana, the sense of comfort, constancy, and cultural identity derived from them demands some scrutiny on the part of food scholars. The nation's grain industry has undergone dramatic changes in the last century. Contemporary consumers continue to take "wheat" for granted as an all-Canadian commodity and rarely have occasion to wonder what cultivar is being grown, where it came from, or by whom it is being harvested.

For much of the country's history, the wheat crop that thrived in its iconic fields, filled its grain elevators, and sustained the faces of its farmers was a venerable variety called Red Fife. In many ways the Red Fife story is the story of the nation itself. The first wheat to really flourish on these shores, it laid the foundation for the railroad, opened the West to cultivation, and helped establish the country's reputation as one of the world's top grain exporters. By the 1950s, however, what was once a household name had fallen into obscurity. There it remained until the last decade, when it was plucked from the edge of extinction by a grassroots initiative of farmers, bakers, and food activists and, once again, was brought to international attention by the culinary crusaders of the Slow Food movement.

This chapter traces the rise, fall, and revival of this pioneering grain, as well as the changing values – monetary and more ephemeral – associated with its

F.W. Schultz's wheat farm, near Rosebud, AB, c. 1920. Photograph by Wm Notman & Son. Courtesy of McCord Museum, VIEW-8606.1.

journey. My goal is to situate Red Fife in relation to the local food culture – as a Canadian-identified product – and to articulate the players and processes that have shaped its story for the last century and a half. As well, my aim is to link the grain to the global food scene and explore the implications of its present renaissance in the context of the wider resurgence of interest in "national" foods, alimentary authenticity, and place-based labelling. Red Fife, like all food products, is a culturally constructed phenomenon. To probe the political, economic, and social structures underlying its (re)commodification, I refer to communications scholar Vincent Mosco's definition of political economy as "the study of the social relations, especially the power relations, that mutually constitute the production, distribution, and consumption of resources."[3] Consequently, the gastronomic practices that support the Red Fife revival are considered here not just as a network for the trade of resources but as a system that communicates the importance of a taste of place in the era of third-stage (or monopoly) capitalism.

At a time when sources of sustenance are increasingly obscured by an industrialized agro-food system, discussions about the need to promote and protect culinary tradition are playing out over formal debating tables, including the parliamentary ones in Ottawa, just as they are over intimate dinner tables around the world. On the international stage, place-based products are being afforded intellectual property protection on an unprecedented scale by the European Union and the World Trade Organization (WTO). At regional levels, the resurgence of interest in farmers' markets, the demand for niche labels, and the popularity of alternative food movements demonstrate marked tendencies towards provenance purchasing on the part of citizen-consumers. Red Fife is far from the only food being repatriated and revalued in the global food marketplace, but it is an exceptionally Canadian example.

PUTTING DOWN ROOTS

If national foods tend to be imbued with historical and cultural significance, Red Fife has no shortage of lore behind it. While Canada's long-standing reputation for cultivation might suggest otherwise, wheat is not native to North America. It originated in the Fertile Crescent, an area of the Middle East hydrated by the Nile, Euphrates, Tigris, and Jordan rivers, where it was such a force in the agricultural revolution – and thus in the upheaval of previous ways of life – that researchers such as Evan Eisenberg have speculated that the forbidden fruit in Genesis was not, in fact, the apple, but rather Mesopotamian wheat.[4] Various cultivars made their way to the New World following colonization and were tested in Canadian climes, but most could not survive the winters or matured too late in the season. Red Fife itself is speculated to have descended from Halychanka, the beloved wheat of the Ukraine, where it has vanished from the landscape, though it is still celebrated in folklore and song.[5] That it arrived from overseas, perhaps as a stowaway, was seen as fitting for a Canadian product, as remarked by R.S. Kennedy in the August 1933 issue of the *Canadian Magazine*: "Red Fife is a true Canadian-born child, although like all of us except the Indians, its ancestor was an immigrant."[6]

The differing tales of how Red Fife wound up on these shores are full of twists and turns, some confirmed and some conjecture.[7] In 1842, a very small amount of the hard spring wheat – as little as a single kernel – accidentally crossed the ocean aboard a boat from Scotland in a shipment of winter wheat originating from Poland or Germany. It wound up in the hands of Ontario farmer David Fife, who, along with its deep ruddy colour, would give the variety its name. Some say the packet was mailed to Fife by a friend who worked in a Glasgow seed house or who simply found it on the docks; some say it was an impure sample; yet others contend that a grain or two dropped into an open package from a hatband. Whatever the case, Fife planted the contents of his missive on his land near Cobourg, Ontario, and was surprised when a few robust heads popped up in the early spring. The glorious plants impressed the farmer, his wife, and apparently the barnyard animals as well – for as legend has it, these healthy specimens would have been munched by the family cow had not a breathless Mrs Fife caught Bessie in the act. To this day, the Fife 1825 log cabin, in what is now Peterborough County, Ontario, stands as a monument to the wheat that would go on to have a tremendous impact on the nation's economy.[8]

Not, however, before another twist occurred in the Red Fife story, which some might find wryly Canadian. Although it was initially sown in Ontario, the variety's full profit potential was first realized south of the border. Canadian farmers gave the grain to American farmers in the Midwest, but they later found themselves asking for some back so that they could seed their own lands with it. A Canadian Department of Agriculture circular from 1883 recorded this blend of fluke and fortune:

> Accidental events can sometimes establish prosperity and create a flourishing economy for a society or an entire country. If an American farmer had not received a small amount of this wheat from David Fife, sowed it, made money with it and revealed its extraordinary value to the press, the Halychanka (Red Fife) wheat might well have been lost to this whole continent. Truly, the development of this wheat in North America owes him a great deal. What a strange, roundabout journey

Wheat wagon at country elevator on the prairies, c. 1927. Courtesy of McCord Museum, MP-0000.25.445.

for a small Ukrainian grain of wheat! From Ukraine to Ontario, from Ontario to the United States, then to Manitoba, and back to Ontario, and then throughout Canada.[9]

Once established, Red Fife put Canada on the map as a quality wheat producer and eventually earned it the title of breadbasket for the world.[10] Red Fife did well in the climate, pushing back prairie grasses and transforming ranchland into viable farmland. It played a key role in the settlement of the prairies in the late 1800s and in the development of towns like Winnipeg, Regina, and Edmonton. As agricultural zones opened up further north and west, rail lines were extended across the Rockies to the Pacific Ocean so that freight loads of golden cargo could scoot across the territory, destined to be shipped overseas. Along with its descendants, most notably Marquis,[11] Red Fife played a key role in increasing the land under cultivation on the prairies from 2.7 million acres in 1881 to 57 million some thirty years later.[12]

In its day, Red Fife was regarded as a fine milling and baking wheat, suited to traditional sourdough breads. Prior to the introduction of the fast-acting yeasts and flavour additives used in commercial baking, its stone-ground flour was valued for its nutty tastes and nutritional worth, both of which would be reduced in grain processed by industrial methods. Classified as a landrace (or open-source versus proprietary seed), also called "folk seeds or farmers varieties, meaning there is a uniform shape but genetic diversity in the seed population,"[13] Red Fife is of the type of grain that has been used by subsistence farmers for the last ten thousand years, but is not one of much value to large-scale trade.

Although it is the genetic parent to modern bread-wheat varieties grown in Canada today, Red Fife was all but forgotten by the end of the 1950s, supplanted by higher-gluten, higher-yield strains better suited to mass-market interests and bred for the earlier maturity sought by cultivators. As a result, Red Fife disappeared almost entirely from the landscape, remembered only by the eldest of Prairie residents.

RIPE FOR REVIVAL

Red Fife would lie dormant until the mid-1980s, when a bag of pure Red Fife seed, some of the last remaining stock, was discovered in a shed on a lonely stretch of prairie road. These seed specimens were transferred to a seed orphanage operated by the Canadian Heritage Wheat Project, under the guidance of agronomist Sharon Rempel. Like sister projects in Sweden, Greece, and the US Dakotas, the orphanage is based on the rationale that heritage varieties (those introduced before the 1960s) are essential to maintaining biodiversity and to opposing corporate control of seed, and that they are therefore of profound ecological and cultural value, even if such values are not reflected in modern trade standards.

Starting with half a pound of seed, Rempel began bulking up on Red Fife and eventually had enough to begin distributing it to farmers by the late 1990s.

Since then, it has cropped up from coast to coast, in Antigonish, Nova Scotia, and Woodstock, New Brunswick, as well as in Hastings, Ontario, and Cranbrook, British Columbia, with the tonnage harvested each year continuing to mount. Like many old wheats, its genetic variability makes it adaptable to different growing conditions and thus suitable for organic cultivation. For those harvesting Red Fife, the plots of land on which it grows represent living artifacts, the furthering of environmental awareness, and pockets of resistance to encroaching agribusiness.

The next chapter in the Red Fife story unfolded on a rainy night in November 2004, when the grain made the leap from cultivator to consumer. On this date, several tonnes of the wheat from the Loiselle family farm (the Loiselles had been growing the crop since 2002 in Vonda, Saskatchewan, harvesting sixty-five tonnes that year) were delivered to Wild Fire Bread and Pastry, a tiny bakery in Victoria, British Columbia. This delivery made Wild Fire the first bakery in Canada to use Red Fife commercially in any quantity in more than seventy-five years. Commissioning and processing wheat directly from organic farms, the bakery ensures a personal connection to the ingredients straight down the line. Wild Fire's loaves are hand-formed and baked the old-fashioned way in a wood-fired oven. According to founding baker Cliff Leir, customers seeking "ethically made great taste" increased the bakery's production 300 per cent since it opened in 2000.[14] Proponents of Red Fife predict that within five years there will be at least two more artisanal bakeries following in Wild Fire's footsteps,[15] and that the flour will be available in stores for home use by the end of the decade.

In the meantime, a granola-meets-gourmet social culture has taken root around the wheat. Largely community-based, these initiatives include the Heliotrust heritage bread wheat conservation project in the Maritimes, which harvested twenty tonnes in 2004; the volunteer-run Seedy Saturday Heritage Seed Exchange events, which are now held on a nation-wide basis; distributors offering Red Fife seed for private cultivation on farms or in personal gardens; the Red Fife Sisterhood, a group of women (including a Fife descendant) who grow the cultivar on the old homestead; at least two museum exhibits that honour historic wheats; and the Slow Food movement's support in getting the wheat back into production by establishing links with artisanal bakeries.[16]

Milling organic Red Fife at Pat Reichart's mill on Saltspring Island, BC. Courtesy of Mara Jernigan, Fairburn Farm.

Red Fife has also gained worldwide recognition at the hands of Slow Food, which took the product under its wing in 2003. Often viewed as the culinary offshoot of the anti-globalization movement, Slow Food is an international and increasingly influential network of eco-gastronomists devoted to preserving and propagating heritage foodstuffs by emphasizing the value of authentic tastes.[17] The Slow Food movement advocates both the enjoyment of traditional foods and the age-old methods of producing them. In supporting alternative agricultural practices and alternative economies, these epicurean ecologists have found themselves very much at the centre of the fight for food sovereignty in political, economic, and cultural spheres.

Taking on the snail as its mascot and proposing that revolution and rosé can indeed go hand in hand, Slow Food presents an unusual profile for a culture of resistance. "We all go to the same place, so let us go there slowly,"[18] founder and left-wing journalist Carlo Petrini has famously quipped. The organization began in 1986, when a group of protesters – armed with pasta instead of placards – gathered in Rome to express their discontent over the opening of Italy's first McDonald's franchise. It has since expanded on the international scene, counting eighty-three thousand members in fifty countries.

Slow Food chapters, or convivia, began cropping up in Canadian cities in 2000 and now dot the country from Halifax to Vancouver Island.[19] Red Fife is one of the movement's poster foods, and in 2003 it was nominated to the Slow Food Ark of Taste, a sort of edible walk of fame cataloguing culturally significant food items and near-forgotten flavours from around the world.[20] Because its near extinction merited Red Fife extra protection, it became the first Canadian product awarded Presidia membership, reserved for top-tier products that benefit from Slow Food business initiatives to bring them back into commercial circulation. Slow Food is keenly aware that setting up market links between potential customers and producers for niche items is an effective way to resist the forces of homogenization. At the 2004 Salone del Gusto in Turin, Italy, a biannual food fair that showcases heritage products and attracts some one hundred and forty thousand visitors, loaves of freshly baked Red Fife bread offered the rest of the world a taste of Canada.

RENEWAL OF THE REAL

For Slow Foodies and other supporters, reintegrating Red Fife into the Canadian marketplace, and into the Canadian consciousness, has brought challenges both concrete and conceptual. In a landscape increasingly dominated by corporate interests, the chain of production, processing, distribution, and retailing has evolved to favour large-scale orders, leaving niche products out of the equation. Wild Fire had to make a significant investment in infrastructure in order to be able to use this particular wheat at all. The shop installed a seven-metre grain silo to store its shipments and its own stone mill to grind them. This represents one major obstacle facing small-scale wheat producers: flour mills are set up for mass production and are no longer equipped to handle small accounts. Independent outfits have disappeared, much like the grain elevators. In the 1930s, there were more than six thousand elevators in operation in Alberta, Saskatchewan, and Manitoba, now there are about eight hundred.[21]

Another systemic problem is that Red Fife has yet to be recognized by the Canadian Wheat Board (CWB) or approved by the Canadian Food Inspection Agency. Technically, that means it cannot be legally grown and sold for human consumption. As an unregistered wheat, it can only be used for feed purposes. In order to be registered, it must earn qualification as a new variety, a strict procedure involving the Grain Standards Commission and trading companies, none of which are geared towards specialty products. According to a CWB official, it is unlikely ever to be approved because of modern expectations about yield and quality, the latter largely defined in terms of disease resistance and conformity. Taste, it should be noted, has never been a quality characteristic in Canadian variety registration.[22] Despite its historical significance, then, Red Fife is essentially traded under the radar.

Also problematic is the task of determining and defending Canada's current culinary identity and just what national foods should taste like. It is not as easy to define traditions in a New World context – or even the word *traditional* – as it is in an Old World context, such as in Italy or other Old World nations, where dishes can be traced back for generations within historically delineated regions. If the United States is indeed a fast food nation and Europe the guardian of Old World values, are we recovering or reinventing traditions in Canada?

Like the iconic images in the calendars described earlier, Canadian wheat calls to mind a time when family farms flourished, when food production took place on a human scale, when the independent farmer led a viable, if tough, way of life. It offers current consumers – especially growing urban populations – a link to an idealized place and time, real or imagined. It suggests not only a specific place but a wider sense of place, based on the idea of a happier past and the "rural innocence" of the pastoral, as Raymond Williams holds in *The Country and the City*. The lure of Red Fife could be a short form of the poetry Williams expresses in his book: "The means of agricultural production

– the fields, the woods, the growing crops, the animals – are attractive to the observer and, in many ways and in the good seasons, to the men working in and among them. They can then be effectively contrasted with the exchanges and counting-houses of mercantilism, or with the mines, quarries, mills and manufactories of industrial production."[23]

Seen in the context of agricultural development in Canada, the bountiful era of the family farm seems rather short lived. Already in the 1800s, independent farmers were complaining that they were being squeezed out by big business, accusing the Canadian Pacific Railway of granting monopolies to grain-handling companies.[24] As early as 1899 and again in 1904, royal commissions investigating the grain trade agreed with farmers that protection was necessary, and their recommendations led to the creation of the first incarnation of the Canadian Wheat Board. Evidently, from the time of initial settlement, First Nations foodways gave way quickly, relatively speaking, to an industrialized agriculture model. Canadians, therefore, may be guilty of the same idealistic thinking as those developed nations that, as geographer scholar Susanne Freidberg comments, "hold tenaciously to romanticized myths of their country's peasant agriculture, even if their peasants largely disappeared centuries before."[25]

Canada's economy, as economist Harold Innis has suggested, has always been outward-looking, with the demands of export very much tied to the notion of nation building: "As long as Canada's policies had to accommodate the commercial policies of the more advanced metropoles such as Britain and the United States, its development remained trapped by the conflict between local institutions and regional needs, between the intense pressures of indigenous political culture and the conflicting values of colonialism and nationalism, between the constant imposition of imperialist needs on a compliant state and the emergence of strong local markets supporting indigenous development."[26] In this New World situation, it seems that Canadian culinary consciousness developed in the context of Canada sending away food to places that had previously been home to many of its citizens, while these citizens, in turn, requested foods from home and recreated them in a new place. It also developed in relation to a growing American agro-food system that was homegrown, perhaps, but ultimately growing towards placelessness.

A green wheat field. Photo: JG Photography.

That said, mythic qualities still surround the Canadian and American farms of yesteryear, and the struggles of reviving Red Fife provide a window onto the changing realities of, and attitudes towards, rural life in North America. And even if the enduring image of the family farm is in part folklorization, it does refer to an era when food production was less centralized. When, precisely, this era existed is more difficult to identify. In 1934, writing on this country's economic nationalism, Innis noted the "increasing disparity between standards of living of urban and rural population."[27] Around that same time, in 1931, Saskatchewan's farm population peaked at five hundred and sixty-four thousand. Three decades later, between 1961 and 2001, the province's farm population declined by two-thirds, and the number of farms dropped by half. Today, wheat, once a major staple of the Prairie economy, accounts for a small percentage of its provinces' exports; likewise, declining prices and higher farm expenses have seen the percentage of farm family income from operations fall from 70 per cent in the 1970s to 40 per cent in 2000.[28]

It is tempting to view such trends in the Canadian food landscape as the inevitable results of economic progress and industrialization. But comparisons with other milieus show them to be reflections of policies tied to cultural values operating within the political economy. By comparison, for example, the rural population hardly declined at all in Europe during the last thirty years. "In contrast to Canadian policy, the European Economic Community has made the continuation of a stable rural population a high-priority social goal," John Warnock points out in his history of Saskatchewan.[29]

A TASTE OF PLACE

There are several reasons why the commodification of traditional foods, which for these purposes I would describe as those having an established link to the land, would appear to have stronger state support in Europe. A key issue is that small-scale output by a group of producers from a specific area has long been validated by the notion of *terroir*. Rooted in the French word *terre*, or land, *terroir* encapsulates the idea that a particular interplay of geography, history, and human factors imbues foods with a particular taste that cannot be recreated elsewhere. In the past, the term was closely associated with European wines; these days it is used in the popular press to describe artisanal foods from different continents – butter, cheese, and chocolate, for example. France has long used the notion of *terroir* to instil pride in those who uphold a peasant-driven mode of production and to promote its own culinary authenticity among citizens and tourists alike. Food scholar Warren Belasco suggests that in doing so "the French also unwittingly established a patriotic model for the current sustainable food movement – particularly the celebration of the 'local' and 'regional' over the forces of 'globalization' and 'McDonaldization.'"[30]

Today, Europeans, and not just Slow Foodies, are increasingly demanding protection for traditionally produced goods and support for the rural communities that create them. Recent reforms to the Common Agricultural Policy reflect "a paradigmatic change from a *quantity* to a *quality* oriented food policy."[31] Hermann Scheer, president of the Agriculture Commission of the Assembly of the Council of Europe, has called for "the abolition of all the government directives that determine the size of apples, pumpkins and so on, since these rules are only to help large distributors and hinder the process of regionalization in agriculture."[32] His statement could apply to a defence of Red Fife against the control regulations imposed by the Canadian Wheat Board.

On the global front, the rationale of *terroir* finds a formal counterpart in recent regulatory initiatives of the World Trade Organization that grant intellectual property rights to specialty food products deemed worthy of market protection. Under the auspices of the TRIPS (Trade-Related Aspects of Intellectual Property Rights) Agreement, the governing body administers a system of formal certifications known as Geographical Indications (GIs), which work much like collective trademarks for certain foodstuffs whose particular quality, reputation, or other characteristic is attributable to their geographical origin. Equivalent to France's Appellation d'origine contrôlée, a highly bureaucratic quality-control system initially used for wines, a GI guarantees an authentic package to consumers, linking product, producer, technique, land, and taste. Although the impact of this system has yet to be fully felt on this side of the Atlantic, such measures have created deep rifts within the WTO – between member countries and also between Old World and New World countries. While many European nations have sought GI certifications for their home-grown edibles, the United States, Canada, and Australia, among others, have come out against extending protections to heritage foods; it remains to be seen whether North American goods such as Red Fife might eventually find a home in the European Union's proposed global database of place-based products.[33]

GI-mandated or not, enhanced global competition since the postwar period has created opportunities for producers of traditional foodstuffs to expose their goods to a wider audience, and shoppers have demonstrated increasing interest in niche items and a willingness to pay more for products legitimated by locationist labelling.[34] As borders between states are blurred and national identities lost or hybridized through the effects of economic globalization, the preservation of local distinctions seems to meet the citizen-consumers' profound need for reassurance of cultural continuity.

It is worth noting that while place-based foods are necessarily produced in limited quantities because of land restrictions, even mass-mediated commodities can offer local distinctions that seem to stand in opposition to the

Red Fife wheat farmer Marc Loiselle. Photo: JG Photography.

dominant food system. In his study of doughnut chain Tim Hortons, Steve Penfold suggests that "[w]e consume American products, yet somehow crave a more 'genuine' Canadian mass culture experience, like a Tim Hortons coffee on a February morning."[35] Like the imagery of the homegrown wheat harvest, the comforting lure of the blue-collar coffee shop that Penfold describes is built on the "constructed folklore of simple people living authentic premodern experiences outside the complications of market capitalism, mass culture, modernism, and so on."[36]

Recent preoccupations with provenance may also be reinforced by millennial health and safety scares. Such scares suggest a demand for a level of quality and accountability not associated with largely untraceable, mass-manufactured edible items. "Marketing food as local or national appeals to assumptions about the qualities of place-based foodways and, more fundamentally, to people's affinities for and identification with place itself," Freidberg notes, adding that "[t]his can certainly help sell food at times when the integrity of places and their foodways appear threatened, both by specific events (like the foot-and-mouth outbreak) and by the institutions associated with globalized food culture (like multinational retailers, fast food chains, or the WTO)."[37]

According to Freidberg, nations seem to start firming up their foodways and attaching more importance to their culinary heritage when that heritage might be about to change. In England and France, "[f]oodways did not become a recognized part of *national* cultural identity – in that they were written about, taught, served and exported as such – until the mid-to-late nineteenth century."[38] Paralleling the current climate, this was a period when anxieties and controversies about food were simmering in response to shifts in socio-economic structures. "With the emergence of an urban bourgeois society devoted to gastronomy – the science of taste – both the French state and French farmers realized food's power as an expression of natural and national distinction – a distinction that strengthened national consciousness around food on both sides of the Channel."[39] Perhaps Canada is simply a hundred years behind in codifying its culinary consciousness.

CONCLUSION: HOME AND AWAY

To promote their own place-based foods and to distinguish between local and foreign, citizen-consumers must first have some idea about what "their" food is and where it comes from. The situation for Canadians is far from straightforward, given that they lack the same kind of entrenched legacy of local distinctions that are rooted in *terroir,* cannot claim a peasant past to deify as France does its *paysans,* and are faced with the American-modelled food industry's tendency to divorce the farm from the fork. If consumers are beginning to adopt localist and locationist leanings in Canada, these tendencies are reflected in non-state spheres, such as in the renewed popularity of farmers markets, which offer seasonal, place-rooted pleasures but also an occasion to shop morally and support producers face to face; in upscale restaurants' practice of identifying regional sources and local purveyors on menus – in Montreal, for example, diners will be offered Mr Daigneault's Jerusalem artichokes, Charlevoix lamb (sourced from the Charlevoix region of Quebec), and Pied-de-Vent cheese made with milk from *canadienne* cattle; in growing interest in food scholarship for academic and general audiences; and in the growing momentum of activist food-based networks, such as Slow Food. However, all this has as yet effected little significant change in agricultural policy or in the granting of government-sponsored appellations for products such as Red Fife.

In closing, it is important to emphasize that the Red Fife wheat revival may have significant political, economic, and social implications for Canada. If Canadians were to be proud to serve a slice of Red Fife bread with Pied-de-Vent cheese and a wedge of heirloom apple to represent their national food-ways, they might also recognize that the integrity of independent wheat cultivators, raw-milk cheesemakers, and small orchards is threatened to varying degrees in the current agro-food system. As a new calendar year begins and Red Fife continues to gain ground across the country, Canadians find themselves in a position to sample, savour, and potentially find new ways to support the tastes of home.

NOTES

1 *Canada* 2006.
2 Hickey, *Faces of Our Farmers*. Profits from this calendar are directed to an educational fund for young farmers in the district.
3 Mosco, *Political Economy of Communication*, 25.
4 Quoted in Belasco, "Food Matters," 3.
5 Red Fife is also sometimes referred to as "Galician wheat" after an area in western Ukraine.
6 Symko, "From a Single Seed," http://www4.agr.gc.ca/AAFC-AAC/ display-afficher.do?id=1181318948130.
7 From interviews I conducted in spring 2005 with Mara Jernigan, Canadian representative for the Slow Food Ark Project, co-coordinator of the Vancouver Island and the Gulf Islands Convivium of the Slow Food Movement, and Sushil Saini, coordinator of the Canadian Heritage Wheat Presidium, in preparation for the magazine articles "Bread Winner," *Saturday Night Magazine* 120, no. 2 (2005); and "Going with the Grain," *Doctor's Review Magazine*. An account of Red Fife's origins is also recited in Dorothy Duncan's *Canadians at the Table*.
8 The original 1825 Fife family log cabin was relocated to Lang Pioneer Village, where the Lang Grist Mill that was used by Fife and his neighbours, is still operational. In addition, a plaque erected in the village by the federal government recognizes the accomplishments of David and Jane Fife, and there is another plaque in Fife's honour on Highway 7 near Peterborough.

9   Symko, "From a Single Seed," 80.

10 For more on Canada's transformation into breadbasket of the world and the early provisioning of early residents, see Dorothy Duncan's *Canadians at Table*.

11 Marquis, a cross between Red Fife and Hard Red Calcutta, was developed by breeder Charles Saunders and first publicly distributed in 1909.

12 Warnock, *Saskatchewan*, 130.

13 Rempel, "Heritage Wheat Project."

14 Leir, personal communication. I have also had the pleasure of enjoying his bread, excellent with just a smear of semi-salted butter.

15 Cliff Leir has since sold his stake in Wild Fire and in the fall of 2008 opened another bakery, Fol Epi, in Victoria. Other bakeries that are or have been experimenting with Red Fife flour in varying degrees include True Grain Bread in Cowichan Valley Village and the Renaissance Bakery in Penticton, BC; Alpine Bakery in Whitehorse, YK; Christie's Mayfair Bakery in Saskatoon, SK; Mill Stone Bakery in Cobourg, ON, which uses wheat grown close to the original Fife farm; and Boulangerie la Vendéenne, which sells its bread at the farmers market in Halifax, NS. Red Fife bread has also been baked and served at the Toronto restaurants of celebrity chef Jamie Kennedy.

16 Further explanation, listings of heritage seed events, and contacts for distributors can be found at http://www.seedysaturday.ca and http://www.seeds.ca (maintained by the charitable organization Seeds of Diversity, which is dedicated to conserving, documenting, and propagating heirloom and endangered plants of Canadian significance). The Living Museum of Wheat is located in Keremeos, BC, http://www.keremeos.com, and in 1999 the Museum of Civilization opened a permanent exhibition devoted to Prairie wheat, including a full-size replica of a Saskatchewan grain elevator (http://www.civilization.ca).

17 For more information on the goals of the movement, see Petrini, *Slow Food: The Case for Taste*.

18 Quoted in Muoio, "We all go to the same place," 194.

19 The locations of the eighteen Canadian convivia include Vancouver, Vancouver Island, Whistler, Calgary, Edmonton, Toronto, Ottawa, Guelph, Windsor (and several other cities in Ontario), Montreal, Halifax, and Whitehorse.

20 In 2003, Red Fife joined two other Canadian products – La Vache canadienne and the Montreal Melon – in the Ark of Taste. The national projects section of Slow Food Canada's website (http://www.slowfood.ca) provides listings of convivia in Canada and links to Presidia products promoted by the Slow Food Foundation for Biodiversity.

21 These figures are from "Wheat Boom," http://www.pc.gc.ca/apprendre-learn/prof/sub/histc-cstor/histc-cstore10_e.asp.

22 From a spring 2005 interview and a press release by Fitzhenry, "Prairie farmers caught in EU/US crossfire at WTO," http://www.cwb.ca/public/en/newsroom/releases/2005/110105.jsp. The CWB, the sole marketing agency for wheat and barley farmers in western Canada, has been busy fighting battles of its own since the North American Free Trade Agreement came into force. As of this writing, the fate of its single-desk system remains to be determined.

23 Williams, *The Country and the City*, 46.

24 Warnock, *Saskatchewan*, 137.

25 Freidberg, *French Beans and Food Scares*, 131.

26 Innis, *Staples, Markets and Cultural Change*, xxii.

27 Ibid., 216.

28 Warnock, *Saskatchewan*, 144.

29 Ibid., 141.

30 Belasco, "Food Matters," 12.

31 Thiediga, "Welcome to the Club?" 5.

32 Scheer, "Region Is Reason," 7.

33 Perhaps the most powerful example of the profit potential and public profile to be derived from GI branding came in October 2005, when the European Court of Justice ruled that the term *feta* is geographic and not generic. Greece won a protected designation of origin for its brine-soaked ewe- or goat-milk cheese in recognition of its specific ecology, history, and savoir-faire. To ensure "the remarkable reputation of feta," foreign producers are no longer allowed to market their cheese under the name feta within the European Union. AP, "Decades-long feta cheese fight decided in favour of Greece," *Globe and Mail, Report on Business*, 26 October 2005, B11. The full judgment of the court (Joined Cases C-465/02 C-466/02 from 25 October 2005) is available online: http://eur-lex.europa.eu/LexUriServ/LexUriServ.do?uri=CELEX:62002J0465:EN:NOT.

34 Barham, "Translating Terroir," 127.

35 Penfold, "Eddie Shack Was No Tim Horton," 52.

36 Ibid., 59. National associations may be disconnected from the origins of the commodity itself, however. Penfold notes that doughnuts were first mass-retailed in the United States, and that despite its ultra-Canadian marketing and its connection to hockey hero Tim Horton, the chain is now owned by an American company.

37 Freidberg, *French Beans and Food Scares*, 218.

38 Ibid., 48.

39 Ibid., 34.

Part Two

What Do Our Food Stories Tell Us about Who We Are or Were?

7

"There *is* a Canadian cuisine, and it is unique in all the world": Crafting National Food Culture during the Long 1960s

RHONA RICHMAN KENNEALLY

INTRODUCTION[1]

In 1972, Sondra Gotlieb, Canadian author, journalist, and broadcaster, introduced her book *The Gourmet's Canada* as a means of offering clarification. "The idea of a good Canadian cuisine is hazy," she explains, "not only in the minds of non-Canadians, but in our own. The coffee shop in Montreal's Dorval airport has an 'international menu,' listing pizza as the specialty of Italy, paella, for Spain, and the hot chicken sandwich as Canada's contribution to the world's cuisine. No, Canada has not so far been considered a haven for gourmets of the world."[2]

Five years earlier, in that same city, a similar haziness had presented itself. In that year, Canada celebrated its centenary through Expo 67, the world exhibition attended by some fifty million visitors. Here, at thirty-two of the exhibition's pavilions, restaurants representing Canada as a whole, Quebec, Ontario, and the Atlantic provinces, as well as countries such as the Soviet Union, Italy, India, and Czechoslovakia, offered versions of their foods for visitors to taste.

These dining experiences were authenticated by allusions to long-standing culinary traditions, by having foods specially imported from the motherland, and by the inclusion of simulated or actual traditional artifacts and decor in the eating spaces. Within this eating environment, two restaurants in the Canada Pavilion offered up distinct versions of culinary identity associated with the host culture. One of these, La Toundra (The Tundra), is memorable for its murals, which were created by two Inuit artists; patrons made contact with "three genuine Eskimo girls [serving] as hostesses" and waiters "attired in Eskimo-inspired costumes with rough Whalebone stitching."[3] The menu was divided into three parts: "Arctic" dishes contained such ingredients as beluga whale meat, arctic char, and buffalo meat; "Canadian" dishes included "Duckling Okanagan" (named for the Okanagan region of British Columbia) and "Ojibwa Kee Wee Sen," a fish dish "as enjoyed by generations of Ojibways braves"; and "International" dishes comprised the third group that nonetheless contained "Pork Chops Hochelaga" (Hochelaga being the name of the First Nations settlement on which Montreal is now situated) and "Canadian Lobster à la Nage."[4] The second restaurant in the Canada Pavilion, called "The Buffet," had "décor like a one-room 'Happening' [a distinctly sixties reference] and huge cages holding 80 singing Birds." It served a synthesis of foods whose origins could be said to emulate either the varying heritages of the Canadian mosaic or the tenets of contemporary cosmopolitan cuisine – "Tourtière" (a meat pie of French Canadian origin), "Seafood Newburg in Patty Shell," and "Curried Seafood."[5] The Canada Pavilion was no mere building at this exhibition; it was the host country's carefully presented repository of architecture, material culture, ideology, and aspiration, created to uncloak a mature, dynamic, modern, and sophisticated nation. Would not most visitors to the Expo site include this monumental series of structures in their list of must-see pavilions? If its restaurants were meant to be equally suggestive of the most exciting – and most representative – culinary creations that the country had to offer, one would have to conclude that a distinctly "Canadian" cuisine was a porous concept.

Yet the assertion of this chapter is that the impulse to construct a distinctly Canadian culinary heritage can be seen as a key generating force behind a few significant cookbooks published during the long 1960s. Food seems to have been perceived, at least by the author/compilers of these cookbooks – public figures familiar to Canadian audiences as authoritative spokespersons – as an effective vehicle through which to ponder a national ethos, despite the fact that Canada, unlike, say, France or Italy, did not possess an automatically recognized gastronomic heritage. Significantly, the impulse to generate a Canadian food culture coincided with a number of other federal government projects intended to create a sense of Canadian identity and patriotic fervour, particularly in anticipation, or as a result, of the centennial celebrations of 1967. These included a new flag (1965) and a new national logo (the wordmark "Canada" with a small Canadian flag over the last "a," making the vertical stroke of the "d" look like a flagpole).[6]

GLOBALIZED FOOD

In a 2005 article entitled "Identity and the Global Stew," Allison James wonders if a "confusion of culinary signposts," emanating from Britain in the twenty-first century due to "an increasingly (global) international food production-consumption system and a seemingly 'creolized' world," can challenge an effective understanding of food as "a marker of (local) cultural identity."[7] Though perhaps not to the same degree, such a jumble had characterized the menus of the Canada Pavilion restaurants in 1967 and was readily apparent in the mid-century cookbooks that will be discussed below.[8] How could all this variety be considered as collectively representing the cuisine of one country? Could Canada be understood as even having a distinct food culture, and if so, how could it be defined? Did visitors to Canada who dined at the Canada Pavilion go home thinking that we regularly ate whale meat, that the Ojibway Nation or other aboriginal groups substantially influenced Canadian cooks, or even that curried seafood was a popular Canadian supper? As will be demonstrated in this chapter, the issue of what *did* constitute Canadian cuisine occupied a number of interested individuals during the middle decades of the twentieth century, in tandem with larger issues related to the construction of Canadian nationalism. Indeed, this issue occupied Canadians to the extent that they were stimulated to create cookbooks that crafted a culinary heritage and established a database of contemporary dishes constructed as Canadian. The intention of this study is by no means to attempt a comprehensive analysis of all Canadian cookbooks of this period, but rather to explore a few pivotal works in some depth in order to determine how their authors both implicitly and explicitly encode the dishes they present to the reader with markers of national association. What will be demonstrated through an investigation of these cookbooks is that the very haziness of a Canadian food identity was, in itself, as Allison James asserts, a significant marker of (local) cultural identity.

Of course, a key assumption in this argument is that cookbooks are critical foci that transmit the cultural values, beliefs, and practices of the society out of which they emanate. Arguments along this line are well established. Susan J. Leonardi explores recipes as "embedded discourse" in her now-canonic article on *The Joy of Cooking*.[9] Janet Theophano articulates a related sentiment and argues that "women's cookbooks can be maps of the social and cultural worlds they inhabit"; consequently, her book reflects a commitment to discover "something about the social networks that gave birth to these culinary inscriptions."[10] Sherrie Inness understands cookbooks as serving political agendas for the women who write them, as a means, for example, of calling for widespread reform.[11] Community or fundraising cookbooks have the additional benefit of enabling an exploration of foods from a descriptive – as opposed to a prescriptive – perspective, inasmuch as they are usually composed of recipes tested and perfected in the homes of their contributors.[12]

That foods themselves – and hence cookbooks – can be vital contributors to the conceptualization of a national identity has also been extensively demonstrated. Arjun Appadurai's analysis of cookbooks in contemporary India has been incorporated into analyses of other nationalisms by subsequent foodways researchers and has also stimulated later examinations of that particular country.[13] Jeffrey M. Pilcher, looking to nineteenth-century Mexico, explores cookbooks as gendered readings of nation. He links his research to Benedict Anderson's concept of a nation as an "imagined community," which Anderson perceives as a "deep, horizontal comradeship," imagined (rather than concrete), since "members of even the smallest nation will never know most of their fellow-members, meet them, or even hear of them, yet in the minds of each lives the image of their communion."[14] David Bell and Gill Valentine also build on Anderson's argument to claim that "the nation's diet is a feast of imagined commensality," and in this way, they interfere with the simplistic isolation of certain foods as "definitionally" belonging to any given nation's cultural repertoire.[15] Intrinsic to this argument is the fact that valorizations of certain foods as traditionally belonging to a certain national heritage are culturally constructed as part of an invented discourse.[16]

Moreover, the designation of foods as "authentic" in light of a particular national gastronomic heritage is similarly based on a selection of criteria that are subject to variation and transformation. Lisa Heldke's perception of the concept offers a useful approach to understanding authenticity in this regard, inasmuch as it "rejects the notion that properties of a dish inhere in the dish, independent of the perceivers, and instead conceives of taste or flavor as a property of the experiential work of the cuisine." In other words, a food preparation can be negotiated as authentic through what she calls "transactions" between the dish (and its cook) and the eater; an exploration of this transaction becomes the means through which an understanding of food culture can arise.[17] Such a definition encourages us to acknowledge and investigate the hybridity inherent in the tripartite menu of the restaurant La Toundra, instead of dismissing it out of hand as "inauthentic," as an unrevealing mish-mash, or, perhaps, as a primarily consumer-driven concession to attract hungry patrons with varying levels of gastronomic curiosity or familiarity. This is especially important, as the recipe books to be presented in this essay reflect similar variations.

CONSTRUCTING A CANADIAN CULINARY HERITAGE

The aim in the selection of the cookbooks for this study was to hone a Canadian culinary heritage out of conditions precisely contrary to those conventionally underscoring a national food history – that is, out of a hodge-podge of diverse eating traditions from numerous regions of the world, brought to Canada through decades of immigration, and in evidence across the country. Moreover, rather than make a case for some kind of sanctioned food elite as the primary underpinning for this heritage – using indicators of gastronomic excellence such as recipes from renowned Canadian restaurant chefs, for example – the authors of these cookbooks tend to compose their food valorizations based on the degree to which the foods were directly connected to the personal, family, or community narratives of the non-professional home cooks (apparently mostly women) who provided the recipes, and to the Canadian regional landscapes out of which these stories (and, sometimes, key recipe ingredients) emerged. Or, some of the cookbook authors have incorporated recipes found in earlier Canadian cookbooks from different parts of the country into a nationally perceived cultural history.

THE COOKBOOK AUTHOR/COMPILERS

All but one of the cookbooks to be explored here have a basic commonality: their authors or titles had solid links to the popular culture of the time. Three of the author/compilers were established media personalities in their own right, and two already had strong associations with food culture. Jehane Benoît was a Sorbonne- and Cordon Bleu–trained expert who was operating a cooking school in Montreal by the fifties, had appeared regularly as a food expert on national radio and television in English as well as in French, wrote food columns for popular magazines, and published cookbooks that were apparently meant to demonstrate her strong connections to at least one sphere of Canada's gastronomic heritage.[18] A French-language cookbook called *Secrets et recettes du cahier de ma grand'mère* (Secrets and Recipes from my Grandmother's Notebook), dating from 1959, was dedicated to Benoît's daughter Monique and granddaughter Susan in a further gesture of cultural continuity.[19] Other cookbooks by Benoît, in English and French, include *L'Encyclopédie de la cuisine canadienne* (1963) and its English translation, *Encyclopedia of Canadian Cuisine* (1964); *The Canadiana Cookbook* (1970) and its translation, *La cuisine canadienne* (1979); the twelve-volume *Madame Benoît's Library of Canadian Cooking* (1972); *Enjoying the Art of Canadian Cooking* (1974); and English and French versions of a microwave cookbook written in the 1970s.

The second established food expert examined here is Sondra Gotlieb. Whereas she had not received formal training in gastronomy, she based her qualifications at least in part on her mother's expertise in the kitchen and on growing up in a family of discriminating eaters, as discussed in her books. At the time she was publishing her works on Canadian food culture – *The Gourmet's Canada* (1972); *Cross Canada Cooking: Favorite Recipes of Canadians from Many Lands* (1976) and its French translation, *Cuisine sans frontières: Recettes préférés de canadiens des quatre coins du monde* (1977) – she was also well known for her work for *Maclean's*, *Saturday Night*, and *Chatelaine*, the major Canadian news, culture, and women's magazines, respectively, and had a weekly radio broadcast on food in Ottawa, where she lived.

Husband-and-wife collaborators Pierre and Janet Berton, producers of only one food study (albeit one that underwent at least three printings, including one revision), also commanded substantial public attention, theirs based on Pierre's popularly celebrated expertise both in the history of Canada and in current affairs.[20] Author of bestsellers on Canadian history beginning with *Klondike* in 1958, Pierre Berton was a journalist for *Maclean's* magazine and a television personality, especially as a panellist on the CBC news quiz show *Front Page Challenge*. The Bertons' *Centennial Food Guide: A Century of Good Eating* (1966) was one of a series of books that comprised the Canadian Centennial Library from Canadian publishers McClelland and Stewart, along with such other titles as *Great Canadian Sports Series*, *Great Canadian Writing*, and *The Making of the Nation: A Century of Challenge*. Whereas the Bertons did not claim professional expertise as food practitioners, their book is peppered with references to their own recipes, meals, and food reminiscences.

To the uninitiated, the author of the *Laura Secord Canadian Cook Book* (1966) would seem to have been the woman whose name appears in the title. This might well have been the conclusion of Canadians during the sixties, because Laura Secord was the name of a national chain of candy stores that sold chocolates and other products under their own brand. However, Laura Secord was a nineteenth-century heroine who put her life at risk to warn Canadians of an imminent attack by American forces during the War of 1812, and she herself had no direct connections to food culture. The authors/compilers of this best-selling cookbook were actually three members of the Canadian Home Economics Association, a national organization established in 1939 and devoted to strengthening the profession of home economists and improving the quality of life for Canadians.[21] Whereas the 2001 reprint of this cookbook mentions that the original version was developed "in partnership" with the candy company, one suspects that the cookbook title was also meant to garner the attention of an extended popular audience. Favourable sentiments would inevitably have been generated by the fact that Laura Secord candy was associated with gift-giving and with family occasions such as Christmas, Valentine's Day, and Mother's Day; a Laura Secord cookbook could thus create positive food connotations to attract readers and reassure them that the food described in the recipes was tasty and unintimidating.

Indeed, only one of the cookbooks mentioned in this study comes from someone who was not very well known when the book was published, although she would subsequently gain fame and culinary recognition as food editor of *Canadian Living Magazine* and as a regular on a number of television programs in the country, including the *Canadian Living Cooks* show on Food Network Canada. Elizabeth Baird's first cookbook, *Classic Canadian Cooking: Menus for the Seasons* (1974) was followed by many others, including *Elizabeth Baird's Favourites: 150 Classic Canadian Recipes* (1984) and *The Complete* Canadian Living *Cookbook* (2004).

THEORIZING A NATIONAL FOOD CULTURE

The mechanisms that underpin the construction of a national cuisine have been of great interest to famed anthropologist Arjun Appadurai, whose study of mid-twentieth-century India has strongly influenced subsequent researchers. Appadurai sees the Indian model of an emerging national cuisine as "what might be expected to occur with increasing frequency and intensity in other societies having complex regional cuisines and recently acquired nationhood, and in which a postindustrial and postcolonial middle class is constructing a particular sort of polyglot culture."[22] In this case, exchanges of recipes of particular regional or ethnic origins are the result of the inter-urban migration of middle-class families relocated for business and other purposes, as women enthusiastically experiment with new dishes obtained either from similarly displaced families of different ethnicities or from the new host environment.[23] This initial exchange, oral in origin and then set down in cookbooks (and, indeed, increasingly practised in restaurants), "clearly reflects and reifies an emerging culinary cosmopolitanism in the cities and towns of India."[24] What are thus "created, exchanged, and refined are culinary stereotypes of the Other, stereotypes that are then partly standardized in the new cookbooks."[25] In such a diverse gustatory environment, Appadurai notes, "perhaps the central categorical thrust is the effort to define, codify, and publicize regional cuisines," thus systematizing culinary traditions ascribed to this ethnic "Other."[26] Out of this "increasingly articulated gallery of specialized ethnic and regional cuisines," a series of permutations and combinations serve to carve out a wider-reaching, national Indian food culture. These admixtures arise from different incentives, for example, out of a nostalgic urge of an emigrant from India to reconstitute a remembered cuisine, or to articulate a colonial perception of Indian food (as a series of curries, for example), or through the authors' choice to cluster kinds of foods (breads, pickles), basic ingredients (vegetables, lentils), or types of meal (snacks, desserts).[27] In this way, overarching assemblies of local dishes are juxtaposed and hence constructed as defining the broader rubric of a national Indian cuisine, which, derived from the perceptions and vicissitudes of each professed expert, emerges "because of, rather than despite, the increasing articulation of regional and ethnic cuisines."[28]

THE CANADIAN EXAMPLE

These findings are instructive because they can serve as a point of departure to understanding the construction of a Canadian national cuisine. Appadurai's observation that such strategies are tied in with "recently acquired nationhood" can be adjusted to the Canadian context, to be seen as coinciding with the centenary discourse that asserted Canada's newly mature status on the world scene. As was the case in the Indian example, all the major Canadian cookbooks explored in this essay perceive the national cuisine as a composite of foods developed in different regions of the country, very often built on the use of local ingredients and exhibiting characteristics of the cultural groups that cooked them. Moreover, the authors/compilers are careful to demonstrate that they undertook substantial research of regional food customs, sometimes even traversing the nation to make contact with the individuals whose recipes figure on the pages.

There are only rare cases where the compilers admit to interfering with a recipe they receive in order to adapt it to a pan-Canadian audience, which suggests that they are concerned with maintaining the authenticity of the original version.[29] Hence, the cookbooks are significant in that they perform the service of capturing recipes that existed previously only in unwritten formats or in written ones that were fragile and minimally transferable (in a notebook, for example), obscure, or of limited focus. Sondra Gotlieb, for example, mentions having made a "gastronomic journey through Canada" prior to writing

The Gourmet's Canada and acknowledges the help of "friends who drove me around from St. John's [Newfoundland] to Victoria [British Columbia]."[30] In *Cross Canada Cooking*, she specifically states, "I needed personal contact; I wanted to find out if there were people who cooked in a manner that bore some relationship to their ancestry or region. I wanted to find out who they were, how they lived, and what the food they cooked in their own kitchens tasted like ... I needed human beings to bring this book to life." She adds that the cooks, in turn, happily cooperated with this project and "prepared the most elaborate meals for a total stranger, because they were proud of their cooking tradition and wished to see it preserved in print."[31] In this book, most chapters are organized around Gotlieb's visit to homes in a particular community – Emmy Lou and John Allan's house in St John's, Mrs Helen Cholakis and her family in their Winnipeg home, or Bhagwant Natt's apartment in Vancouver, where she was exposed to Newfoundland, Greek, and Indian food, respectively, in the company of the hosts' family and friends.[32] Not surprisingly, then, at the end of the book, Gotlieb confesses that her greatest wish "was to describe how the men and women in this book enrich our country with their different cultures and skills. Interesting as their recipes are, they are not as important as the people themselves."[33] Hence the recipes are meant to serve as conduits to an understanding of the individuals who make up the collective community of Canada.

The authors of the *Laura Secord Canadian Cook Book* also undertook original research, their representatives "scouring every province" to find suitable recipes and collecting over a thousand in the process.[34] This book, too, has a few recipes whose names refer directly to individuals or to particular cultural groups or locations – "Mary's Polish Bread," "Barkerville Gold Digger's Special," "Wolfe Island Cheese Soufflé," or "Dutch Speculaas." When the recipe names are generic, the descriptions that introduce them often associate the dishes with a particular region or group. Hence, we learn that "Christmas Pudding" comes from Stratford, Ontario; "Buffalo Birds" are buffalo burgers as made in Fort Smith, Northwest Territories; and "Maple Ginger Cake" was once prepared on a television cooking show broadcast from Sydney, Nova Scotia.[35]

Publisher Christopher Ondaatje introduces Jehane Benoît's *Canadiana Cookbook* as being "based on an exhaustive search for traditional Canadian recipes through material accumulated over the years, much of it never published before." He adds that the book's very success comes from "the intermingling of different cultures, different geography," as well as the simple use of simple ingredients, albeit cooked "with care and imagination."[36] There are twelve chapters, one for each of the ten provinces and two territories, beginning with Quebec, then Ontario, and then fanning outward – first east, then west, then north. Chapter subsections are quick indicators of regional food engagement. The subsections in Manitoba's chapter, for example, are titled "The Native Story," "A Taste of Honey," and "Western Mennonite Sweets and Pickling." The first includes recipes for "Pemmican," "Indian Wild Rice Casserole" and "Pioneer's Bannock"; the second expands on Benoît's praise of honey from the Red River district and provides recipes such as "Honey Crunch from St. Boniface"; and the third offers Mennonite recipes for "Pincherry Jelly" and "Bohnenikra," the latter made with wax beans, two tins of tomatoes, and a bottle of ketchup.[37]

Pierre and Janet Berton's *Centennial Food Guide* is essentially organized chronologically, and its assertions of accuracy and representative diversity are built on a historic, rather than on a primarily geographic or regional, contextualization of the recipes that appear throughout the work. Nevertheless, the different regions of the country are invoked in an admixture that is ultimately nationally oriented. Here, the recipes are not the book's sole raison-d'être, but rather act as one of a number of means of constructing the desired Canadian culinary history. Other support material includes images and quotes from journals and other documents that bring food practices to life; these are embellished with historical material that reverberates in revealing ways with what they present as the Canadian food culture of their own day. For example, in a chapter on the temperance era in Canada, they juxtapose old recipes for "Pioneer Blackberry Wine" (taken from the *Canadian Illustrated News* of 1871) and "Dandelion Wine" (from *The New Galt Cookbook* of 1898) with their own recipe called "How the Authors Make Hard Cider."[38] In this book, the Bertons' own gastronomic cooking practices may appear idiosyncratic – monosodium glutamate figures prominently in most of the recipes of their own derivation – but it is hard to challenge the authority with which the book's narrative, and the recipes in the margins whose provenance is clearly indicated, established a pan-Canadian food heritage.

The only, and quite remarkable, exception to the pattern of using regional practices to construct a national food culture comes from Elizabeth Baird. Like the other authors/compilers, she devoted years to studying Canada's cooking heritage, a heritage consisting of "printed cookbooks ... local women's groups' collections and recipes, handwritten personal collections, newspapers, magazines, pamphlets, libraries, and innumerable private kitchens." But, despite its name, Baird's *Classic Canadian Cooking* is not, as she explains, primarily meant to address the food culture of an entire nation. Instead, "classic Canadian cooking" refers to the cooking of Upper Canada (Ontario), such as it evolved in the 1800s and early 1900s. This she differentiates from cooking traditions in the Maritime provinces and in Quebec, each of which developed and flourished autonomously. Her justification for the seemingly national appellation of "Canadian" is not entirely convincing and actually anticipates some slippage away from her own criteria, evident in the recipes and menus themselves. She claims that limiting her focus to the cooking of Ontario would have been too restrictive, "because the tradition has been developed and is known over a much wider area of the country." Does "known" mean "practised," one wonders? She adds that "East Coast [Maritime] cooks would not use the term 'Canadian' to describe their cooking tradition, nor would the cooks of Quebec," although, as we have seen, Jehane Benoît does not seem uncomfortable with the term as a descriptor for Quebec cuisine. Moreover, the recipes that Baird assembles as menus do not always adhere to the regional restriction she imposes: one is for "Atlantic Fish Chowder"; a "New Year's Buffet" includes Oka cheese from Quebec as well as "Nova Scotia Oatcakes"; and her recipe for baked beans is presented as a hybrid of Quebec and Maritime versions.[39]

Seen in the light of Appadurai's findings, these cookbooks illustrate interesting cultural characteristics. Like India's, the emerging cuisine of Canada is one in which regional cuisines are undisguised formative contributors.[40] Appadurai cautions, however, that in the assimilation of such regional bodies of food heritage, "fairly complex compromises" have to be undertaken in order to make food practices, ingredients, and other aspects of the recipes palatable and accessible to eaters outside the host region. For example, certain foods or flavours or cooking implements might be omitted, substituted, or modified, and techniques simplified or standardized. In other words, there would have to be efforts, on the part of the authors/compilers, to make the recipes appear less remote, more accessible, and more integral to a holistic understanding of what constitutes Canadian cuisine. He adds that in Indian cookbooks – that is, in those displaying clear intentions to define a national food culture for India – "the selective process is much more obtrusive, and whole regional idioms are represented by a few 'characteristic' dishes, which frequently are not, from the insider's perspective, the best candidates for the role."[41] In the Canadian examples, whereas fidelity to the original cooks' tastes, ingredients, and methods was almost always an apparent priority, attempts were usually made to offset the remoteness or exotic aspect of a region or the obscurity of the cooking practices of a particular cultural group. This was achieved in part by the emphasis put on both the prowess of the authors/compilers (their ability to discern appropriate and representative recipe choices) and their direct connection with the contributors of the actual recipes.

The unabashed way that the authors/compilers trumpet their success in defining a national food culture seems meant as further reassurance. The dust jacket of *The Canadiana Cookbook* asserts that "one of Mme. Benoit's [*sic*] lifelong ambitions has been to prove that Canada has a cuisine of which we can be proud. Her awareness of history makes her views on traditional Canadian cooking particularly authoritative. Now she has produced her proof – *The Canadiana Cookbook*, based on traditional recipes gleaned from every corner of Canada, recipes she has personally tasted and tested before allowing them to appear in this cookbook."[42] The *Laura Secord Canadian Cook Book* also hails its own success in this regard: "One thing we did prove conclusively: there *is* a Canadian cuisine, and it is unique in all the world." This is true notwithstanding the heterogeneous origins of this heritage: "Some recipes, brought from the Old Country generations ago, are still made exactly as they were in Europe. Others have been adapted to the foods and the way of life in Canada. We found recipes that are the result of several Canadian-European alterations. And there are many dishes, 'born in Canada,' that had never been served in any other country!"[43] In the last chapter of *The Centennial Food Guide*, entitled "Towards a Canadian Cuisine," the Bertons recount a debate during which they argued in favour of the existence of "a distinctive national dish" against those who claimed that any dish that could be mentioned could be said to have been derived from elsewhere. Their response: "[T]o say ... that *soupe aux pois* is not typically Canadian because other peoples also make soup out of peas is to say that ravioli isn't Italian because it derives from the Chinese *won tun*." They then proceed to devise three categories of Canadian native foods: the "natural dishes, unchanged since Indian times," including Saskatoon berries, fiddleheads, and maple syrup; "Canadian species," such as Malpeque oysters, Winnipeg goldeye fish, and Brome Lake duckling; and "distinctive Canadian concoctions," including pemmican, tourtière, and baked beans (the latter even if Boston claims the dish as its own, since baked beans were prepared in Canada before the era of the Pilgrim Fathers). A Canadian cuisine does exist, the Bertons affirm, because "there are pockets of specialized eating right across the country from Saltspring Island in B.C. (spring lamb) through the Mennonite country of Ontario (smoked sausage) to Lunenburg, Nova Scotia (potato soup). Such traditional fare, adapted and revised over the years, can now be said to be as Canadian as sour-dough biscuits or – well, as corn on the cob, for instance, a distinctive national dish which, like so many others, we have tended to call 'American' by default. But corn was eaten in Canada by white men as early as it was eaten in the American colonies."[44] The Bertons go on to underscore this position by presenting excerpts of writings that confirm the relevance of their gastronomic assertions. For example, John Clare, a Toronto novelist, remembers the pickling season in the 1920s in his hometown of Saskatoon. These texts are complemented by recipes for dishes defended as intrinsically Canadian, including "Rapee Pie, a Famous Acadian Dish"; "Coquilles Eskimo"; and, curiously, "Curried Fillets of Arctic Char," with half a teaspoon of curry powder and half a cup of white wine.[45]

What, then, are the salient characteristics of Canadian cuisine, understood region by region, woven into these cookbooks? Canadian cooking is, it seems, multicultural in derivation. Even Elizabeth Baird, whose narrow focus necessitates the exclusion of the food of cultural groups arriving in central Canada after the early 1900s, happily acknowledges the "very diverse ethnic cooking traditions which survive and prosper across this country," making it "easy for all of us to cook Chinese, Italian, Scandinavian, and East European dishes with ingredients and produce that are often fresh and easily available." And she acknowledges that German immigrants to Ontario contributed to the "classic Canadian tradition" itself.[46] The Bertons' *Centennial Food Guide* has a recipe for "German Wine Soup" from 1900 and one for "Pineapple Fritters," with curaçao, from 1870, both from old Canadian cookbooks, not to mention the Bertons' own recipe, "How to Make Pork Egg Foo Yong at Home."[47] Ontario and the Prairie provinces (Manitoba and Saskatchewan in particular) are presented as having the greatest multicultural variety. The chapters in *Cross Canada Cooking* that Gotlieb devoted to these provinces include recipes from Mennonite and Jewish communities, Italy, Hungary, Romania, Poland, Austria, Czechoslovakia, Macedonia, Greece, Iceland, Japan, and Ukraine. In the *Laura Secord* cookbook, recipes from Manitoba alone include "Dutch Kringle Bread," "Greek Easter Bread," "Makiwnyk" (Ukrainian), "Beef Stroganoff," "Vinarterta" (Icelandic), and "Red River Scotch Broth."[48] Benoît is more restrained in *The Canadiana Cookbook*, where she has a few recipes of non-British or non-French cooking heritage, such as "Dutch Treats," Mennonite foods from Ontario and Manitoba, Ukrainian "Buckwheat Kasha Casserole," and "Chop Suey" from Saskatchewan – the latter explained by the passage across the prairies of Chinese labourers who worked on the Canadian Pacific Railway.[49] Benoît's multicultural engagement is much more diverse in her *Library of Canadian Cooking*, where such recipes appeared as "Chicken Kiev," "Chinese Barbecued Chicken," "Flemish Hare Casserole," and "Polish Mazurka Cookies"; the book's "Dictionary of Cooking Terms" includes entries for advocaat, Bombay duck ("cured raw fish with a very strong odor"), yerba mate tea, and Xeres (sherry).[50] We can see, then, that just as Canada was fashioning a Canadian citizenry out of men, women, and children whose ethnicity, race, or country of origin reflected global parameters, the cookbooks synthesized a Canadian food paradigm out of the broad assemblage of the food habits, tastes, aesthetics, and experiences of these individuals.

How do these cookbooks construct a cooking culture that can be identified as cumulatively Canadian? How do they show an overarching Canadian ethos? Justifications are built in various ways. First, cookbooks are shown as integral to a wider conceptualization of Canadian culture and history. This is most obvious in the Bertons' *Centennial Food Guide*, which is all about creating "an anthology of writings about food and drink over the past hundred years, together with divers recipes ... curiosa and illustrations culled from old records, the whole being seasoned with the personal prejudices and enthusiasms of the authors" – Pierre being one of the foremost experts on Canadian history within the realm of Canadian popular culture.[51] Visual illustrations play an important role in this pedagogical process, one example being a two-page spread of advertisements for cookstoves dating from 1863 to 1966.[52]

Similarly, Jehane Benoît adds a soupçon of history to *The Canadiana Cookbook*. She notes that she first read of the "Indian recipe" for Roast Young Wild Goose in what she calls "an old journal *The Jesuit Relation*, in the Quebec City Archives." The *Jesuit Relations* are the narratives of the Jesuit missionaries who visited New France in the seventeenth century, and they are rich accounts of the experiences of explorers and their relations with First Nation communities. In the chapter on Ontario, Benoît introduces Mennonite culture as being similar to that of "the pioneers in French Québec" in that "they had land-clearing and barn-rising 'bees,' where their wonderful foods were prepared by women to feed their working men."[53]

Sondra Gotlieb, too, works to bring food culture under consideration across a wider realm. For example, she explains that Newfoundland's unique terminology and pronunciation of English, as well as its cooking traditions, are all direct results of that island's geographic isolation, the accents and vocabulary resembling "those of English and Irish seamen of three hundred years ago." She attributes the link between the Icelandic and Manitoba food cultures to the fact that Winnipeg had, at one time, "more Icelanders than Reykjavik." She further justifies the Icelanders' impact on the province by explaining that in 1877 the Republic of New Iceland was carved out of a piece of Manitoba, complete with constitution and ruling council and with Gimli as its capital; it existed for one year before being reabsorbed into Canada. And in her description of eating habits in the Maritime provinces in *The Gourmet's Canada* (1972), she decries Danish overfishing of Canadian waters.[54]

Elizabeth Baird, who devotes a chapter to each of the four seasons, begins each one with a historical contextualization or other type of expansion that encompasses culinary practice. These include a description of the sugaring process by renowned author Catharine Parr Traill; a reference to fishing as possibly being the second sport of choice in Canada, after hockey; the observation that Thanksgiving was created as a Canadian public holiday by Sir John A. Macdonald (the country's first prime minister) in 1879; and famous Canadian writer/settler Susanna Moodie's depiction of Christmas Week in 1853.[55]

The *Laura Secord* cookbook, too, is instructive. The reader is told that suet puddings were habitually made in large quantities in November and buried under the snow to keep over winter – hence the "Wascana Suet Pudding," named for the "man-made lake of Regina, Saskatchewan, the capital city of the province with the most freezers per capita." "Skidaddle Ridge Drop Cookies," on the other hand, "frequently [eaten] by hunters of this region," were named after a hideout used during the American Civil War by Republican draft dodgers who had "skidaddled" out of the country.[56]

A comprehensive Canadian cuisine is also unified by the use of exceptional ingredients that are specific to or available in abundance in Canada, as well as by food practices that cross regions or communities. Elizabeth Baird tied menu selections to Canadian harvest times, arguing that "just by following the rhythm of the seasons, we can turn unmatchable Canadian produce into elegant Canadian cooking." She mentions "justly famous" Canadian bacon, praises western wheat as "the world's finest grain," and calls wild rice "one of Canada's most precious culinary products." She also claims that the best corn fritters are from Canada because they are made with stiffly beaten egg whites. One commonality that she notices as well is that there "still remains an old urge in many Canadians not to waste and to make at least a few jars of jam or pickle for winter."[57] The quality of bacon in Canada is also mentioned in the *Laura Secord* cookbook, along with beef and pork in general, which "are of exceedingly high quality"; fresh or smoked pork is presented as being able to withstand freezing for up to two months "because the scientific feeding of Canadian hogs bred for high meat quality ensures a more stable fat." East Coast oysters are admired for their "great abundance, large size and excellence."[58] *The Centennial Food Guide* also mentions bacon as exceptional ("why else would New York restaurants make a fetish of identifying it?"); Canadian cheeses are "the finest in the world"; and Winnipeg goldeye "owes its flavour to a secret smoking process that belongs to Manitoba."[59] Gotlieb flags both ingredients and food practices: "wild rice, good beef and lamb, salmon (six kinds), New Brunswick rainbow trout, grayling from the northern lakes, pickerel and whitefish unequalled anywhere, berries (from the bakeapples of Newfoundland to the saskatoons of Saskatchewan), and real, black, sturgeon caviar." She is able to isolate two common links between all the communities she visited, "whether Ugandan Indian or Irish Newfoundland, [namely] warmth, hospitality, and good food." More specifically, she uncovers a consistency in the "tradition of wrapping dough around meat, vegetables and fruit," since "Canadians from every culture come from thrifty stock," and she cites evidence ranging from Acadian *poutine à trou* to Jewish blintzes and Japanese tempura.[60]

The cookbooks even contain references to intercultural hybridities that illustrate what occurred when members of the same cultural group distributed themselves across the country. "Kitchener Kartoffel Kloesse" is one variation of potato dumplings that found its way to Ontario along with German settlers; Acadians from Moncton, New Brunswick, also appropriated the dumplings, served them with sugar and molasses as a New Year's treat, and called them *poutine râpée*.[61] The personal cookbook of Hilda Zinck of Lunenburg County, Nova Scotia, was singled out by Sondra Gotlieb as "a perfect example of the culinary cross-pollination that occurs in our country"; the contents include "Dutch Mess" and sauerkraut soup, as well as Anglo-Celtic dishes, including scones and cottage pudding. Gotlieb concludes that the communities of German and Scottish descent "lived side by side" for two centuries, so "naturally their cooking styles mingled." Gotlieb also connected a recipe for "Cold Water Schnecken" (brought from Hungary by Mrs Mikos) to similar ones she found in a Manitoba Mennonite, Jewish, and Austrian cookbook during her research.[62] In the *Laura Secord* cookbook, the authors themselves create hybrid cuisine when they use a recipe for *makiwnyk*, a Ukrainian sweetdough bread, as the basis for Chelsea buns, cinnamon ring, and Hungarian coffee cake.[63]

Another recurring theme in all the regions of Canada around the time these cookbooks were published was the push-pull between the valorization of cooking as a retrospective activity, whose excellence in the present builds on a respect for tradition and adherence to practices passed down from generation to generation, and such incursions of modernity that manifested themselves in the kitchen during this period through the use of prepared foods, technological aids, and so on. As we have seen, the recipes in these books are consistently linked to history and to ancestral precedent, and indeed, Canadian food culture, such as it was being fashioned, is underscored by this basic conceptualization. But the cookbooks also consistently show signs that modern tendencies were beginning to displace some old-fashioned ones.

In *Classic Canadian Cooking*, for example, Elizabeth Baird laments the advent of industrial food practices and complains in particular about distribution systems that ship unripe fruits and vegetables across great distances rather than stocking stores with fresher local produce that tastes better and is healthier. Among other time-tested suggestions, she also recommends using homemade bread for turkey stuffing and making homemade candy for Halloween.[64]

A number of Gotlieb's recipes evoke and give preference to the practices of earlier times: one contributor still buys flour in 100-lb bags and bakes bread and rolls three days a week; and a recipe for "Chicken Fricot" begins with the instruction "Find two hens and chop each one in four (after they are killed)." And she complains about incursions of "modern" cookbooks that omit such puddings as "junkets, flummeries, [and] fools made with rice, cornstarch and semolina," and decries the poor quality of kosher-style food served in Montreal and Toronto, because it is "cursed by modernity and has become an industry instead of a culinary art," since Jewish grandmothers no longer "bang the blintz skins out from their special six-inch frying pans."[65]

In one of the chapters in *The Centennial Food Guide* – "The Big Change" – the Bertons reproduce images of diet food cans and note trends towards "informality" and "gimmickry" such that "food crazes sweep the land as regularly as the monsoons hit Asia."[66] They then devote another chapter to "Certain Reservations about the Future": "[T]he day will come when the average housewife will select nothing but pre-cooked and pre-packaged meals"; after these meals, "the flick of a ... switch will send the garbage (including the disposable plastic plates) hurtling off down a special chute." In short, "The Art of Cooking ... [will be] replaced by the Art of Stirring. As a result, we [will] have no further need for our taste buds and it is my conviction that babies of the future will be born without them ... There will never be any need to switch from Pablum." All would not be lost, however, because eventually the bloom would fall off the rose and "Mum may start to yearn for an old-fashioned kitchen and an old-fashioned chopping board."[67]

Still, modernity is not presented as totally anathema. Sondra Gotlieb reports being told by Joan Wong, who prepared a Chinese meal for her, that she bought all her ingredients at Loblaws (a supermarket) except the cloud ears;[68] the Bertons include a recipe to make potato cakes out of instant potato flakes; and the *Laura Secord* cookbook has a recipe for "Sweet and Sour Pineapple Chicken" whose flavour is "exactly right" thanks to the Vancouverite who supplied it and recommended a cup of prepared pancake mix for the batter. Here, too, can be noted a recent trend towards buying chicken parts rather than a whole chicken, the news that "sometimes a plastic lemon filled with juice replaces the fresh fruit" in "a Canadian fisherman's knapsack," and the observation that jellied salads are "the darlings of today's buffet table."[69] The most obvious indicators of a modern component of Canadian cuisine in terms of technology appear in Jehane Benoît's *Library of Canadian Cooking;* in a section on "Electric Frying-Pan Cookery," Benoît recommends an electric mixer-blender, electric coffee grinder, electric frying pan, and electric kettle for a bride's trousseau.[70]

As Appadurai warns, however, the construction of this Canadian food heritage does not come without certain costs, namely an "obtrusive" selection process that necessitates "fairly complex compromises," whereby "whole regional idioms are represented by a few 'characteristic' dishes."[71] This is apparent in the cookbooks owing to the very fact that only a finite number of recipes from any one region could be included in the collections. One such regional idiom can certainly be observed in the way some of the cookbooks treat the food of Quebec. Despite the multicultural nature of the province at the time – especially that of Montreal – the province of Quebec is almost exclusively presented as having substantially monolithic culinary practices, emanating mostly from its French-speaking settlers and their descendants, essentially independent of contributions from other cultural groups. Jehane Benoît, easily the most experienced critic on the cuisine of this region, seems initially to take a more expansive position and equally flags the English and French origins of Quebec's gastronomy, claiming that "[b]ecause of two founding countries, Québec traditional foods are sometimes very French, sometimes very English, or a mixture of both." Yet of the seventy-three recipes that she includes in her chapter on the province, thirty-two have French names that suggest French affiliation, three have generic names (that is, they do not show adherence to either a French or an English heritage) but are listed as derived from French cuisine, eight are said to link directly to the kitchens of Benoît's family, twenty-six have generic names and no specific French or British connection, two come from sources other than British or French ones (one uses seasonings inspired by a German cook; the other has First Nations associations), and only two are noted as British derivatives, one of these said to reflect a First Nations linkage.[72] Sondra Gotlieb articulates a common stereotype in reference to Quebec, that "French Canadians believe that cooking and eating are important occupations. The English and French are our 'founding nations,' but it is only the French who can claim the heritage of truly loving and respecting food." She constructs a virtually exclusively French-derived food tradition in Quebec, making only fleeting references in *Cross Canada Cooking* to the availability of Oysters Rockefeller and Italian meringue at a Montreal dining club and bakery, respectively; to kosher cooking in Montreal (mentioned above); and to the "ethnic" cohort of Hungarians, Jews, and Italians – one of the "three solitudes in Montreal" – the ingredients for whose recipes could be had in certain stores in the city.[73] In the *Laura Secord* cookbook, mention is made of "the keen interest of modern French Canadian homemakers in adapting recent recipes to suit their highly developed interest in fine cuisine." Of the thirty-one recipes attributed to Quebec, fifteen have French names or declared French roots, thirteen are generic, two are of neither origin (recipes for "Russian Coulibiac" and "Italian-Canadian Pizza"), and only one, "Old Fashioned Doughnuts," is nominally British derived, supplied by a cook of Scottish heritage.[74] The Bertons do not divide the cuisine of the province along English/French lines, but they do state categorically that "the best regional cooking is still to be found in Quebec, where it is easier to get a good meal than anywhere else in Canada."[75]

It is also possible to recognize in the cookbooks the "food-based characterizations of the ethnic "Other" predicted by Appadurai.[76] First Nations cultures are presented as having exotic tastes and methods; for example, it is stated in the *Laura Secord* cookbook that "Eskimos [sic] relish blueberries preserved in fish oil, but the more southerly residents of Canada prefer them made into jam with sugar."[77] Sondra Gotlieb, in *Cross Canada Cooking*, titles her chapter on Chinese cuisine "Tiger's Testicles," having noted this ingredient in an herbal store in Vancouver's Chinatown. Whereas most of the individuals with whom she talks about food are presented as serious and sensible, she lauds Harvey Lowe, born in British Columbia and educated in Shanghai, as the "yo-yo champion of the world (London title 1932)" and notes that he "is thinking of opening a Russian-style restaurant right in Chinatown, using Hong Kong chefs to make borsch and shashlik, and a Russian orchestra with balalaikas and mandolins to serenade the guests." She adds, "How fitting this will be for

Pender Street I'm not sure, but Harvey Lowe, who's never been beaten in loop-the-loop on two continents since 1932 and plays mah jong until 2 a.m. almost every night, is not a man to be pigeon-holed."[78] Another curiosity is that the French translation of *Cross Canada Cooking*, published in Quebec by Pierre Tisseyre (whose declared mandate was to create convergence between English and French Canada), uses entirely different illustrations than the English version. Situated at the beginning of each chapter, some of these illustrations further exoticize the cooks around whom the chapter is built. Mme Salvatore Di Cecco of Toronto, for example, is replaced entirely, in the caricature, by a moustachioed male, a chef adding flour to one end of a bizarre, gear-laden machine to create (presumably) pasta at the other end. Perhaps the image is meant to represent *Mr* Di Cecco, who was a commercial pasta-maker. The chapter devoted to Greek food practices has a drawing of a sheep sitting on the open oven door of a kitchen range, knitting (herself?). Reference is made, in that chapter, to a woman who cooked a sheep's head for her husband and to a Mrs Cholakis, who in the 1930s insisted that her sons wear a shirt and tie to school even though other kids beat them up for wearing "Sunday clothes everyday." Perhaps the drawing is perceived as a synthesis of the two stories. Gotlieb herself, in her own narrative about growing up Jewish in Winnipeg, is drawn standing, like Alice in Wonderland, before a giant refrigerator stocked with her mother's super-abundant food.[79]

Gotlieb, like the other cookbook creators, implicitly makes distinctions between Quebec and the rest of Canada, despite the overall nationalist agenda of her work. She dwells on difference to some extent when she reports that "Quebec" eats less frozen food, eighty times more molasses, and three times as much fresh orange juice as the rest of Canada, and "prefers fruit-flavoured candies to mint-flavoured ones."[80] Her chapter on Quebec in *Cross Canada Cooking* is unique in not beginning with an account of her experiences with the cooks or other members of the particular community being studied in the environment where the food was cooked and eaten. Instead, she reports having attended four dinners in "officially registered dining clubs in the province"; she describes a Christmas dinner at the home of Montrealers André and Francine Ouellette, which took place in Ottawa, Ontario; and, in one of the recipes, she makes a passing reference to a meal in the summer cottage of Anita Cadieux, "wife of one of Canada's senior diplomats," although it is unclear whether the visit was part of this cookbook project or not. The recipes in that section come from the Ouellettes, Cadieux, and *A French Canadian Cookbook* by Donald Asselin. The chapter certainly does not connote the same degree of intimacy with the local food culture as the others. One possible explanation is that Gotlieb may not have spoken French at that time and hence chose to interview Quebecers who could speak English to her.[81]

THERE IS A CANADIAN CUISINE

Paul Magee, in his editorial introduction to a special issue of *Postcolonial Studies* devoted to food, makes the suggestion that "we [should] treat cookbook writers as cultural theorists in their own right, and take seriously their claims."[82] The cookbook authors/compilers investigated in this chapter worked hard to precipitate commonality out of diversity – of ethnicity, geography, race, etc. – through the medium of food. What is important to recognize is that at the very moment they were making this attempt, precisely the same thing was happening in many arenas of culture and society in the evolution of Canada as a nation. Significant transformation was certainly occurring demographically. The sixties and seventies were a period of substantial population expansion in Canada (from 18.2 million in 1961 to 24.3 million by 1981), owing both to the baby boom as well as to mass emigration from other countries to Canada.[83] These demographic changes, alongside certain other factors – an overall liberalization of politics and behaviours, the rise of a "youth-centered counterculture," and the emergence of "newly energized collective minorities" in the country – contributed to a potentially transformative cultural dynamic.[84] Given, as Doug Owram asserts, that during the long decade of the 1960s "no phrase had more power or meaning ... than 'participatory democracy,'" traditional value systems were subjected to new seismic forces.[85]

At the same time, government-derived top-down strategies to redefine Canada as a thriving, modern postcolonial culture were well underway, as were efforts to construct a paradigm of nationalist rhetoric as a means of asserting cultural distinctiveness and sovereignty, especially in light of the concurrent flurry of mass culture generated by its southern neighbour.[86] Indeed, by the end of the 1960s, the "search for an identity through cultural policy" had been reformulated as a conscious effort to "redesign the nation" itself to reflect these new expectations.[87]

Social commentators have characterized the long 1960s as a powerful and stimulating historical moment in the construction of a national identity; they have specifically pointed to the centennial celebrations, including Expo 67, as having been a means of strengthening Canadian nationalist sentiments among the citizenry. Kuffert, for example, describes the planning of small-scale centennial events throughout the country – often government-sponsored – in parallel with the large-scale celebration of Expo in Montreal, as the "preservation of local, regional, and 'ethnic' folkways."[88] And Jeffrey Cormier concludes that all of these centennial activities "served to increase both personal feelings and public manifestations of Canadian nationalism, pride and patriotism" and were instrumental in generating the Canadianization movement of the late 1960s and 1970s.[89]

The orchestration in the sixties and seventies of a national, Canadian culinary heritage can be seen as having been a means of taking charge to define, or redefine, the nation in a particular way, consistent with the wider-reaching agendas of the time. To that end, this orchestration signalled what seems to have been an abiding desire, at least among the cookbook authors/compilers discussed above, to overwrite a contrary perception – that Canadian foodways can, ultimately, only be understood as a variety of culinary heritages, each emanating from a different ethnic group, region, and so on. Their quest is a difficult one, for the latter point of view may well prevail (for a number of reasons) as the more automatic response of food researchers. Sidney Mintz, for example, dismisses the parallel possibility of framing an "American" cuisine, at least for now, apparently basing his criteria for such a cuisine on the need for localized tastes and practices to be somehow transformed in the process of becoming Americanized: "On the one hand ... the regional cuisines [evident throughout the country] have tended to lose some of their distinctiveness in the dilution and 'nationalizing' of regional specialties. On the other, I do not believe that any genuine national cuisine has emerged as yet from this process."[90]

The purpose of this study, however, is not to take a position concerning whether or not some collection of dishes can justifiably be called a "Canadian" cuisine, but rather to consider and elaborate on the conclusions drawn, at the time, by certain spokespersons who believed they were in a position to make such a determination, who felt the need to pose and investigate questions about what that cuisine might constitute, and who publicized their findings. It is their resolution – that Canada could be conceptualized as having a commonality based on food (regardless of whether or not we might consider the conception accurate) – that is the issue at hand. Given the historical context – accelerated immigration and the increase in population, pre- and post-centennial patriotism, and other transformations in Canadian culture – it seems understandable that Berton, Gotlieb, et al. should have sought to find parameters to encompass the country's diverse cultural groups within some rubric of Canadian-ness.

The Canada Pavilion at Expo 67, like the cookbooks, suggested a willingness on the part of Canadians to be culturally inclusive, at least on the surface, even if the resulting complexity ultimately undermined a straightforward definition of what it meant to be Canadian. In a country the size of Canada, inhabited by so few people, Canadian-ness would have to remain an abstract concept or, at best, an aspiration.

NOTES

1 Funding for the research supporting this paper was provided by the Social Sciences and Humanities Research Council of Canada. I am also indebted to Bruno Paul Stenson and Sara Spike for their significant assistance.
2 Gotlieb, *Gourmet's Canada*, 9.
3 Rasky, "Wondrous Fair," 9; Bantey, *Bill Bantey's Expo*, 20.
4 Menu of La Toundra Restaurant.
5 Oliver, "Man and His Menu," 43–4; *Répertoire*, 22.
6 For further reading on the design of both the flag and the wordmark, see Large, "Flag for Canada," 40–50.
7 James, "Identity," 373.
8 The following cookbooks form the essence of this analysis: Elizabeth Baird, *Classic Canadian Cooking: Menus for the Seasons* (1974); Jehane Benoît, *The Canadiana Cookbook: A Complete Heritage of Canadian Cooking* (1970) and its translation, *La cuisine canadienne* (1979), as well as *Madame Benoît's Library*

of Canadian Cooking: Over 6,000 Easy to Prepare Recipes, 12 vols (1972); Pierre
and Janet Berton, *The Centennial Food Guide: A Century of Good Eating* (1966);
Sondra Gotlieb, *The Gourmet's Canada* (1972) and *Cross Canada Cooking:
Favorite Recipes of Canadians from Many Lands* [sometimes titled *Cross
Country Cooking*] (1976) and its translation, *Cuisine sans frontières: Recettes
préférés de canadiens des quatre coins du monde* (1977); Sally Henry, Lorraine
Swirsky, and Carol Taylor, *The Laura Secord Canadian Cook Book* (1966; reprint
2001). Citations to the *Laura Secord* cookbook are to the 2001 edition.

9 Leonardi, "Recipes for Reading," 340.

10 Theophano, *Eat My Words*, 13.

11 Inness, *Secret Ingredients*.

12 See, for example, Bower, "Cooking Up Stories," 29–50; McDougall, "Voices,
Stories, and Recipes," 105–17; Ireland, "Compiled Cookbook," 111–17.

13 Appadurai, "How to Make a National Cuisine," 3–24. See also Nandy, "Changing
Popular Culture," 9–19.

14 Pilcher, "Recipes for Patria," 209. See Anderson, *Imagined Communities*, 6–7.

15 Bell and Valentine, *Consuming Geographies*, 169.

16 Ibid., 177.

17 Heldke, "But Is It Authentic?" 390, 392.

18 Library and Archives Canada, "Revolutions in the Kitchen," in *Bon Appétit:
A Celebration of Canadian Cookbooks*, http://collectionscanada.ca/
cuisine/002001-5060-e.html.

19 See also *Jehane Benoît dans sa cuisine* (1955). Some of the recipes in *Secrets et
recettes* link Benoît directly to this food heritage; her grandmother, for example,
is presented as stating that gastronomy is "part of our folklore." And when
descriptions of recipes include comments that associate a dish with the monthly
arrival of the priest to the grandmother's household or refer to one of the dishes
as associated with Christmas Eve Midnight Mass, there is a further anchoring of
Benoît and her subject matter within the embedded culture of Catholic Quebec.
Benoît, *Secrets et recettes*, 8, 32, 98.

Curiously, on the inside of the dust jacket flap at the back of the book, the
reader is told that this book stands as evidence of the fact that "a Canadian
cuisine" really does exist, is neither a "myth" nor an "invention"; the proof is
demonstrated on the back of the dust jacket, as a reproduction of a page from
the grandmother's actual notebook – which the reader who looks carefully can
discover to have been written in English. Are "Canadian" and "Quebec" synonymous of the same geographic region in this work, as is sometimes the case in
the complex historiography of the area? Was Benoît's grandmother an English

speaker and hence not a native participant in that province's cherished French-derived heritage? Regardless of the answers to these questions, Benoît's extraordinary popularity as a food critic was sustained for decades afterward.

20 That this cookbook had three printings suggests its popular success. The two versions that appeared in 1966 have identical titles, colophons, and text but different covers (one with a photo of an old-fashioned larder, filled with fresh fruits and vegetables as well as antique-looking jugs, bowls, and other kitchen implements; the other with CANADA in capital letters, "1867" appearing over the word, and "1967" appearing below it, all encircled by a swirling ornamental device built out of a series of little gold maple leaves). A revised edition, published by Pierre Berton Enterprises Ltd and printed by McClelland and Stewart, appeared in 1974 and was retitled *Pierre and Janet Berton's Canadian Food Guide.*

21 Bannerman et al., "Canadian Home Economics Association 1939–1989," 2–6.

22 Appadurai, "How to Make a National Cuisine," 5.

23 Ibid., 6.

24 Ibid., 7.

25 Ibid., 7, 9.

26 Ibid., 15.

27 Ibid., 18–19

28 Ibid., 19, 21.

29 For example, Sondra Gotlieb includes a recipe for "Sugar Plum Fruit Cake" given to her by Mrs Zinck of Lunenburg County, Nova Scotia, and, in its introduction, admits to a dislike of the cup of candied diced pineapple that it calls for. She includes the pineapple in her version, but notes that, for her own version, she replaced it with apricots and also added an extra half-cup of brandy. Gotlieb, *Cross Canada Cooking*, 30–4, 36.

30 Gotlieb, *Gourmet's Canada*, Preface, n.p.

31 Gotlieb, *Cross Canada Cooking*, 7; Gotlieb, *Cuisine sans frontières*, 7.

32 Gotlieb, *Cross Canada Cooking*, 11–14, 93–6, 138–40.

33 Ibid., 159.

34 Henry, Swirsky, and Taylor, *Laura Secord*, [9].

35 Ibid., 17, 54, 130, 114, 66, 104.

36 Ondaatje, Preface, [7].

37 Ibid., 144–54.

38 Berton and Berton, *Centennial Food Guide*, 48–55.

39 Baird, *Classic Canadian Cooking*, 3, 21, 151, 167–8.

40 Appadurai, "How to Make a National Cuisine," 5.

41 Ibid., 17.

42 Benoît, *Canadiana Cookbook,* dust jacket.

43 Henry, Swirsky, and Taylor, *Laura Secord,* [9].

44 Berton and Berton, *Centennial Food Guide,* 106–7.

45 Ibid., 110–19.

46 Baird, *Classic Canadian Cooking,* 3. She even includes a recipe for Swedish tea rings (148).

47 Berton and Berton, *Centennial Food Guide,* 58, 45, 81.

48 Henry, Swirsky, and Taylor, *Laura Secord,* 13–15, 42, 120. See also Gotlieb, *Gourmet's Canada,* 99–131.

49 Benoît, *Canadiana Cookbook,* 65, 70–8, 154, 159–60.

50 Benoît, *Library of Canadian Cooking,* 3:196, 3:226, 7:591, 12:1105, 12:1107, 12:1111, 12:1114.

51 Berton and Berton, *Centennial Food Guide,* [3].

52 Ibid., 86–7.

53 Benoît, *Canadiana Cookbook,* 51–70.

54 Gotlieb, *Cross Canada Cooking,* 12, 101; Gotlieb, *Gourmet's Canada,* 44.

55 Baird, *Classic Canadian Cooking,* 14, 50, 81–2, 136.

56 Oddly enough, the cookies require one cup of canned fruit cocktail. Henry, Swirsky, and Taylor, *Laura Secord,* 119–25.

57 Baird, *Classic Canadian Cooking,* 2, 43, 10, 93, 127, 51.

58 Henry, Swirsky, and Taylor, *Laura Secord,* 57, 34, 88.

59 Berton and Berton, *Centennial Food Guide,* 47, 107.

60 Gotlieb, *Gourmet's Canada,* 10; Gotlieb, *Cross Canada Cooking,* 8.

61 Henry, Swirsky, and Taylor, *Laura Secord,* 146.

62 Gotlieb, *Cross Canada Cooking,* 32, 79.

63 Henry and Swirsky and Taylor, *Laura Secord,* 15.

64 Baird, *Classic Canadian Cooking,* 2, 85, 131.

65 Gotlieb, *Cross Canada Cooking,* 42–3; Gotlieb, *Gourmet's Canada,* 74–5, 200–1. The Bertons lament the passing of puddings, too. See Berton and Berton, *Centennial Food Guide,* 78.

66 Berton and Berton, *Centennial Food Guide,* 78–9.

67 Ibid., 122–3.

68 Gotlieb, *Cross Canada Cooking,* 150.

69 Berton and Berton, *Centennial Food Guide,* 91; Henry, Swirsky, and Taylor, *Laura Secord,* 80, 79, 89, 161.

70 Benoît, *Library of Canadian Cooking,* 12:1099. See also 3:251–5.

71 Appadurai, "How to Make a National Cuisine," 17.

72 Benoît, *Canadiana Cookbook*, 10. See the chapter on Quebec for the recipes (10–48). Inexplicably, despite the almost exclusively English/French bifurcation that she establishes for the province, Benoît writes that "[b]ecause of the early trade routes, Nova Scotia and Quebec have more food traditions than the rest of Canada." What kind of traditions does she mean? Benoît, *Canadiana Cookbook*, 94.

73 Gotlieb, *Cross Canada Cooking*, 46–8.; Gotlieb, *Gourmet's Canada*, 155. The term "two solitudes" comes from Montreal writer Hugh McLennan and refers to the English- and French-speaking communities in Quebec, which he sees as two autonomous entities.

74 Henry, Swirsky, and Taylor, *Laura Secord*, 105, 52, 56, 26.

75 Berton and Berton, *Centennial Food Guide*, 107.

76 Appadurai, "How to Make a National Cuisine," 15.

77 Henry, Swirsky, and Taylor, *Laura Secord*, 139.

78 Gotlieb, *Cross Canada Cooking*, 148–9. Another eccentric in the book is Erskine Lyons, who had assisted his parents in preparing for a party Gotlieb attended in his house by "melting and gluing candle stubs together so that his parents would have longer, more elegant ones for their dinner table." He had also threaded the *yaki-niku* on skewers before broiling them – *yaki-niku* is a kind of Japanese pork kebab. Erskine was fifteen, wore blue jeans, had long hair, and is reported as saying, "There is nothing adults do or say that can surprise me anymore." Erskine's "nonchalance" is then linked to his "multi-cultural heritage" (a half Scotch-Irish/half American-Jewish father and British Columbia Japanese mother); as a result, "Erskine, (named after his Scotch grandmother), can make Chelsea buns, (when he feels like it), and fries Japanese tempura in schmaltz. (Schmaltz is duck, chicken or goose fat Jewish people used to put in chopped liver, before they heard of cholesterol.)" Gotlieb, *Cross Canada Cooking*, 148–9, 84–5.

79 Gotlieb, *Cuisine sans frontières*, 48, 65, 72–3, 99. See also page 106.

80 Gotlieb, *Gourmet's Canada*, 48.

81 Gotlieb, *Cross Canada Cooking*, 46–60.

82 Magee, "Foreign Cookbooks," 3.

83 Statistics from Avery and Hall, *Coming of Age*, 205. On the 1960s and the baby boom, see Owram, *Born at the Right Time*, esp. 159–84.

84 Bumsted, *History of the Canadian Peoples*, 368.

85 Owram, *Born at the Right Time*, 229.

86 Cavell, "Cultural Production," 6.

87 Kuffert, *Great Duty*, 6; Elder, "Canada in the Sixties," 4.

88 Kuffert, *Great Duty*, 218.

89 Cormier, *Canadianization Movement*, 45.

90 Mintz, "Eating American," 29.

8

Regional Differences in the Canadian Daily Meal? Cookbooks Answer the Question

ELIZABETH DRIVER

INTRODUCTION

Today we cherish the differences among Canada's regions. We look for the characteristics that signify regions, such as local ingredients, artisanal foods, and the settlement of particular cultural groups. Diversity, not just in matters of food, is the catchword of the early twenty-first century. In the past few decades, numerous books have appeared that combine archival documents, old photographs, reminiscences, and recipes to present a food history that is unique to a region. In 2000, Anita Stewart aptly summarized our contemporary approach to Canadian food in her award-winning *The Flavours of Canada: A Celebration of the Finest Regional Foods:* "Canadian cuisine is about celebrating our magnificent differences, our roots and our ethnicity. It's about possibilities and how we as a people continue to welcome immigrants from all over the earth and in doing so permanently enrich our food ways. It's about creating the best from our local ingredients ... [and] proudly joining together as a people at a national table to share the flavours of Canada."[1]

Given the vast geographical expanses of Canada, one would expect marked regional differences in food. But are these differences as strong in the daily meal of the average family as today's food writers often suggest? Is it possible that regional differences are, and always have been, the exception rather than the rule at Canadian dinner tables? Were regional differences always as apparent in Canadian culinary literature over the course of the twentieth century as they are today, and if not, when did they begin to manifest themselves and be articulated in cookbooks? While carrying out the research for *Culinary Landmarks: A Bibliography of Canadian Cookbooks, 1825–1949*,[2] I looked at over 2,200 individual works and noticed little regional variation in the form and content of the daily meal in works published before 1950. So homogeneous did most recipe collections seem that on the odd occasion when I noticed a regional characteristic, I made sure to document it. This chapter examines the regional differences in the daily meal across Canada in the first half of the twentieth century, as revealed in the pages of a selection of English-language cookbooks recorded in *Culinary Landmarks*. I do not have definitive answers to all the questions posed above, but patterns emerge as one looks more closely at the texts.

For the purposes of comparison, I assembled English-language cookbooks from each province, where possible, published in three different periods, circa 1900, 1925, and 1950. I chose these years to allow for a quarter-century gap for evolving food habits and to avoid books compiled during the two world wars and the Depression, where common nationwide concerns about food shortages and economy might skew the results. I chose community cookbooks (also known as fund-raising or charitable cookbooks) because I believe they reveal most accurately the food people eat in a specific location.[3] As well, I avoided home economics texts, which tend to be prescriptive, and advertising cookbooks, which are designed to sell products. The fact that no French-language community cookbooks appear to have been published up to 1950 is a barrier to making the same examination of French sources.[4] In Canada, community cookbooks, from their first manifestation in the last quarter of the nineteenth century to 1950,[5] were generally produced by organizations of women from the dominant culture, that is, English-speakers of British origin, usually Protestant. I took the "daily meal" to be the main meal of the day – the iconic family dinner, when the average constellation of parents and children sit around the table together. Most Canadian cookbooks were produced for the average family.

CIRCA 1900

In cookbooks from the turn of the last century, there is a striking uniformity in the recipe selections. Starting with books in the East and moving west, I looked at *Jubilee Cook Book,* by the Ladies' Aid Society of the First Methodist Church, from Charlottetown, Prince Edward Island, 1897; *My Pet Recipes* from St Andrew's Church, Quebec City, 1900; *Recipes* from the Broadway Tabernacle in Toronto, 1900; *Tried and True Cook Book* from the First Congregational Church, Calgary, 1910; and *The King's Daughters Cookery Book* from Victoria, British Columbia, 1904. Had these books been stripped of their publication information revealing place of publication, it would have been difficult, if not impossible, to identify the province of origin.

Charlottetown's *Jubilee Cook Book,* an item of only 72 pages, does not define categories of savoury food, but it does have specific sections for cakes, puddings, jellies, and biscuits, plus a section that contains a variety of recipes, including several fish and shellfish recipes for dishes such as fresh codfish chowder, fresh lobster (scalloped or in croquettes), and oysters (scalloped or fried). The text's salmon recipes, incidentally, use canned salmon; the recipe for "Blueberry Drops" presumably uses local blueberries. For such a small volume, a large proportion of it is dedicated to the "Walnut Cake," with a total of six recipes. The cookbook's recipe selection raises questions: Are the fish recipes a sign of distinctive seaside cookery? Do the multiple recipes for walnut cake indicate a particular preference in the Maritimes? The answer is no to both questions. Most of these recipes are also found in the cookbooks from other provinces.

Every one of the selected cookbooks from the turn of the last century has a significant selection of fish recipes, and like the Prince Edward Island book, they are mostly for cod, lobster, oysters, and salmon. Usually, the cod is salt cod and the salmon canned. Admittedly, the Victoria book has the most extensive selection of fish recipes, including eels, halibut, whitefish, crabs, and clams, but I found an equivalent range of fish dishes in a 1907 cookbook from the small Alberta town of High River,[6] which offered fresh broiled shad, fried

SCOTCH CAKE.

Half pound butter, quarter pound sugar, one pound flour. Mix butter and sugar together. Work in flour.

Mrs. D. Farquharson.

WALNUT CAKE

One cup sugar, half cup butter, two eggs, half cup sweet milk, one and one-half cups flour, one and one-half teaspoons baking powder, one large cup chopped walnuts.

Frosting.—One and one-half cups white sugar, half cup water, white of one egg.

Mrs. D. Farquharson.

FRENCH PUDDING

Make sponge cake and cook in cake ring mould. Turn out and frost any color you choose. Fill centre with a nice jelly broken up, with french cut up in it, put whipped cream on top, and serve with boiled custard.

M. W. D. McKay

WHITE CAKE

Whites of nine eggs beaten stiff, two even coffee cups sugar, three-quarters cup butter, three-quarters cup milk, three and one-half of sifted flour, two heaping teaspoons baking powder, quarter teaspoon vanilla. Work butter and sugar together until it drops apart, then add flour, milk and whites alternately until all are used, reserving one tablespoon milk to blend baking powder. Beat hard for fifteen minutes before adding baking powder, then stir well. Do not cut for twelve hours at least, and will be better after twenty-four hours. This cake depends on being put together exactly as the recipe calls for, and may be used either as layer or loaf cake.

Mrs. B. Rogers

SOFT GINGER BREAD

One cup molasses, half cup sugar, half cup butter, one egg, half cup milk, one tablespoon ginger, one teaspoon soda, flour enough to thicken.

Mrs. McLeod, (D

A page with one of six recipes for walnut cake in the *Jubilee Cook Book,* published by the Ladies' Aid Society of the First Methodist Church, Charlottetown, PEI.

whitefish, baked trout, and halibut, plus sardines "from a box" and smoked salmon. A recipe in a 1900 cookbook from Barrie, Ontario – also far from salt-water fishing grounds – called for "2 good sized fine freshly boiled lobsters."[7]

Nor are walnut cakes exclusive to Prince Edward Island. There are walnut cakes in all the selected books – as many as five in each of the cookbooks from Toronto and Victoria – and although the Calgary book has only a chocolate-walnut cake, its High River neighbour has four walnut cakes. Many other recipes are common to all or most of the cookbooks I examined, whether they be for soups such as tomato, celery, cream of pea, and potato; the main courses of spiced beef, pressed tongue, and game; or the "Lemon Pie" or "Velvet Cream" that might end the meal.

Are there any signs at all of regional differences in these turn-of-the-last-century cookbooks? There are some recipes identified by national origin, for example "Scotch Cake" in Charlottetown and "Genuine Irish Stew," "Scotch Haggis," and "Kedgeree" (an Anglo-Indian dish) in Quebec City. And there is the "Bobotee"[8] in Victoria, but it is not identified as a South African dish. These national dishes might indicate a concentration of people from the dish's country of origin or they might be dishes that have simply entered the mainstream, crossing the boundaries of cultural groups within a province or across the country, as is likely the case for Cornish pasties. It is possible to discern an overt British sensibility in the Victoria cookbook in the recipes for "Beef-steak Pudding," "Scotch Mince Collops," and "Good Plum Cake (English)," but these recipes are also common to the other 1900 cookbooks. Moreover, the British recipes are offset in the Victoria book by American "Maryland Biscuit," "Southern Corn-Bread," and "New Orleans Ochra Gumbo." *The High River Cook Book*, too, has recipes identified as American, such as "Wisconsin Cake" and "Wyoming Cake." Perhaps this awareness of origins also has to do with a western population that was composed mainly of newcomers in contrast to the population in the more settled eastern part of the country. In the Quebec City text, the only French Canadian elements I found are Madame A. Grenier's recipe for "Croquignoles," a deep-fried braided dough, and Madame J.T.'s recipe for "Turbot à la crème au gratin." The Quebec City book generally represents the cooking of a group of women with refined tastes who fancied "Consomme à la Toledo" more than "Potato Soup" (a mainstay in the other books), and who considered beans "a nice winter vegetable, but [when] cooked with pork as 'baked beans,' ... too strong for daily use." When searching for recipe origins, one must be wary of reading too much meaning into recipes with a Canadian place-name: "Manitoba Pudding" in the Quebec City book is very similar to the "Montreal Pudding" in the Toronto book; "Muskoka Chocolate Cake" in the Toronto book is not the same as "Muskoka Cake" in the Victoria book, which contains no chocolate! And I have yet to find a text published in Manitoba, Montreal, or Muskoka where the local inhabitants identify these recipes as their own. Beyond the volumes examined for this paper, there are occasional examples of regional differences in early twentieth-century cookbooks; for example, there is a brief section on "Chinese Cookery" in a Vancouver Gas Company publication of about 1909, acknowledging the city's growing Asian population.[9]

CIRCA 1925

At the quarter-century mark, as for 1900, regional expression in Canadian cookbooks remained limited and the same general uniformity in recipe selection held true. Looking at the texts alone, without the benefit of publication information, it might be possible to identify some, but not all, of the provinces of origin of the following books: *The P.L.A. Cook Book* from St Andrew's Church, St John's, Newfoundland, 1925; *The Modern Cook Book for New Brunswick* from the province's Hospital Aids and Moncton's L'Assomption Society (a Catholic group), 1920; *Our Best Recipes* from the Montreal Amateur Athletic Association, 1925; *Moore Park Big Sister Circle Cook Book,* Toronto, 1925; *Harmsworth Community Cook Book,* in aid of the Virden Hospital, Manitoba, 1924; *Cook Book* of the B.B. Circle at Westminster Church, Regina, [1927]; *The Cook's Friend,* by the Stony Plain Women's Institute, Alberta, 1930; and a 1930 cookbook from the Creston Women's Institute in British Columbia.

The P.L.A. Cook Book, from St John's, Newfoundland, is a good example of the ambiguous nature of regional expression in culinary manuals of this period. Sometimes the text appears to reflect traditional Newfoundland foodways; at other times, new Canada-wide fashions in taste seem to trump tradition. As one would expect, the Newfoundland cookbook has a substantial fish section, with homely recipes. The instructions for "Fish and Mashed Potatoes in Casserole" begin in the following manner: "This is a nice way of using

FISH

COD STEAKS WITH TOMATO PUREE

Mrs. William Clouston

Cut 3 or 4 slices of cod into cutlets, remove skin and bones, sprinkle with lemon juice, pepper and salt, and put in buttered fireproof dish. Bake in moderate oven 30 minutes, turning fillets once, moisten with a little dark stock. Rub 4 large tomatoes, when cooked, through a sieve, mix with juice 1-2 lemon, pepper, salt, add liquid in which fish was cooked, stir well, heat, pour over fish. Chopped mushrooms may be used instead of tomatoes, and filleted sole or plaice instead of cod.

FISH AND MASHED POTATOES IN CASSEROLE.

Mrs. McKeen

This is a nice way of using canned flaked fish or left over cooked fish of any kind. Method: Free the fish from bone, break into flakes and season with salt and pepper. Make a cream sauce, using a pint of milk boiled with one small onion sliced, strain and add the milk to a tablesp. each of flour and butter that have been blended in a small saucepan. Stir until smooth and thickened, season with salt and a little cayenne or paprika. Line a buttered casserole with a thin layer of mashed potato and put in the fish. Pour the sauce over, cover with buttered crumbs and bake in a moderate oven half an hour.

A page from the *P.L.A. Cook Book,* published by the Ladies' Aid Society of St Andrew's Presbyterian Church, St John's, NL, 1925.

canned flaked fish or left over cooked fish of any kind."[10] And the "Bottled Fish and Salmon" recipe explains how to preserve excess amounts of fish for less bountiful times. The restricted availability of vegetables on "The Rock" is evident in the vegetable section, where there are only five recipes for potatoes, two for onions, and two for mixed-vegetable dishes. The first recipes in the "Beverages" chapter are for dandelion, blueberry, and rhubarb wines – the ingredients free for the picking. There are a good number of steamed puddings – a satisfying hot dessert to dispel the damp cold of the maritime climate and just as welcome at the end of a meal in what was still a British colony as in the Mother Country, which experienced similar weather. Molasses, part of the sugar trade between Newfoundland and the West Indies going back to the eighteenth century, is a sweetener in "Molasses Pie," in five gingerbreads or ginger cakes, and in the "Marble Cake," where molasses is used in place of chocolate. Yet, the homely fish recipes, steamed puddings, fruit wines, and molasses are not exclusive to Newfoundland, and alongside these humble dishes are "Waldorf Salad" (which originated in a New York hotel) and eleven chocolate cakes – more chocolate than molasses-flavoured ones! In 1925, chocolate cakes were popular in all the provinces, just as steamed puddings were standard everywhere, although one can observe a little less use of molasses in desserts in cookbooks west of Quebec.

It was not unusual to make homemade wines and non-alcoholic beverages, such as the "Blueberry Wine" in the New Brunswick book and the "Choke Cherry Drink" in the Manitoba book. Moreover, the Newfoundland "Supper Dishes," such as "Swedish Omelet," "Chop Suey," "Cornish Pasties," and "Pomme de Terre au Gratin," are just as multicultural as in any other book of the period. As for the bottling or canning of fish, the custom certainly extended beyond Newfoundland: the New Brunswick cookbook also has instructions for bottled fish; Ontarians in the Huntsville area bottled fish, especially suckers;[11] and prairie farmers of Central European origin homecanned mullets from Lake Winnipegosis according to a Manitoba government report of 1939.[12] As for typical recipes or ingredients in the 1925 cookbooks from provinces other than Newfoundland, there seems to be a preference on the Prairies for brown sugar–based pie fillings, and oddly, there is no pork in the Manitoba or Saskatchewan books, except for salt pork in the latter's recipe for "Canadian Baked Beans." Nothing in the Ontario cookbook sets it apart from the others.

The title of a single recipe in the New Brunswick collection is a sign of an emerging sense of regional identity in cookbooks: "Chicken à la New Brunswick." The recipe is for creamed chicken on toast, which with Madeira or Sherry is also known as "Chicken à la King," and which is also found in the Québec, Ontario, and Saskatchewan books. The recipe cannot be distinguished in any way from other creamed chicken recipes, but whoever named it felt that it represented New Brunswick cooking. Similar regional and national identifications are found in the Montreal book, where the chef of the St James Club contributed "Habitant Pea Soup," that is, soup of the *habitants*, the original French settlers, and another person submitted "Pea Soup (Canada's Second Name)," the parenthetical description drawing attention to the soup as a national dish. The slim differences that may exist between one regional dish and another become evident on a page of *Our Best Recipes,* where full directions for "Boiled New England Dinner" (an American regional dish) are followed by this single line of instruction for "Jiggs' Dinner" (a Newfoundland main course): "Corn beef cooked as above but only cabbage added the last hour of cooking."[13] Cookbooks from this period begin to show signs of the flood of European immigration to the West. In the Alberta book, Mrs Oppertshauser contributed "Cartoffel or Potato Cake" and "Danish Raisin Pastries." In the Manitoba book, there is a recipe for "Icelandic Kisses," which the contributor, Mrs Tinney, may have picked up from an Icelandic neighbour (Icelandic immigration to Manitoba began in the 1870s, when the area was still part of the Northwest Territories), just as Mrs Hayes's recipe for "Iceland Fruit Cake" in the Creston cookbook may have come from the Icelandic community in the Kootenays. The first edition of the only Canadian collection of Icelandic recipes to appear in the first half of the twentieth century was produced by the First Lutheran Church in Winnipeg in 1929.[14] What the Creston cookbook calls "Back East Doughnuts" shows the movement of people and their recipes from one region to another.

CIRCA 1950

By mid-twentieth century, one sees increasingly in Canadian cookbooks an effort to express regional cuisines. In *The New Brunswick Cook Book* of 1938,[15] Aida McAnn, a freelance writer and journalist, married provincial history with sections for Acadian, Yorkshire, Loyalist, Irish, and Scottish dishes, and for local ingredients (potatoes, apples, strawberries, blueberries, rhubarb, fish, game, even dulse). McAnn was ahead of her time in the way that she defined the province's cuisine by immigrant groups and local ingredients, although it must be noted that her publication was not a community cookbook and may have been a by-product of her work for the New Brunswick Travel Bureau. A year later, in 1939, a church in Grand Pré, Nova Scotia, published a fundraiser that included a chapter of "Recipes for Nova Scotia Apples,"[16] and a few years after that, a church in Kentville, Nova Scotia, published *Cook Book with Special Apple Recipes.*[17] There is nothing distinctive about the apple recipes, but the books drew attention to an important provincial agricultural product.

The "Black Whale" Cook Book: Fine Old Recipes from the Gaspé Coast Going Back to Pioneer Days broke new ground in 1948 by using art and narrative to create a context for the recipes. As the preface states, "In undertaking to present this cook-book, the 'Black Whale' [a craft shop in Percé] is following its policy of gathering and preserving the rich lore of the district." The book is a valuable resource of the English and French culinary history of the Gaspé. There is information, for example, about outdoor bake ovens and a description of the butcher cart, pulled by a dog, delivering beef, mainly, because most of the farmers killed their own sheep and pigs – the beef, one learns, is not butchered "to any recognized city pattern." The "Black Whale" cookbook and craft shop were partly initiatives of rich anglophone summer vacationers from Montreal to help economically depressed Gaspesians through sales of heritage products to the tourist trade.

In contrast, in 1939, in the Saguenay region of Quebec, the Women's Association of Arvida First United Church produced *International Cook Book,* which expressed the identity of their new town entirely in their own words.[18] The construction in 1925 of a smelter by the Aluminum Company of Canada had attracted employees of different backgrounds.[19] Not only does the book's title convey the many origins of the people who came to work at the plant, but the recipes bear the name and nationality of the contributor, often described as Canadian, but also as Finnish, Russian, German, Slovakian, Ukrainian, Swiss, English, Danish, American, and Scotch.

On the prairies, recognition in print of Central and Eastern European foodways was slow. There had been a handful of Ukrainian- and German-language cookbooks from presses serving these populations[20] and a 1941 English-language cookbook from a Ukrainian church in Edmonton that included Ukrainian "national" recipes and special Christmas fare,[21] but it was not until the late 1940s that recipes of other than British or American origin began to appear with any frequency. The most striking example of this new development was the 1946 *Co-op Cook Book*, from the Outlook Women's Co-operative Guild in Saskatchewan, which presented a section on what it called "Foreign Recipes" for such dishes as "Norwegian Lefse," "Finnish Herring Salad," and "Ukrainian Pyrohy" – all recipes that apparently came directly from the women's respective immigrant groups.

POST-1950

In 1953, there appeared for the first time in a Canadian cookbook a chapter called "Regional Dishes." It was the last chapter in the new edition of *Nellie Lyle Pattinson's Canadian Cook Book,* revised by Helen Wattie and Elinor Donaldson. Pattinson's *Canadian Cook Book* was a popular general trade book. First produced as a classroom text in 1923, it became a reliable reference in the home kitchen through twenty printings up to 1949. Requested by the publisher to update her text in the early 1950s, Pattinson declined, partly because of ill health, but also because she felt she was not abreast of new food fashions.[22] Wattie and Donaldson introduced their new chapter of "Regional Dishes" with the statement: "In Canada there are people of many nationalities: those whose grandparents came years ago to begin a new life and to become Canadians, those who have come recently for the same reason. With each group have come recipes which have been changed and adapted until they, too, are Canadian. So that *The Canadian Cook Book* may justify its name, a sampling of these recipes is included."[23] The selection is comprised of what we now think of as iconic regional dishes, such as cod tongues from Newfoundland and cabbage rolls from the Prairie provinces, and the Ontario section highlights, as had not been done before, ethnic foods from that province – Italian, Scottish, English, German, Irish, Dutch, and Jewish.

The idea of a regional identity in food took hold, and as Canada's hundredth anniversary approached in 1967, the Canadian Home Economics Association (CHEA) decided to mark the centennial by asking its members to "scour every province to find recipes distinctive to different regions" for publication in *The*

Laura Secord Canadian Cook Book.[24] There was, however, no rigorous effort by the editors to define regional cooking. Although the brief introductions to the recipes made a regional connection where one could be found, the editors sometimes resorted to devising fanciful names to tie a dish to a location: for example, "Calgary Pumpkin Pie," "Capilano Rye Bread," and "Wolfe Island Cheese Soufflé." The idea conveyed is of a nation with colourful foodways that are directly rooted in specific locations. Yet, the impression is misleading – Wolfe Island, near Kingston, Ontario, has a historic cheese industry, but it is not known for its soufflés!

In 1969, when Wattie and Donaldson produced a "completely revised and enlarged edition"[25] to replace their 1953 overhaul of Pattinson's *Canadian Cook Book,* they dispensed with the separate chapter on regional dishes at the back of the book. Instead, the regional dishes "appear in suggested menu form in Chapter I," and the recipes were "transferred to the general chapters according to their category."[26] The integration of the recipes in the general chapters signalled to readers that the recipes were now considered part of the mainstream repertoire of foods for the daily meal. Similarly, creating menus of these dishes and placing the menus in the "Planning and Serving Meals" chapter at the front of the book (albeit at the end of that chapter) gave the material a prominence it had not had before. This time, however, Wattie and Donaldson used the heading "Our Heritage Food" and expanded on their justification for including the regional content. As in the 1953 edition, they state that the recipes had come with each new group and "have been changed and adapted until they, too, are Canadian."[27] However, in 1969, they add a geographic explanation: "As each group moved across the country they made use of the native foods and so regional recipes became part of the Canadian heritage."[28] The menus that follow create thumbnail portraits of particular regional and ethnic cuisines. Under Ontario, the text lists "all these people [who] built Ontario and established her food customs."[29] The people include, for example, "the Italians who came in the railway building era" and whose menu comprises "Antipasto," "Chicken Cacciatore," "Rice Zucchini," "Escarole Salad," and "Peach with Burgundy."[30] Under British Columbia, one learns that the Okanagan Valley is renowned for its fruit and the coast is a rich fishing ground; the menu includes "Crab Curry Canapé," "Halibut Turbans," "Broccoli," "Scalloped Tomatoes," and "Peach Berry Pie."[31] I am not convinced that these menus, or any of the others in "Our Heritage Food," represent accurately – or even approximately – what an Italian family in Ontario (peach with burgundy?) or a British Columbian family (crab *and* halibut in one meal?) typically ate then, or now. Rather, the menus seem to be a distillation of the editors' perception of regional food characteristics. In the act of distilling the "essence" of the regional foods, Wattie and Donaldson have excluded common foods eaten routinely by many families across the country. In 1969, it was not a new idea to create a menu that expressed regional (or national) identity. For a long time, chefs had been creating menus for high-class hotels (especially national railway hotels) or for special banquets and diplomatic dinners to showcase local ingredients and specialties,[32] but it is doubtful that families ever sat down to eat a complete "regional" meal as defined by the chefs' menus or by Wattie and Donaldson.

CONCLUSION

In the last three decades, books have appeared that draw on a variety of sources to help readers better understand the food history of a province or region, such as (to name but three) Marc Lafrance and Yvon Desloges's *A Taste of History: The Origins of Québec's Gastronomy*, 1989; Beulah Barss's *The Pioneer Cook: A Historical View of Canadian Prairie Food*, 1980; and from British Columbia, *The Raincoast Kitchen: Coastal Cuisine with a Dash of History*, 1996. Yet, to varying degrees, it is still sometimes the case that what may be evocative food writing does not capture Canadians' shared food experiences, whether for a special occasion or for the everyday meal. Furthermore, a text may veer to the fanciful, as did the invented geographic recipe names in *The Laura Secord Canadian Cook Book* and the hypothetical "heritage" menus in the 1969 edition of Pattinson's *Canadian Cook Book*.

The fascination with regionalism continues, driven by such factors as culinary tourism initiatives and other promotional efforts of provincial departments of agriculture and tourism, an increase in locally made artisanal foods, the popularity of the Slow Food movement (which advances the concept of *terroir* for food as well as wine), and a body of culinary literature that highlights regional differences. Underlying all these factors is, I believe, a pervasive ideology that values difference over sameness. The question remains, however, whether the daily meal of the average family in Canada today differs in any significant way from one region to the next. For if, as this examination of Canadian cookbooks from the first half of the twentieth century indicates, regional differences were limited at a time when food production was more local, there was less international trade, and there was no powerful mass media, why would regional differences be more pronounced now? Regional variations in food are exciting to experience and may be a reason for celebration, but to appreciate them fully, it is also necessary to recognize that which we have in common.

NOTES

1 Stewart, *Flavours of Canada*, 13.
2 Driver, *Culinary Landmarks*.
3 For the reasons, see Driver, "Home Cooks," 43–4.
4 To compare English and French culinary texts from the same category, one would have to turn to the food pages of women's magazines or to home economics manuals (for example, the first editions of Pattinson, *Canadian Cook Book*, and *Manuel de cuisine raisonnée*, and there are other pairings for later timepoints). It would be revealing to ask what these sources share, as well as how much they differ. Although this chapter examines the cookbooks themselves as evidence and does not delve into the underlying reasons, it is important to note that developments in the United States (industrial, cultural, and educational) influenced both English and French populations in Canada. The popularity in Quebec of Canadian editions of Fannie Farmer's *The Boston Cooking-School Cook Book*, whether in English or as *Livre de cuisine de Boston*, underscores this impact (French editions were issued in 1941, 1944, 1945, 1949, 1965, and 1973).
5 The first community cookbook published in Canada was *The Home Cook Book*, "published for the benefit of the Hospital for Sick Children."
6 *High River Cook Book*.
7 *Royal Victoria Cook Book*.
8 Bobotie is a baked dish of curry-flavoured minced meat, topped with custard.
9 *Modern Household Cookery Book*.
10 *P.L.A. Cook Book*, 24.
11 See Ralph Bice's books about the town of Kearney, near Huntsville.
12 *Commercial and Home-Canning*.

13 *Our Best Recipes*, 29.

14 *Cook Book.*

15 McAnn, *New Brunswick Cook Book.*

16 *Grand Pre.*

17 *Cook Book with Special Apple.*

18 Arvida is now part of the city of Jonquière.

19 Now Alcan Inc.

20 As well as printing recipes from their respective homelands, these books some-times also aimed to help the cook adapt to Canadian ways. Michael M. Belegai, for example, in *Ukrains'ko-angliiskyi kukhar* (Ukrainian-English cook), divides his text into (translated) "Old Country" and "Anglo-American" recipes that he selected from the 1913 *Five Roses Cook Book,* an advertising vehicle for a Canadian flour company, and the 1887 *White House Cook Book,* an American title published in Toronto editions in about 1900. Belegai, *Ukrains'ko,* 5–124, 125–220.

21 *Tested Recipes.* An equivalent and equally rare example of a cookbook from a minority cultural group in Ontario features Scandinavian specialties: *Favoured Foods,* compiled by the Fireside Group of the Scandinavian Canadian Club of Toronto, undated but a fundraiser for "war and welfare work" during the Second World War.

22 Discussion with Wattie during the course of research for *Culinary Landmarks.* Nellie Pattinson was born in 1879 and died on 30 April 1953.

23 Pattinson, *Nellie Lyle Pattinson's Cook Book,* 460.

24 Although prepared by the CHEA, the book was funded by, and named after, Laura Secord Candy Shops.

25 Described thus on the front cover.

26 The quotations are from Wattie and Donaldson, Foreword, [v].

27 Ibid., 54.

28 Ibid.

29 Ibid., 55.

30 Ibid., 56.

31 Ibid., 58, 59.

32 The practice, in fact, can be traced back to the nineteenth century. A menu for a dinner given in Ottawa on 12 April 1876 by Sandford Fleming, engineer-in-chief, Canadian and Intercolonial Railways, for "a few professional friends," featured dishes from across the nation, as reported in *Canadian Illustrated News,* 3 June 1876: "Dominion pea soup. // Newfoundland – Cod, come by chance, oyster sauce. // Nova Scotia – Halibut, anchovy sauce. // New Brunswick – Restigouche

salmon, Matapedia sea trout. // Prince Edward Island – Oyster patties, Cotelette de Shediac. Homard de Cobequid, Ris de Veau à la Baie Verte. // Quebec – Dindon bouilli, sauce au celeri. Langue. // Ontario – Roast beef, potatoes, tomatoes, parsnips, sweet corn, green peas, asparagus. // Manitoba – Poules de prairies, garnis de sauterelles. // Keewatin – Pemmican of the Saskatchewan. Beaver Tail. Cariboo tongue // British Columbia – Pouding au Continent, sauce à l'Ile de Vancouver, Rocky Mountain Ice cream. // Dessert-Coffee, &c." For menus devised by Chef John Rayburn for a visit of the Prince of Wales to Brockville, Ontario, in 1927, in which he aimed to express the "theme of … loyalty to the British Crown" and to "emphas[ize] … the integral part of Canada in relation to the British Empire and to the world," see *Culinary Chronicles* (newsletter of the Culinary Historians of Ontario) 44 (Spring 2005): 8–10. In about 1937, the Nova Scotia Bureau of Information encouraged the province's hotels to *Set a Good Table!* for visitors by serving "distinctive Nova Scotian menus," such as those printed in the booklet. Further research would uncover many other examples.

9

The Cookbooks Quebecers Prefer: More Than Just Recipes

MARIE MARQUIS

INTRODUCTION[1]

Quebecers are facing a rather ironic situation. On the one hand, they behave like other North Americans insofar as they constantly seek convenience and time-saving tricks at mealtimes, and hence devote less and less time to cooking.[2] On the other hand, they are flooded, like never before, with books, magazines, and television shows about cooking. We can therefore assume that the cookbook is still present in the household, but which cookbook and what functions does it fulfil? According to Laura Shapiro, the presence of a cookbook in a household does not reflect what takes place in the kitchen on a daily basis, but one can conclude that the book is more than a simple reference or source of inspiration or entertainment.[3] Indeed, "[p]opular cookbooks tell us a great deal about the culinary climate of a given period, about the expectations and aspirations that hovered over the stove and the dinner table, and about the range of material and technical influences that affected home cooking."[4]

A study of domestic practices performed in the kitchen can begin with the various entries found in cookbooks. According to Jean-Pierre Poulain, analysing the reasons behind the selection of a preferred cookbook reveals the nature of those practices.[5] Asking someone to name their preferred cookbook will usually lead that individual to recall a domestic practice. If this individual is also invited to justify that practice, then we learn not only about the preferences of the individual, but also about his or her motivations, values, and behaviours.

In October 2004, the Montreal daily newspaper *La Presse* asked its readers to answer the following question: "What is your favourite cookbook and why?" Readers were invited to respond by e-mail, and the most impressive letters would qualify their authors for a contest. Two weeks later, 363 e-mail responses had been received. Of these, 343 were analysed so that the reasons for the choices might be understood.[6]

All respondents were residents of Quebec. It was possible to deduce from the first names of the participants that 88 per cent were women. The age of the respondents could not be determined, although some stated it either explicitly or implicitly by, for example, mentioning their role as mother or grandmother, thereby identifying their stage of life. Some also identified themselves as cookbook collectors.

REASONS FOR THE CHOICES OF PREFERRED COOKBOOKS

Beyond identifying their preferred cookbook, the participants explained the reasons behind their choice. We arranged this information under the following topic headings: ease of execution of recipes; presence of information about food items and nutrition; recipe sources; and a close association between cookbook and family. We then grouped the preferred cookbooks into specific categories: cookbooks associated with a chef, a religious community, or a women's organization; those edited by a food company; those linked to a charismatic character; health-oriented cookbooks; those edited by a newspaper food columnist; and those associated with women's magazines.

Ease of Execution of Recipes

"Ease of execution" has to do with how easily a cook can prepare a meal within a limited amount of time, a requirement that goes hand in hand with the expectation that the final result will taste good. Several contestants stated that recipes that were easy to prepare enhanced their limited culinary ability.

> My preferred book is indisputably Daniel Pinard's ... Because I do not cook much, I needed to feel that the recipes could be prepared easily ... Also, because I needed to feel that I could omit such and such ingredient without serious consequences, so that I could replace it with something else ... it gave me the confidence to tackle recipes that I would never otherwise have dared to make. (No. 168)[7]

Many respondents, taking into account the intangible dimension associated with reading a recipe, preferred a cookbook that contained illustrations that guided them through the various steps of a recipe. Illustrations of the preparation process were reassuring and were seen as a training aid, and an illustration of the final result confirmed that the recipe was a good one. Sometimes, both the illustrations and the recipes were inspiring, going beyond being merely cooking references:

> First of all, a good cookbook must be illustrated – gastronomy, or the appetite, starts with the eyes; if a dish is beautiful to look at, it is mouth-watering. Then comes the desire to prepare it and share it with family and friends. When I started to cook, I could barely boil water, but this beautiful book made learning easy. My mother gave it to me when I moved into my first apartment, and said, "If you can read, you can cook." (No. 97)

Finally, ease of execution is related to the number of ingredients and their accessibility. Other criteria for ingredients are that they be near at hand, can easily be found in the grocery store, and can be bought with the knowledge that they will be used for more than one recipe. With experience, cooks will personalize a recipe with the addition of ingredients of their choice:

> The list of "super simple" ingredients in general contains fewer than 10 items, and ALL of them are already present in our pantry. So, no more foods purchased that are for only one recipe and that will end up gathering dust in the pantry. (No. 203)

The Presence of Information about Food Items and Nutrition

Beyond being a collection of recipes, the cookbook is also a useful source of information on the origins of foods, food values, and how foods can be combined in menus for various occasions. A concern for health can motivate the search for some of this information. Much of the information, some of it anecdotal, serves as a cultural complement to the recipes in the traditional cookbook:

> Complicated? Not at all ... this book offers a lot of information on food: its composition, its value, its importance for health. It allows us to discover affinities between foods as well as incompatibilities. (No. 67)

The metaphors the respondents used in describing the cookbooks also illustrate their faith in this source of information:

> To answer your question concerning the best cookbook, I believe that it is definitely *The Joy of Cooking* ... This bible contains absolutely everything. (No. 41)

Recipe Sources

The sources of the recipes in the respondents' preferred cookbooks vary from traditional *québécoise* cuisine to international cuisine. Some participants enjoy books that teach them something about the history of women in Quebec, while others like those that satisfy their thirst for culinary adventure:

> This book is a hymn to our ancestors. These women not only cooked, but also had to plan throughout the year. To plan according to the availability of certain ingredients and to organize food production following their arrival. (No. 187)

> Although my library is rather well-stocked on this topic, there is one book I will never abandon. It is *Le guide de la cuisine tradition-*

nelle québécoise … I like the traditional kitchen. One could also call it "comfort" cuisine. I refer to this book when I want, for example, to prepare good pies as our mothers did, and pancakes, stuffed cabbage, and even candies made with potatoes. (No. 183)

A Close Association between Cookbook and Family

The topic of a preferred cookbook prompted respondents to speak of childhood memories, memories of happy moments and loved ones. Several of them reported having nostalgic thoughts of the kitchen and of family meals. There was evidently a strong link between the cookbook and the important stages of life, such as birth, marriage, and death. As well, references to women – mothers, aunts, and grandmothers – were omnipresent in the respondents' remarks about their preferred book:

> When I moved into my first apartment – this is more than twenty years ago – my grandmother, who was also my godmother, knowing my great culinary talents … offered me the *Encyclopédie de la cuisine* by Jehane Benoît. (No. 224)

> Every time I use it, I can't help but smile and think of her. She loved to discover new recipes and make them for us, both for ordinary dinners and for special evenings. So much nostalgia in a book that appears so humble! (No. 113)

> Last year, my brother died. Cooking was his favourite pastime … I had to think very hard before giving his copy of the *Encyclopédie* to someone who would make the best use of it. (No. 118)

The cookbook represents comfort and conjured up powerful metaphors, like the feather bed, the home base, or a grandmother's wrinkled cheeks:

> This cookbook has been my reference, my feather bed for a long time. When I open it, I have the feeling of standing beside Grandma Élodie in the kitchen. (No. 187)

It was my father who gave it to me a few years ago. He had used it a lot himself. This small book is a home base for me; it is comforting. (No. 102)

It is old, torn, and wrinkled, like a grandmother's cheeks. Some pages are missing. It is heavy. (No. 332)

The most tangible expression of the link between cookbook and family is indisputably the family cookbook, a handwritten collection of recipes that is transferred from generation to generation, usually from mother to daughter:

This book reminds me of so much, which is why I consider it to be the best. My mother was an excellent cook and she did everything she could to pass on to my sister and me her love of cooking and recipes ... she would seat me on the kitchen counter, right beside the famous cookbook, so that I could help her. Of course, I couldn't read at the time, but I would have recognized my mother's cookbook among thousands of others. I knew that when she picked it up, I was going to beat eggs, or eat chocolate nuggets as soon as she turned her back to me, and of course, I knew that I would soon be tasting one of her marvellous recipes. I believe that this recipe collection always had a particular significance for me, because every time I take it out of the cupboard, it means that I will spend a nice moment with my mother. She did not manage to make me enjoy cooking as much as she did, and I seldom cook, but when I see this book, I always want to turn the pages and cook. I will always remember the day when I was able to write one of my own recipes in this book. I considered that to be an honour. My preferred cookbook doesn't have an attractive cover or tempting illustrations, but I consider it to be a very good book anyway, because it is my mother's. (No. 270)

The book ended on November 30. A recipe for "very good scones" was written there in clumsy handwriting. The pencil had replaced the pen. My mother always collected recipes, and even when she could no longer find the energy to cook, she still felt the pleasure of writing them down, so that some day one of her small daughters would find a forgotten aroma there. (No. 85)

The cookbook that I regard as the best – and also as the most beautiful and precious to me ... is a simple black binder, with loose-leaf sheets, which I received as a gift from my teenaged daughter three years ago. Every time I see it, I smile broadly, and in my heart as well. On the gold-coloured cover with a red frame, she glued words cut out of newspapers and magazines to compose a short text which ends with the words, "I love you, Mum!" which moves me every time I look at it. She took the time to rewrite my favourite recipes, those that I had been collecting on bits of paper for some thirty years ... It will be part of my history, her history, and her family's history. Perhaps she will add to it and give it, who knows, to her own daughter. So, from daughter to mother and from mother to daughter, our love for one another and our love of the cuisine will remain. (No. 125)

Finally, a reference to an old book published by nuns in 1878 deserves mention, since this book – though not handed down from one generation to another – has been preserved for more than a century:

I believe I have the most complete cookbook, and maybe the oldest: *Directions diverses données par la Révérende Mère Caron, supérieure générale des sœurs de la charité de la Providence* was written to help us become good cooks, and it was the textbook for a course given at the Couvent du Sacré Cœur, *chemin* Chambly ... My small daughter made her first cookies with a recipe taken from this book. I found it in a cottage that we bought several years ago. (No. 61)

PREFERRED COOKBOOKS

Table 9.1 presents the preferred cookbooks grouped (as noted above) in specific categories: cookbooks associated with a chef, a religious community, or a women's organization; those connected with a food company; those linked to a charismatic character seen on television; health-oriented cookbooks; those

TABLE 9.1   QUEBECERS' PREFERRED COOKBOOKS

Categories	Titles
Cookbooks associated with a chef	*L'encyclopédie de la cuisine canadienne,* by Jehane Benoît (1963) Pol Martin cookbooks (1971)
Cookbooks associated with a religious community	*La cuisine raisonnée* published by La Congrégation Notre Dame (1945) *La cuisine de Monique Chevrier, sa technique, ses recettes* (1978)
Cookbooks associated with a women's organization	*Qu'est-ce qu'on mange?* (several volumes published since 1989), edited by Les Cercles de Fermières du Québec
Cookbooks connected with a food company	*La cuisinière Five Roses,* edited by Lake of the Woods Milling Company Ltd (1915)
Cookbooks linked to a charismatic character seen on television	Cookbook by Josée di Stasio (*À la di Stasio,* 2004) and those by Daniel Pinard (*Pinardises: Recettes & propos culinaires,* 1994 and *Encore des pinardises,* 2000)
Health-oriented cookbooks	Books edited by the Dietitians of Canada, including *Nos meilleures recettes* (2002)
Cookbooks edited by a newspaper	*La bonne cuisine de Perspectives,* by Margo Oliver (1967), a selection of recipes from a food writer which appeared in the newspaper *La Presse*
Cookbooks associated with a women's magazine	Cookbook associated with the women's magazine *Coup de Pouce* (1985)

edited by a newspaper food columnist; and those published by a women's magazine. The dates in parentheses refer to the years the books mentioned were first published; some have been republished, and others are the first in a series of books published by the same author.

L'encyclopédie de la cuisine canadienne by Jehane Benoît. I got this encyclopedia, booklet by booklet, week after week, from Steinberg's grocery stores in 1964, the year I was married. There were twelve booklets in all. This cheap way of obtaining an important cookbook enabled me to read it from cover to cover … The idea was to buy the booklet of the week. And that gave me the time, as a young woman at the beginning of my married life, to read it completely and to look forward to the next one. (No. 138)

My preferred book is *La cuisine raisonnée* by the Congrégation Notre-Dame. I have had it since 1962. I find it practical, with simple and economical recipes. I raised my daughters with this cooking, and if somebody asks me for cooking tips, this is where I find them. This book is invaluable. It is the oldest one I have. (No. 60)

For me, it's *Qu'est-ce qu'on mange?* This book encourages us to test simple and delicious recipes. I believe that it helps us to break away from daily routine … The book is also a historical reference and, to some extent, a tribute to the women of Quebec, as this masterful work was written by the Cercles de Fermières du Québec, founded in 1915. (No. 169)

My preferred cookbook is unfortunately unavailable now. It is an old version of *La cuisinière*, which was published by Lake of the Woods Flour Mills Ltd. In this book is everything a new cook needs to know, from explanations of meat cuts to making jams. It also has the cooking times for various meat cuts, the basic recipes with variations for pancakes, and recipes for breads, pies, cakes, etc. This was the first book of recipes I used … I always return to it, both for the small, day-to-day dishes and for my dessert recipes. It has been used so much that its hardcover is falling to pieces. (No. 263)

I sometimes have friends over for supper, and I feel better if I have already seen the recipe prepared on television. My choice of recipes is sometimes influenced by the fact that I literally fall in love with her [Josée di Stasio's] guests [in the TV show], but that has nothing to do with the book. Her book is terrific. For entertaining a group of adults, it is unbeatable. Josée di Stasio is a woman with great culinary ideas and a friendly approach. (No. 185)

My preferred cookbook is *Nos meilleures recettes* [Our best recipes], compiled by the Dietitians of Canada. It contains 450 simple recipes, the ingredients for which can often be found in our pantry. I also like the dieticians' advice on food alternatives to increase food value. I tested several recipes on my three children, all of which were a success and suited their tastes! The photographs are beautiful and each recipe comes with a trick from the chef who prepared it. (No. 219)

Finally, several respondents wrote about things they might have done or thought in connection with their preferred cookbook, such as offering it as a gift, speaking about it favourably with others, envisioning whom they might bequeath it to, should the occasion arise, and so on:

I could not live without this book, I always recommend it to my friends, and I will even give it for Christmas this year, to my sister-in-law who is moving into an apartment! What better way to learn how to cook! (No. 1)

When I wanted to give the *Five-Roses* [*sic*] cookbook to my daughter, some twenty years ago, I could only find a reprinted version of this marvellous book; mine is more complete and is covered with food stains! I fix it when it tears and take it with me when I go to the cottage. (No. 100)

DISCUSSION

The responses to the question posed by *La Presse* suggest that cookbooks, whether in the form of books, personal collections, or newspaper cuttings, act as reference material, sources of memories, and guides for travel and health, among other things.

The answers having to do with ease of execution are interesting. One might expect that less-skilled cooks would be inclined to avoid cooking, and instead buy ready-to-eat food products, or to limit the amount of time spent putting a meal together. However, according to Shapiro, cookbooks as they have evolved (introducing measurements in recipes – cups and teaspoons – for example) have not put an extra burden on cooks, but rather have been the means to their needing less preparation time and having good results.[8] The cookbook, in Shapiro's estimation then, is designed to free its readers as much as possible from moments of hesitation or uncertainty in the kitchen. Therefore, it seems that anticipated ease of execution, illustrations, and a limited number of accessible ingredients enhance the speed of execution.

The data collected led us to reflect on the act of cooking and on the way cooking skills are transferred. Cooks learn from watching and doing rather than from reading alone.[9] The respondents' mention of the importance of the illustrations and additional explanatory comments that appeared in some of the books, as well as in some of the handwritten recipe collections, is a concrete indication of the value of this modern way to transfer knowledge. It should be noted that recipes dating from the beginning of the twentieth century also included illustrations, in the form of drawings or sketches, but with the advent of television, cookbooks began to include images that, in their format, imitated the close-up of the television screen.

The transfer of knowledge through direct observation of cooking techniques, as with a daughter watching over her mother's shoulder, is undoubtedly less prevalent in the twenty-first century than in the early twentieth century. As Lise Bertrand explains, data collected in Quebec enable us to confirm the loss of culinary skills and the loss of the transfer of knowledge.[10] This primary source of a trans-generational transfer of cooking skills has come under tremendous pressure, it is generally thought, because of the increasing demands placed on mothers in different spheres.[11] Interestingly, the loss of culinary skills is not a new phenomenon in Quebec. Indeed, on 20 June 1890, *La Presse* published an article stating that it was becoming impossible to find domestic cooks, the thrust of the piece being that housewives themselves would have to take on the task. However, to do so, they would need to know how, but they had no one to learn from.

The fact is that while cooking is linked to positive memories, these memories may be idealized in terms of the cooking event and the people recalled. Our desire to collect cookbooks that remind us of our childhood may be linked to the concept of personal nostalgia, a past that has not only been lived but also idealized. The generally positive comments from respondents related to family and the kitchen in days gone by support Harvey A. Kaplan's definition of nostalgia as "warm feelings about the past, a past that is imbued with happy memories, pleasures, and joy."[12] A function that could be further explored is how this overall positive attitude towards the past could help an individual "maintain a sense of connectedness with parts of [the] self over time, and with other people through life."[13]

Interestingly, the subjects in this study tended to talk both about what cookbooks meant to them personally and about the role of cookbooks in the food experiences of others. For example, whereas some wrote about the pleasure of reading a cookbook or of possessing more than one, others wrote about cooking for a group, of sharing new dishes, or of cooking for a special event. As noted by Risto Moisio et al., home cooking can have a different function depending on the generational perspective – that is to say, it can be self-oriented for the young cook and other-oriented for the middle-aged.[14] However, the limitations of our data do not permit us to analyse home cooking with respect to the age of respondents.

The preference for and interest in international cuisine expressed by some respondents indicate that Quebecers are opening up to different ethnic foodways, and may demonstrate an interest in gastronomy for its own sake, setting aside the issue of diet. The letters of some participants reflect a real interest in food and its origins, without any reference to health or to the fears and anguish that food can generate.[15] As stated by Faustine Régnier, if culinary exoticism allows a cook to travel, it can also involve a voyage in time.[16] The history of the products or the dishes makes it possible to introduce this historical dimension, a kind of history of the exotic. This often presents itself in the form of anecdotes that further enhance the effect of exoticism. Culinary exoticism (what Kauffman might call a "passion cuisine") is undoubtedly associated with creativity, and it provides a break from daily food preparation,[17] from a routine made up of repetitive tasks that respondents might more readily associate with domesticity.

Although mostly specific to Quebec, the most popular cookbooks in the study are similar in type to the most successful cookbooks elsewhere in North America, which are either associated with chefs or cooking schools (e.g., the

Cover of *La cuisinière Five Roses*. Courtesy of Centre d'histoire de Montréal.

Boston Cooking School), linked to charismatic personalities (e.g., Julia Child), written by newspaper food columnists, put out by magazine publishing companies (e.g., *Better Homes and Gardens*), written by television celebrities, intended to advertise a product (e.g., Jell-o), or compiled by food manufacturers (e.g., General Mills).[18] It is surprising that very few fundraising cookbooks were mentioned by our respondents, since these play a significant role in cookbook traditions.

What is also surprising is the publication date of some of the preferred cookbooks. *La cuisinière Five Roses* was first published in 1915, and the first edition of *La cuisine raisonnée* was published by the Congrégation Notre Dame in 1945. As suggested by Caroline Coulombe, the re-editing of these books seems to have reinforced their relevance to the domestic practices of today's Quebec kitchens.[19]

In terms of the limits of this analysis, we may now know which cookbooks are preferred by Quebecers and we may understand the reasons behind their choices, but we have learned nothing about how frequently these preferred books are used or how many of their recipes have been prepared. Shapiro, for instance, has mentioned that many home cooks may use only two or three recipes from the cookbook they consider their favourite.[20] Although certain authors maintain that we should pay more attention to what appears in the cookery columns of magazines and to what actually occurs in the domestic kitchen, rather than to what appears in the pages of cookbooks, the letters received by *La Presse* indicate to us that cookbooks are still in use at home.[21]

Finally, we should emphasize that the results of the *La Presse* exercise are specific to Quebecers. The study of the domestic practices of consumers is a relatively young discipline, and the analysis presented here serves only to disclose a field of research rich in information. The study of recipes, whether from cherished cookbooks or from cookery columns or articles in newspapers or magazines, offers ways of exploring not only culinary traditions but also their evolution.[22]

NOTES

1 The author thanks *La Presse* for agreeing to give her the e-mails received from the participants.

2 Green, "Parsing the Demographics," 32–35; Sloan, "Top 10," 22–40.

3 Shapiro, *Something from the Oven.*

4 Ibid., xix.

5 Poulain, *Manger aujourd'hui.*

6 The original letters were in French; the quotations from them in this document have been translated into English.

7 The number is the case number associated with each letter.

8 Shapiro, *Something from the Oven.*

9 DuSablon, *America's Collectible Cookbooks.*

10 Bertrand, "Consommations alimentaires," http://www.stat.gouv.qc.ca/publications/sante/pdf2004/enq_nutrition04c5.pdf.

11 Caraher et al., "State of Cooking in England," 590–609.

12 Kaplan, "Psychopathology of Nostalgia," 465–86.

13 Batcho, "Personal Nostalgia," 411–32.; Baumeister and Leary, "Need to Belong," 497–529.

14 Moisio, Arnould, and Price, "Between Mothers and Markets," 361–84.

15 Fischler, "Gastro-nomie et gastro-anomie," 189–210.

16 Régnier, "Le Monde," http://www.lemangeur-ocha.com/uploads/tx_smilecontenusocha/Regnier_Exotisme_culinaire.pdf.

17 Kaufmann, *Casseroles.*

18 DuSablon, *America's Collectible Cookbooks.*

19 Coulombe, "Entre l'art et la science," 507–33.

20 Shapiro, *Something from the Oven.*

21 Mennell, *All Manners of Food.*

22 Coulombe, "Entre l'art et la science," 507–33; Segers, "Food Recommendations," 4–14; Mennell, *All Manners of Food.*

10

Home Cooking:
The Stories Canadian
Cookbooks Have
to Tell

NATHALIE COOKE

INTRODUCTION[1]

In an initiative endorsed by one former Canadian prime minister, two provincial premiers, seven mayors, and one provincial member of Parliament, Canadians from coast to coast were asked to participate on 3 November 2005 in M&M Meat Shops' National Family Dinner Night. Families were not only challenged to dine together (and preferably on M&M meat products, quite naturally), but also to support and foster the value of the dinner experience. M&M's tips for this included not muting the sound of the television but turning it off altogether; smiling and laughing; talking, which means, as M&M Meat Shops pointed out, talking with the kids too; and even eating dinner "backwards" – with dessert first.[2] The initiative, not to mention the high-level political support it attracted, was prompted by widespread concern over the disintegration of the institution of the family meal in Canada and by the corollary sentiment – that the family meal is valuable. In his endorsement of this initiative, then prime minister Paul Martin writes: "This is a perfect occasion to promote the fundamental values that lie at the heart of Canadian communities, and that are essential to the well-being of our nation."[3]

Studies from Columbia and Harvard universities cite the "family-dinner deficit" as a contributing factor to "childhood obesity, teen substance abuse, poor academic performance and increased household stress."[4] Why don't families eat together? In part, the explanation lies in the lack of family time thanks to the predominance of two-career households and the kids' extensive involvement in after-school programs.[5] According to recent US Bureau of Labor Statistics data, "78% of women with children between the ages of 6 and 17 work outside the home."[6] In short, the demise of the family meal is a function of what Misty Harris, in a 2005 article entitled "We Don't Eat Together, and Are Paying for It," calls the reality of the "modern family."

Let me summarize by teasing out three key points implicit in this line of thinking:

1. The institution of the family meal is disintegrating in North America in general and in Canada specifically.
2. This disintegration is a shame, because the family meal hour is a comforting ritual that is beneficial to our health and well-being and especially to the health and well-being of our children.[7]
3. The culprit responsible for this disintegration is "modern" times (although, I might add, many working mothers, wracked with guilt, might find themselves shouldering some responsibility).

At some level, all three of these statements seem to resonate with what we feel about the state of affairs at the Canadian dinner table. But when I began to scrutinize the evidence more closely, they began to seem more mythic than factual.

MYTH ONE: THE INSTITUTION OF THE FAMILY MEAL IS DISINTEGRATING IN CANADA

According to a January 2004 Gallup poll, there is a significant statistical discrepancy between food practice in the United States and that in Britain and Canada. Whereas only 28 per cent of Americans said that they eat dinner together as a family seven nights a week,[8] 38 per cent of the British and a full 40 per cent of Canadians claimed to have such regular family dinners. In addition, a further 40 per cent of Canadians stated that they ate dinner together with their family four to six nights a week. Therefore, only 20 per cent said they had fewer than four dinners with their family each week.[9] These statistics demonstrate that the institution of the family dinner is not nearly as weak as Harris's 2005 article "We Don't Eat Together" might suggest.

If contemporary practice is not exactly what we have suspected, neither did historical practice, I will now argue, live up to the high standards we have assigned to it. More specifically, during the early decades of the twentieth century, dinner functioned primarily as a means of feeding the household's breadwinner, or perhaps even the potential breadwinner – food being the way to a man's heart, after all.[10] It is only at mid-twentieth century that the focus on dinner seems to have shifted towards the children. By the mid-1950s, the iconic image of the nuclear family sharing food at the family table was established and was soon echoed in advertising and television. The 1953 revised edition of Nellie Pattinson's famous *Canadian Cook Book,* now titled *Nellie Lyle Pattinson's Canadian Cook Book,* for example, as well as the home economics curriculum it complemented, has switched from presenting recipes based on individual portions to offering those based on four portions, in what is described as the "family" menu. But, even then, it is quickly pointed out that the recipes can be halved.

The content of cookbooks of the 1960s, however, suggests that children, and specifically teenagers, were often difficult to get to the table and, furthermore, that they were interested in different fare from that of their parents. The family dinner now included packaged and pre-prepared food, one of the main causes of the shift being, as already noted, a perceived time deficit. The shift was also brought about by product, packaging, and technological advances, as well as by the invention of alternative foods to meet people's nutritional needs during the war, when recipes for "mock" food were ubiquitous. A slice of Prem luncheon meat on a dinner table might have looked different to people shortly after World War II than it does to us now; then, it might have been read as a symbol of sustaining modernity, whereas today it might be read as evidence of artificiality or unnaturalness. But I suspect that those "modern" packaged foods were also served because they appealed to teenagers. The 1961 revised edition of the *Canadian Cook Book* includes a new and fairly large section on "Treats for Teens." The editors explain that this section is in keeping with trends, and judging from the recipes for variations of hot dog wieners, one might guess that those trends include the increasing popularity of processed food and an increasing informality of food presentation. The 1977 *Canadian Cook Book* indicates that the trend towards informality has continued. In this edition, the diagram of the formal dinner table settings that had adorned the early sections of the *Canadian Cook Book* since it was first published in 1923 has disappeared; in its place are suggestions for informal get-togethers, both indoors and outdoors (on a picnic table). Gone, too, is the section on "Treats for Teens." One wonders if the teens have left the nest and the family table, just as the family table has left the dining room.

MYTH TWO: THE FAMILY DINNER HOUR IS A COMFORTING RITUAL THAT IS BENEFICIAL TO OUR HEALTH AND WELL-BEING

From evidence in the *Canadian Cook Book* alone, we cannot be sure how reluctantly teenagers have sat at the family dinner table, but there is overwhelming evidence that those responsible for preparing the meal have seldom – at any point in this century or the last – ascribed to the idealistic notion that the family dinner is a pleasant and calming ritual for all. In 2004, the Leger Marketing Group found that "21% of married mothers consider putting dinner on the table to be the most stressful activity in their day."[11] The many pages devoted to planning the family meal in early Canadian cookbooks suggest that such stress is nothing new.

There seem to be four particular sources of anxiety for the housewife. (My examples will all be drawn from the first half of the twentieth century, because similar statements are so prevalent in recent years that they do not bear enumerating.) The first cause for anxiety – the selection of food products to be used – could plague the cook even before she entered the kitchen. At the selection stage, the housewife was faced with two challenges: the food had to be within her budget and it had to be of good quality. Here, one remarks a notable difference between cookbooks at either end of the twentieth century: in the 1990s, there was far less concern with the cost of food than with its long-term cost to our health and to the Medicare coffers. The issue of food quality was, just as now, of critical importance, and in the decades before rigorous food regulations, the housewife's ability to discern good food from bad was what stood between her family and ill health. As one 1914 house wife related, "Such a terrible amount of adulteration goes on that you don't know what chemicals and useless things you may be eating, unless you are sure that the firm you are buying from is honest."[12] At the dawn of this century of consumerism, food selection was not only the housewife's business, but also serious business:

> How is a busy mother to gain the necessary knowledge that will help her determine which foods are best for her family? In exactly the same way that a buyer in a large business conducts his affairs – by constant, careful watching, sampling, comparing and testing. The buyer takes his trade journal, and through its text or advertisements learns of new articles in his line, and immediately investigates them. He is aware that standard names widely known, have a reputation to support; that the firms which use them have spent thousands of dollars impressing their names, trade marks, or catch-phrases on the public and cannot afford to deviate in any slight respect from established quality; that he can rely on their products. New articles must be given a trial and their value estimated.[13]

What precisely to do with a food once it had been obtained was a second source of anxiety for housewives, one that cookbooks could remedy. Before the advent of cooking mixes and packaged and processed foods, cookbooks (like the *Canadian Cook Book*) were broad in focus and typically provided an introduction to the basics of cookery, familiarizing their readers with the cuts of meat, cooking temperatures, or the ways of yeast. And while we might assume that the product innovations of the 1950s assuaged the housewife's culinary anxieties, we could justifiably argue that they created an economy of rising expectation and thereby aggravated the very anxieties they were claimed to quell.[14]

The final two challenges that the housewife faced when preparing the family meal both related to the question of time management. The first and most oft repeated in our own day has to do with the housewife's lack of time. This complaint swells like a chorus through women's magazines of the last half of the twentieth century. A relatively early example of the sentiment as voiced from the point of view of a career woman, from November 1949, goes like this: "A 'For Rent' sign hangs on my office door. It is the symbol of a decision. I would like to shout from the roof tops that the married woman cannot have both a career and a happy husband."[15] The anonymous author goes on to write:

> Then no matter how well you think you have organized your house-
> hold with domestic help there are those days when you get home tired
> enough to scream, a crammed brief case under your arm, to find that
> the part-time help has not come because some of her relatives arrived
> in town.
>
> Dishes are still in the sink, beds unmade, and your own visiting
> relatives, just blown into town, waiting in the living-room for the
> smart little super-woman that you are to turn out a full-course
> dinner. And brother it had better be good.[16]

Assuming that the article is indeed, as it claims to be, written by a career woman on the verge of leaving her job, would she have signed her name to the article today? I suspect the answer would be yes, unless the job she planned to leave was that of a regular columnist for the magazine in which the article appeared!

But time was also a concern for women who did not have paid work outside the home. They, too, found themselves to be very busy, torn between the demands of the family and the community, as well as those of the dinner table. In 1929, *Chatelaine* editor Byrne Hope Sanders sent her Christmas issue to women who "spend hour after hour in hot kitchens cooking and boiling, and roasting and baking, and emerge flushed but smiling" and to "women who, with families of their own and many responsibilities, find the time to help pack bales, decorate bazaar booths, and prepare the parcels that go out to the poor on Christmas Day."[17] But in that same December 1929 issue, an article for the "modern chatelaine" begins: "Christmas, which is looked upon as the merriest feast day of the year, is, unfortunately, often quite the reverse for the housekeeper."[18]

So far, my examples refer to the rituals of preparing the family dinner. One might justifiably argue that "dinner" connotes a meal of a certain complexity deserving of significant thought and preparation, and perhaps warranting

Christmas gathering, 254 Olivier Ave., Westmount, QC, 1899. Photograph by Alfred Walter Roper. Courtesy of McCord Museum, MP-1977.76.99.

anxiety. The *Oxford English Dictionary* makes a distinction between dinner and supper: while dinner is "the chief meal of the day," supper is the "last meal of the day … formerly, the last of the three meals of the day (breakfast, dinner, and supper" and a term "now applied to the last substantial meal of the day when dinner is taken in the middle of the day, or to a late meal following an early evening dinner."[19] Canadian Margaret Visser, explaining the distinction within the context of the 1990s, writes: "'Supper' now means a light evening meal that *replaces* dinner; such a meal is especially popular if people have eaten a heavy lunch. 'Dinner,' in North America, increasingly means any evening meal, light or heavy; the word 'supper' is used less and less, and 'dinner' can now be quite swift and small."[20] While these definitions suggest a certain consensus, there remains a level of confusion over the use of both terms – and this is without the further complication of the word "tea," which in Canadian parlance over the course of the twentieth century might have referred to a late-afternoon meal of such delicacies as sandwiches, scones, and cakes. As Mark Morton notes, "No doubt many guests have arrived for a Sunday dinner much earlier or later than the host intended thanks to the ambiguous nature of the word *dinner*: a guest might understand dinner to be the meal eaten at noon (followed hours later by supper); a host might understand dinner to be the meal eaten at six o'clock or so (having been preceded at noon by lunch)."[21] Canada's Food Guide seems to distinguish between the two meals in terms of their menu rather than their timing. In the 1950 version, dinner "at noon or at night, was meat, fish, or poultry with potatoes, one other vegetable and dessert"; supper or lunch included "cheese, egg, or other protein plus a vegetable and bread."[22] For the purposes of this study, however, which focuses on the ritual of the principal family meal of the day, served and shared by the family at the home table, either term may apply.

One might assume that supper, which is understood to be less formal than dinner, would involve less anxiety on the part of the person producing it. But when it comes to preparing the everyday meal, as opposed to the formal and ceremonial Christmas dinner, the challenge has less to do with the complexity of the task than with motivating oneself to do it. In her 1938 article "Supper Dishes," Helen Campbell notes that "[s]ome women never think of supper until the last minute, and then get in an awful flurry or fall back on unending repetition."[23] In a 1934 article also entitled "Supper Dishes," Frances M. Huck looks at that daunting question: "What *shall* we have for supper?" Acknowledging the existence of moments "when it appears that there are no new answers," the author stresses planning menus ahead.[24] But planning does not solve every dilemma. What do you do when you have to prepare a hot meal on a hot summer day, for example. Estelle Carter Macpherson's solution to this particular conundrum, offered in 1926, is to prepare the evening meal in the morning: "By following this method, the housekeeper may come in from an afternoon at bridge, tennis or motoring and, in the time it takes to freshen her toilet and arrange the table for dinner, the food will be ready."[25] Judging by this, we'd have to conclude that the *Maclean's* reader of 1926 was not a career woman. But, like a career woman, she preferred not to spend laborious hours in the kitchen. As Campbell expressed in her 1931 article on the more challenging "Sunday Dinner" – the weekly meal that was one notch above the evening meal in terms of complexity and ceremony – labour-saving strategies and simplicity were key (just as they are now):

> We should be most unpopular were we to suggest a Sunday dinner which would make a great demand on the housekeeper's time and effort ... With a little wise planning the simple meal which finds favor with most of us today can be prepared without spending the morning hours in the kitchen ...
>
> Heat control devices with which many ovens are equipped are a boon to the housekeeper. She has simply to adjust this, pop the roast in the oven and the meat cooks while the family [members] are at church ... [T]he clever woman can, by taking thought and by a choice of excellent products of her own country, prepare a delicious meal at a moderate cost with a minimum of time and effort.[26]

MYTH THREE: THE CULPRIT RESPONSIBLE FOR
THE DEMISE OF THE FAMILY DINNER RITUAL
IS "MODERN" TIMES

Implicit in the contemporary conception of dinner is the sense that the dinner hour, or the family mealtime, is especially beneficial for children (what they eat may be secondary). Yet cookbooks from the earliest decades of the century, by contrast, suggest that dinner is intended to benefit those who consume it, and most crucially, the man of the house. Cookbook writers/compilers across the years agree that dinner is a valuable institution, but they think this for very different reasons. Anne Clarke, writing in 1899, is concerned about the cleanliness of food: "Uncleanliness produces disorder, and disorder confusion. Time and money are thus wasted, dinner spoiled, and all goes wrong."[27] For Clarke, dinner is the nutritional fuel of the family itself. It is important to keep dinner on track, she believes, because it is the mainstay of the labourer's energy and it is that energy that enables him to support the family. She writes:

"To cook well, therefore, is immensely more important to the middle and working classes than to the rich, for they who live by the 'sweat of their brow,' whether mentally or physically, must have the requisite strength to support their labor. Even to the poor, whose very life depends upon the produce of the hard earned dollar, cookery is of the greatest importance. Every wife, mother, or sister should be a good plain cook. If she has servants she can direct them, and if not, so much the more must depend upon herself."[28]

The meal hour envisaged by Clarke – a form of pit stop for the working machine that is the labourer's body – differs dramatically from the more idealized supper envisaged by contemporary experts who worry about "dinner-deficit" and articulated explicitly as early as 1934: "The man of the house cuts short his interviews. 'We can discuss that later. It must be nearly supper time.' The children appear from play. 'Mom, isn't it nearly supper time?' One of the grown-up 'children' back for a week-end suggests: 'Supper time? Let's set the table in the kitchen.' And so it's supper time – the very phrase is intimate and homey. It's the happiest hour of a winter's day, and it takes no very great perception to see how readily the family reacts to its lure."[29]

There are two difficulties with blaming modernity – both having to do with the vexed term "modern." First, "modern" has both positive and negative connotations, and second, despite promising to describe a particular historical period, the word actually describes a movement that spans continents and decades. The term "modern times" suffices as an example for both complications. In the years after Charlie Chaplin's iconic film of that name, one could not help but realize that the qualifier "modern" was decidedly ambivalent, and the term itself came to describe a moment of change rather than a particular moment in time.

From the pens of cookbook authors, the adjective "modern" suggests something very positive. The modern housewife is to be lauded, and the modern cookbook praised for keeping her informed and up to date. The term seems to have gained real currency in Canadian cookbooks in the 1920s, when even the IODE (International Order of Daughters of the Empire – surely a group we do not usually think to be on the cutting edge, but rather to be concerned with upholding timeless values) compiled *The Modern Cook Book* in 1924.[30] Today's readers will find it ironic that this "modern" book looks to the past as well as to the future, carrying ads for the decidedly modern convenience of the electrical range but also for gas and coal-fired stoves.[31] Nevertheless, the section on "vegetarian" dishes indeed suggests an instinct for things to come.

Other uses of the word "modern" can be traced through the succeeding decades. With the 1930s comes Purity Flour's elegant revision of its cookbook, *The Masterpiece of Modern Kitchen Lore* (1932). The 1940s bring the National Pressure Cooker Company's *Modern Guide to Home Canning* (1947). And although the 1953 revision of the *Canadian Cook Book* does not put the word "modern" on the cover, it has added a section on "Treats for Teens" – as already noted – as well as sections on "Appetizers," "Pressure Cookers," "Oven Cooked Meals," and "Freezing," to "conform with modern trends."[32]

Modern times, as the *Canadian Cook Book's* sections on "Freezing" and "Pressure Cookers" suggest, brought with them modern things. But, again, "modern" things were not exclusive to a single decade. "When the housewife has at her command modern contrivances for cooking at the table," writes Nellie Regan as early as 1926, speaking of the chafing dish, "suppers may be made quite an event." She goes on to suggest that the hostess should involve her guests in the meal preparation: "Usually the guests enter into the fun of the affair and the supper proves to be the best part of the evening's entertainment."[33] Although she does not suggest inviting guests into the kitchen to participate in meal preparation, as do today's culinary gurus, the notion of preparing the meal at the table, in front of and perhaps with the help of one's guests, certainly marked a transitional step in our (and I will not use the word "modern") times.

Another transitional step in the trend towards delegating meal preparation responsibilities was signalled in a 1930 article on "Picnic Suppers" by Helen Campbell, which draws upon the "new woman" stereotype of the early decades of the twentieth century. Campbell begins by noting that "[i]f there are men in your party, you will be sure to have one who delights to prove his ability as an outdoor chef. Or, if there is a boy scout, let him do his good deed in this way and watch his efficiency."[34] But, perhaps more telling than this comment about delegating outdoor cooking tasks to men is how quickly she reclaims that responsibility for women, despite the usual association of the housewife with the kitchen as opposed to the outdoor grill: "Not that they are necessary

Millar family picnic, Brady's Falls, QC, c. 1900. Photograph by Charles Howard Millar. Courtesy of McCord Museum, MP-1974.133.127.

by any means, for the present-day athletic girl is well versed in the ways of the open, and can build a fire and prepare a meal with anyone."[35]

"Modern," it seems, is a term invoked to imply innovation and progress, and innovation and progress are understood as being carried out in opposition to something. Surely, in the realm of cookbooks, to suggest that something is "modern" is to conjure up its opposite – food trends that are passé, antiquated, outdated. However, instead of using these terms, the Canadian cookbooks and articles that I have examined contrast "modern" trends and "new" menus with "traditional" ones. Their choice of oppositional terminology is deliberate and, for the purposes of my investigation of the disintegration of the valuable institution of the family dinner, telling.

Notice, for example, the nostalgia evoked by Campbell in an article that ostensibly claims to be praising "modern" notions of "lighter" dining at Thanksgiving: "Modern ideas of feast days and feasting are all for the lighter touch. Ponderous meals which leave the diners too full for utterance are not popular in these days when there's so much to talk about. Nor is over-richness favored by those who strive to keep their figures trim and their minds keen for games or conversation afterward. How, then, strike a happy balance between the splendor of the old days and the simplicity of an ordinary occasion?"[36] This citation is from 1936, lest one think that the desire to achieve a balance between lighter fare and a traditional menu (one that, in its original incarnations, would have involved very rich foods) is particular to our own day.

And from 1928: "If there is one day in all the year when the Old and the New meet, that is surely Thanksgiving Day. None of us is so modernized as to be willing to forego the outstanding traditions of the Thanksgiving Feast; but neither are we willing to serve a dinner which is a vast labor to prepare, a heavy menu to wade through, and too complicated for service in the average home where the mistress – if she is not actually the cook – must supervise and assist with anything in the nature of a special occasion."[37]

What intrigues me in these invocations of modernity is the nostalgia for tradition – the "splendor of the old days" and the "outstanding traditions" of the past.[38] Jessamyn Neuhaus identifies the 1950s as a time when the family dinner became invested with symbolic importance: "In particular, cookery instruction for women emphasized that dinner – the main meal of the day served in the evening – should be 'the most important meal of the day.' Women should carefully and painstakingly prepare excellent dinners every day and, in addition, help to ensure a pleasant and relaxed atmosphere at the dinner table."[39]

In the postwar era, when Americans came to fear a nuclear holocaust, "cookbooks upheld the family [home] as the antithesis of a nerve-wracking world," and "Americans turned to the familiar image of the family unit, safe and well fed, protected under the wing of the 'angel of the house.'"[40] However, M. Frances Hucks's rapturous description of supper time in 1934 suggests that the symbolic investment of the family dinner hour began decades before in Canada,[41] and I suspect also in the United States.

Paradoxically, this discussion of idealism, nostalgia, and ghosts of dinners past brings us back to our current concern about the disintegration of the institution of the family dinner ritual. Despite the perceived benefits of the ritual of the family meal, the evidence, gleaned from cookbooks and polls, suggests that this institution has *always* been a struggle – both for those who have prepared it and for those who have partaken of it. But it has also been seen to be a worthwhile struggle. We may think that we are perceiving, in today's concern for the family dinner, a response to its demise, but I suggest that we are actually seeing a continuation of the ritual – one that involves conscious effort on the part of all participants, not to mention on the part of a cook with some culinary know-how and the desire and authority to bring everyone to the table.

Canada's food narratives tell us that challenges have been a part of the family dinner tradition throughout the twentieth century, at the very least. Indeed, concern over the demise of the tradition has been a part of the tradition and, perhaps, the thing that has accounted for its continuation.

NOTES

1 A version of this chapter was presented at a conference on "The Daily Meal in Canada" held at the McCord Museum (4 November 2005). Excerpts were also included in a paper, entitled "Beaver Tails, Bannock and Butter Tarts: Practices and Politics of the Daily Meal in Canada," presented at the Weatherhead Center at Harvard in March 2006. The author gratefully acknowledges the Social Sciences and Humanities Research Council for its support in funding research related to Canadian food history, and the Max Bell Foundation for fostering the ongoing inquiry into Canadian food policy at the McGill Institute for the Study of Canada.

2 M&M Meat Shops, "M&M Meat Shops Hosts," http://www.mmmeatshops.com/en/aboutmm/mediaroom/fall2005_dinner.asp.

3 Martin, "Letter," http://www.mmmeatshops.com/en/aboutmm/mediaroom/pdf/Prime%20Minister%20Paul%20Martin.pdf.

4 These studies are mentioned in Harris, "We Don't Eat Together."

5 Harris makes a slightly different point in her article by suggesting that the *perceived* lack of time is also a contributing factor. She writes: "A survey released

this week by Decima Research for the Holmes Group (marketer of Rival and Crock Pot slow cookers) indicates more than half of Canadians believe they don't have time to plan or execute a dinner event for family and friends. A full 30% cited dinner preparation as the most stressful element behind such a gathering. A separate survey of Canadian women, released by Leger Marketing for Palm Canada, similarly found 21% of married mothers consider putting dinner on the table to be the most stressful activity in their day."

6 Kiefer, "Empty Seats," http://www.gallup.com/poll/10336/ Empty-Seats-Fewer-Families-Eat-Together.aspx.

7 Stephen Covey's bestselling book, *The 7 Habits of Highly Effective Families* (New York: Golden Books, 1997), transforms this assumption into a well-supported conclusion.

8 The term "dinner" has complex connotations (which this study explores) but also a range of denotations. Although the chapter will expand on the meanings of dinner, a preliminary working definition of dinner might be taken from Alan Davidson's *The Oxford Companion to Food* (1999): "the main meal of the day, whether eaten at mid-day or in the evening" (250).

9 Kiefer, "Empty Seats," http://www.gallup.com/poll/10336/ Empty-Seats-Fewer-Families-Eat-Together.aspx.

10 Ronald Larson, speaking of American foodways, identifies World War II as a pivotal point in foodways history. He notes that prior to the war dinner was timed according to the needs of the labourers of the household. Whereas a rural family would sit down to the main meal of the day at midday, for example, an urban family with a father who spent the day in the office would sit down to dinner in the evening: "When most of the US households lived in rural areas, dinner was the midday meal and supper was a smaller meal served after the field work was done. With increasing industrialization, meals began to conform to business schedules and the noon 'lunch' break was short" (Larson, "When Is Dinner?" 39). Elaine McIntosh writes: "At least until World War II, whether a person referred to meals as breakfast, dinner, and supper or as breakfast, lunch, and dinner, quickly identified the individual as being of rural or urban origin" (McIntosh, *American Food Habits*, 154). As Johanna Mäkelä confirms, "A tendency to eat fewer meals can be detected all over Europe during the twentieth century because of changing working and living conditions" (Mäkelä, "Cultural Definitions," 10). Furthermore, Kittler and Sucher remark that "[i]n Europe, a large main meal is traditionally consumed at noontime ... while in the United States, the main meal is eaten in the evening" (Kittler and Sucher, *Food and Culture*, 15).

11 Harris, "We Don't Eat Together."

12 "Why I Am Faddy," 35.

13 "Housewife's Business," 28.

14 One of the best-known articulations of this dilemma appears in Ruth Cowan's touchstone study *More Work for Mother* (New York: Basic Books, 1983).

15 "Careers and Marriage Don't Mix," 32.

16 Ibid.

17 Sanders, "To the Chatelaines," 16.

18 Reid, "Planning," 20.

19 *Oxford English Dictionary*, 2nd ed., s.vv. "dinner," "supper."

20 Visser, *Rituals of Dinner*, 160.

21 Morton, "Dinner," 111.

22 Neering, *Canadian Housewife*, 207.

23 Campbell, "Supper Dishes," 50.

24 Hucks, "Supper Dishes," 61.

25 Macpherson, "Warm Dinners," 53.

26 Campbell, "Sunday Dinner," 71.

27 Clarke, "Introductory Observations," 8. Clarke's concern with cleanliness here may largely come from the sponsor of her cookbook – Eclipse soap, in this case. This book is essentially *The Dominion Cook Book*; but it appears under other names, and supported by other sponsors. See, for example, the 1899 *Surprise Cook Book*, sponsored by Surprise soap. Many thanks to Elizabeth Driver for her assistance with this citation.

28 Ibid., 7.

29 Hucks, "Supper Dishes," 61.

30 IODE, *Modern Cook Book*.

31 Ibid., 2. *The Modern Cook Book* contains ads for gas ranges (65), Westinghouse electric ranges (14); and Rosedale coal ("the leisure moment is yours when you use Rosedale Coal in the Cook Stove") (25).

32 Pattinson, "Foreword," v.

33 Regan, "After-the-Show," 74.

34 Campbell, "Picnic Suppers," 75.

35 Ibid.

36 Campbell, "For the Thanksgiving Dinner," 50.

37 Adam, "Thanksgiving Dinner," 75.

38 It is worth noting that the ghosts of dinners past include notions of a "real" dinner; these notions linger in the background of the actual dinner consumed in the present moment. As Laura Shapiro rightly points out: "The flavor of

Swanson's [TV] dinners – entrancingly metallic, as if tray and turkey were one — clings even now to the palate memory of anyone who encountered those magic meals in childhood. But contrary to the industry's expectations, they didn't replace cooking. Children ate them when their parents were going out, and husbands made do with them when their wives weren't home. A TV dinner occupied the time and space of a meal and fulfilled its function, but nobody confused a TV dinner with the real thing" (Shapiro, *Something from the Oven*, 19).

39 Neuhaus, *Manly Meals*, 223.
40 Ibid.
41 Hucks, "Supper Dishes."

11

Affective Histories: Eating "Chinese" across Canada and the World

SNEJA GUNEW

INTRODUCTION

Cultural analysts have noted that representations of food in films, books, and on television have become increasingly popular. Food, as Roland Barthes noted decades ago, functions as a semiotic system in its own right, providing a means for decoding a culture's idiosyncrasies.[1] This paper is concerned with the intersection of food and ethnicity, particularly in memoirs where specific tactics are employed to convey a "'feeling' of difference."[2] The notion of affective histories is meant to suggest histories that attempt to communicate what a culture feels like from the inside, by invoking its grammar of emotions – hence the use of food and the idea that, by way of recipes or culinary anecdotes, a reader/viewer may temporarily occupy the position of cultural insider. But while a plethora of ethnic cookbooks provide accounts of the celebratory aspect of these histories, there is a growing tendency to use food's appeal as a means of conveying more complex dimensions of diasporic histories, including deprivation, racism, and other structures of unbelonging. My

中國憲政黨駐美總支部同人歡宴蔡廷鍇將軍大會

Hin-Jing Society of America, dinner for Gen. Tsai Ting-Gai in Montreal(?), c. 1925. Courtesy of McCord Museum, MP-1987.41.15.

focus in this chapter is on diasporic "Chineseness," where this term carries no prior, self-evident meaning.

In her memoir/recipe book based on her family's life in cafés and restaurants in British Columbia and Saskatchewan, aptly titled *Chow*, Janice Wong begins with an anecdote about her Canadian-born father, who once speculatively eyed a peacock in Stanley Park and wondered what it would taste like (an anecdote with shades of Timothy Taylor's novel *Stanley Park*). The tale's exotic nature and the entrepreneurial flair of Wong's father stand in stark contrast to how daily meals were provided by Chinese cafés and restaurants across Canada throughout the twentieth century. As Wong recounts, these places were effectively the first "ethnic" eateries in Canada, particularly in rural small towns. However, as filmmaker Cheuk Kwan, whose work traces the phenomenon of Chinese restaurants across the world, reminds us in his portrait of "Noisy Jim," most of these so-called Chinese places were also hyper-Canadian in their efforts not to tease Canadian palates unduly with anything alien or exotic.[3] Their offerings remained resolutely Western, and if Chineseness strayed onto the menu it was thoroughly worked over to function within the imagined limits of non-Chinese tastes. It is a story comparable to that of other settler colonies, like Australia, where the history of Chinese communities and families has also been creatively conveyed through cooking, as exemplified by Annette Shun Wah (a media personality), who published her book *Banquet* as a way of imparting a semi-popularized history of Chinese immigration to and settlement in Australia.[4]

One might speak of this approach to history as affective history; generating affect through food works by mobilizing the senses and emotions to produce in the readers or viewer a sense of empathy or fellow feeling – a process that has also been termed the "transmission of affect."[5] Affective history aims to go beyond the facts and events of immigration and settlement in order to impart the ways in which people actually felt while living through these events, particularly in the case of Chinese Canadians whose histories were permeated by racisms of various kinds.

ICONIC FAMILIES

Food and family are closely intertwined, and in a prior study I trace this trope by analysing Kylie Kwong's cooking show.[6] Kwong is the Australian Chinese chef being marketed worldwide by the Food Channel. I suggest that Chinese cooking and diasporic Chinese restaurants have become globally charged with functioning as performative sites that display the recovery of those family values that the West has supposedly misplaced. I argue that the Kylie Kwong series might be described as the search for not simply family but hyper-family.[7] The series is choreographed around Kwong's own family history, particularly in earlier episodes, which introduce us to her brothers, mother, extended family, and niece, as well as to the uncle who runs a noodle factory; in addition, we are referred to her great-grandfather, described as the patriarch of the largest Chinese family in Australia. Kwong herself functions as a reassuring auto-ethnographer who is both inside and outside her inherited Chinese culture. With her familiar Australian accent and her assurance that none of her relatives actually speak Chinese, she inducts viewers into an "alien" cuisine and culture, domesticating it into their everyday practices. The senses of the viewers are engaged in tempered ways – new but not too new. In the final episode of that first series, friends and family gather together in a climactic feasting and commensality.

In the sole Canadian episode in his documentary, Cheuk Kwan explores Noisy Jim's café in Outlook, Saskatchewan, as it becomes the hub of family extending into community. We begin with shots of Jim, retired but still opening up the café for its new owners every day because he enjoys helping out. He refuses to accept money for this service, for doing so would curtail his sense of being a free man able to make choices. His ability to see himself this way stands in contrast to his earlier life, which was punctuated by the repeated recognition that there was a small repertoire of possibilities for exercising choice. The café is open during all European holidays and thus provides a service to the community that no other restaurant does. It also belongs to the history of male Chinese immigrants who were recruited to do the work others shunned, such as the "women's work" (laundry, cooking) in the pioneer camps that spread across the West. Kwan contextualizes this lack of choice as running parallel to the infamous history of Chinese rail-workers, whose labours helped link up the country and who often paid with their lives for this privilege. In repayment, these men were unacknowledged in histories of Canada's railroads. They were also subject to the head tax of 1850–1903 and the Chinese Exclusion Act of 1923–47; both of these led to the rupture of families, as women could not come over and join their male partners. Hence, we have communities of aging bachelors, an example of which is so poignantly described in Wayson Choy's novel *The Jade Peony*. It is largely through fictional writings that these histories have become part of the general Canadian consciousness over the last decade.

Traditionally, the transmission of affect privileges the face. Feelings are communicated via facial expressions, and a universality across the face's range of expressions is generally assumed. Viewers are encouraged to believe, for example, that Noisy Jim's character emerges through close-ups of his face. He is dedicated to service and to remaining free to choose to exercise this option. He speaks of "serving the community," including refusing to view the Chinese café next door as a rival. When asked about the details of his life as a "paper son,"[8] Jim's face initially shows a habitual reluctance to speak about such dangerous secrets in public. Given the Chinese head tax and the Exclusion Act, it is not surprising that the industry of paper relations thrived. We are given a brief history of Jim's travels across the country to Outlook, afraid to leave the train and fearing blackmail because of his secret. But this history does not seem to have left him with any residual bitterness towards Canada. When questioned about his allegiances, he emphatically states the individualist's credo: "I'm myself; I am me!" Names are not transparent signs of affiliations or genealogies, but the revelations traditionally associated with close-ups and interviews are clearly not ones that Jim willingly allows; he illustrates this when he takes out a toy gun and points it at the camera in order to convey what it feels like to be "shot." For him, personal interrogations are intrusive, and he defines himself far more firmly in terms of immediate family and members of the community. His customers, for example, speak of how Jim demonstrates his trust of others by giving them keys to the café so that they can come in and make their own breakfast. In an interview, Jim's daughter reveals that as children she and her siblings resented having no leisure time but in retrospect she is grateful for the discipline and values inculcated into them. Jim himself clearly states that he did not want any of his children to follow in his footsteps – not for them the long hours and low pay. The final accolade is the community's presence at Noisy Jim's funeral; the film's recording of this event is interspersed with footage of an archival film in which a younger Jim performs the role of quintessential rural Chinese cook – simultaneously flamboyant and familiar. The film's final shots are both an evocation of a stereotype – showing the constraints of a social symbol – and a celebration of the idiosyncratic individualism that blazes through these fetters.

HYPHENATED DWELLING

What happens inside these inhibitions and behind the stereotypes attached to the Chinese café in rural towns is unpacked in certain ways by Fred Wah's brilliant *Diamond Grill*, a text of linked prose poems he describes as "biotext." Reminiscent of Dylan Thomas's paradigmatic evocation of the voices of a small Welsh town in *Under Milkwood*, Wah's text gives a sense of the multiple voices inhabiting a fractured temporality and geography. Space jostles with place as the one transforms itself into the other by way of private memories. On the one hand, we have Nelson, British Columbia, a space iconically represented by the place of the café itself and its swinging hyphenated door, which divides public and private spaces (functioning analogously as public and private histories) – in front, public interaction with and service to the community; at the back, the kitchen itself, dominated by a cook who serves authentic Chinese food only to the other Chinese helpers. Uncannily (in the fullest Freudian sense), this text too, like Noisy Jim's funeral, is referenced by a dialogue with the dead and, in particular, with a dead father.[9] The autobiographical narrator is both the child who wishes to distance himself from the burden of being perceived as a visible minority and the son who is attempting to speak with a dead parent because he had not done so sufficiently in life. One painful episode concerns a time the son rejected his father's food: "Dad doesn't cook much with ginger but whenever I accidentally bite into a piece of ginger root in the beef and greens, I make a face and put it aside. This makes him mad, not because he doesn't think ginger is bitter but because I've offended his pride in the food he prepares for us. Ginger becomes the site of an implicit racial qualification."[10]

This is a scene echoed in the fictional kitchens of many "ethnic" households – children reject the old country of their parents by refusing their cooking. In a harrowing scene in Madeleine Thien's eponymous story "Simple Recipes," the narrator states: "I miss the way we sat down together, our bodies hungrily leaning forward while my father, the magician, unveiled plate after plate."[11] That scene of familial nostalgia was torn apart by the son's brutal refusal of food and the father's equally violent retaliation. Clearly, this was not simply a battle about food and taste but about assimilation as the price of belonging. Wah's economical short prose poem ends with the suggestion of a more balanced accommodation by having the son acknowledge his later love of ginger: "This knurled suffix of gradated foreignicity, gyna gendered and warped up tighter than a Persian rug-knot, hardly explains how ginger's almost nicer than being born – but that's just taste."[12]

But what relates a sense of separateness to a sense of embodying traces of other bodies – ancestral incarnations? Wah's father is given his own history and presence in these poems. He was born in Canada to a Chinese father and a mother of Scots-Irish descent. Exiled to China long enough to return as a non-Canadian, he was interned in immigration cells in Juan de Fuca Strait for three months.[13] Lost between worlds, Wah's father was habituated to none and was always self-conscious concerning his outsider status. There is, for example, the unbearably painful poem where he functions as a kind of stage Chinaman whose lapses in verbal expression entertain the locals:

When he joins the Lions Club and has to give an initiation speech,
he gets my mother to help him write something up. She says he's very
nervous about this event; worried that he might flub it, make a fool of
himself, the only Chinaman at an all-white dinner meeting. But there
he is, with his little speech on a piece of paper in front of all these
Baker Street nickel millionaires in the Hume Hotel dining room,
thanking these guys for inviting him to join their club, thanking them
for making Nelson such a wonderful place to live and raise his family,
and then thanking them for this meal with the wonderful *sloup*. We
always kid around at home when he says *sloup* and he laughs and, we
suspect, even says it this way intentionally just to horse around with
us. But here such a slip just turns him copper red (the colour you get
when you mix yellow with either embarrassment or liquor). So when
he hears himself say *sloup* for soup he stops suddenly and looks out
at the expected embarrassed and patronizing smiles from the crowd.
Then he does what he has learned to do so well in such instances, he
turns it into a joke, a kind of self put-down that he knows these white
guys like to hear: he bluffs that Chinamen call soup *sloup* because, as
you all know, the Chinese make their café soup from the slop water
they wash their underwear and socks in, and besides, it's just like
when you hear me eating my soup, Chinamen like to slurp and make a
lot of noise.[14]

In this instance, affect – as a kind of ancestral shame – links father to son, but in some of the other poems the son inhabits the body of the father in more benign ways and identifies gestures and expressions in himself and his own children with the father, as in the following passage: "When I fish now sometimes, his body extends out of me holding the rod, fingers on the line just so, glassy gaze, vertical invisible layers, the line going deep into the lake or flung out onto the surface glaze of river current, layers of darkness, invisible fish, fading."[15] In this reconceptualization of corporeality, mapped as much by affect as by any physical attributes, food plays a curious role. A number of the poems incorporate recipes, as though food allowed entry into a sensorium where time functions in non-linear ways and taste and smell transport one to a past in the present. In some poems, the father remembers forgotten meals from his sojourn in China; he feels his tongue start to move as his mouth waters at the palpable flavour of words.[16] In one poem, the Chinese grandfather enjoys soup made out of burnt rice crust, a taste the narrator found difficult to appreciate in his youth; on the facing page is a foolproof rice recipe that ends with the recipe for this soup – "How taste remembers life,"[17] and in a subsequent era of reconciliation, the narrator reveals his belated esteem for "a dark-coloured soup that is sweet and can be eaten with relished meditation."[18] The conceit running through these poems – that foods awaken a kind of dormant racial memory – runs perilously close to the kind of essentialism that many critics have discarded precisely because it functions as a standard rationale for racisms of the past. But there is another way of looking at it. In recent studies of mourning and melancholia, critics have taken up Freud's distinction between healthy mourning, which relinquishes the lost object, and melancholia, in which instance the lost object remains encrypted in the body, entombed as a petrified and petrifying presence over several generations. In other words, such melancholia can be bequeathed to later generations.

Anne Anling Chen's study *The Melancholy of Race: Psychoanalysis, Assimilation, and Hidden Grief* takes this distinction in complex directions when she argues that racial melancholia is a combination of rejection and desire on the parts of "whites," whereas the racial "other" desires an unattainable perfection, meaning a total assimilation that can never be achieved. Along the way, forms of primary and secondary identification produce a collectivity that is not so much about racial memory as about becoming part of the social realm through the structures of narcissism as detailed in classic psychoanalysis. Rey Chow follows some of these ideas in her important study of "ethnic abjection." Such abjection, she argues, is the result of "thwarted narcissism," when subjects are denied the recognition of the dominant social group's gaze.

In her work on Chinese Canadian restaurants, Lily Cho takes up some of these theoretical structures to suggest (in what is partly a critique of Chow's position) that abjection in the form of homesickness and nostalgia may carry within it the seeds of what will form collectivity in diaspora. Her question is: What do Chinese subjects in diaspora have in common? What unites them? She argues against the prescriptiveness inherent in Chow's argument, which assumes that a cure for homesickness and nostalgia is necessary. As Cho argues, through an analysis of Wah's text, "I locate a form of resistance in the refusal to mourn, to be cured of sadness."[19] Arguing for a history that the body remembers at a corporeal level, Cho suggests that such a memory may be shared at a common rather than individual level, a type of archive of sensory memories. In this scheme, food can trigger these common memories, memories held in common. As Wah puts it, "Juk is even better than bird's nest soup, though both soups share an intrinsic proprioceptive synapse: memory."[20] These memories of collective tastes may explain the overwhelming popularity of cookbook memoirs. Ancestral tastes remain cradled in living bodies, giving them collective heft.

THE TOTEMIC MOTHER

Finally, I would like to turn from the sacrifice of the totemic father to the sacrificed mother. To explain this formulation, I should point out that much immigrant literature deals with the pathos of the sacrificed father, and Chinese Canadian literature is no exception. As suggested earlier, the stories of Chinese men being forced to do so-called women's work can be interpreted as another stage of racial humiliation. Humiliation linked to racialization is a theme that also runs through Janice Wong's memoir, *Chow*. Although her father was born in Victoria, this Canadian birth did not give him more options. As Wong puts it, "When Dad was a teenager, the British Columbia Government offered Chinese nationals one-way passage back to China, with the condition that they never return to Canada. Before the end of the Second World War, Chinese people in Canada were excluded from the privileges of official citizenship. They were unable to vote, unable to enter the professions – barred from teaching, medicine, law, engineering."[21]

Judy Fong Bates's novel *Midnight at the Dragon Café*, set in small-town Ontario during the 1960s, deals with further reverberations of Chinese Canadian "secrets." The protagonist Su-Jen/Annie negotiates the challenges of small-town racism while her family, proprietors of the town's Chinese café, present a model façade of respectability. Born in Hong Kong and having spent the first few years of her life there, Annie – with her mother – is summoned from this relatively comfortable and cosmopolitan life to Canada, where the father, who is much older than the mother (for both parents it is a second marriage), has bought a shabby café. The mother "eats bitterness" from the very beginning of her move to Canada, as she is forced to work in unaccustomed ways in the seedy eatery, which caters mainly to the local community of bachelors from the steel mill: "To the people in Irvine, we must have seemed the perfect immigrant family. We were polite, hard-working, unthreatening, and we kept to ourselves. As far as the townspeople were concerned, there was nothing about us that would upset the moral and social order that presided over them. Even when things started to go wrong, we blended so seamlessly into their everyday life, we remained invisible."[22] What "goes wrong" is that the adult son born of her father's first marriage arrives to work in the café and a relationship develops between him and his stepmother. Because she shares a room with her mother, Annie witnesses and gradually comes to understand the nature of this relationship. While watching her half-brother and mother prepare their favourite foods for each other, she also observes the growing sadness and humiliation of her elderly father, who is forced to endure the good wishes of the townspeople for his wife's pregnancy and subsequently, when a son is born, the congratulations of his peers in Toronto's Chinatown. The family's isolation contributes to these miseries. The mother, a cultured woman, is deprived of the social relations that had been part of her life in Hong Kong, and once the affair begins, she has no one in whom she can confide, except when her family makes the occasional journey to Toronto to see relatives. In a beautifully orchestrated description of gossiping mah-jong players, Bates deftly reveals the social pressures that constrain the mother and force her to keep her secret. It is a secret that Annie (without understanding its import) conveys in her description of the wedding of her half-brother and his bride, who has been imported from China. In the course of the festivities, the mother is unable to eat; weeks later, Annie overhears her parents fighting: "For the next few days a heavy silence hung between my parents. I saw it in their clenched jaws and stiff movements. But one night as I was helping my mother clear the dishes from the supper table, my father touched me on the shoulder. His face was drawn, but his voice was steady, 'Su-Jen, you finish that. Let your mother go upstairs and rest.' My mother looked at him for a moment, her body seemed to sag, but her face was like stone."[23] There is family reconciliation of a kind at the celebrations marking her new brother's first-month haircut – a moment when children officially become part of the family. Her father welcomes the child into the official, public family, whose relations are as substantial as all those paper social ties that were generated to combat racist legislation. The novel ends with Annie finally understanding that both of her parents had sacrificed their own lives in order to enable their children to be successful. It is a revelation not unlike the final recognition accorded to Noisy Jim by his family and community at his funeral.

The affective histories of this diasporic group were partly written in the daily meals they provided for innumerable small-town Canadians, but the gastronomic translations they perpetrated in order to stay in business and erase the conspicuity of their food gathered force in their repressed corporealities. Reading their texts (cookbooks, memoirs, novels, poems) makes us realize what we/they were missing out on during all those decades. Now, when these ethnic eateries have finally entered the public domain in their full splendour, they can unfurl their cuisines with fewer restrictions. Yet we know that for all the years that these dishes were served in the interstices behind the kitchen door, after hours, or in the lodgings above the family restaurants, they always were a secret part of everyday life, imbricated in the affective histories of Canada. Whereas through those early decades these offerings were laced with raw anxieties, now they are acknowledged as comfort food that has simmered over generations.

NOTES

1 Barthes, *Elements of Semiology*, 27–8.
2 For an extended analysis of the politics of ethnicity, see Gunew, *Haunted Nations*.

3 The episode is one of a fifteen-part series titled *Chinese Restaurants,* made by Cheuk Kwan. There is one episode set in Canada that forms part of the "Three Continents" trilogy.

4 See Shun-Wa and Aitkin, *Banquet.*

5 See Brennan, *Transmission of Affect.*

6 Gunew, "Retraining Tongues for Eyes."

7 The Kylie Kwong series is accompanied by a book but was preceded by an earlier publication on which I draw for my information. See Kwong, *Recipes and Stories.*

8 It was common practice to evade the Exclusion Act by using the documents of deceased Chinese Canadians to bring in other Chinese. As Peter Li points out, "real and fictitious birth certificates indicating a Chinese-Canadian parent were sold to prospective immigrants" (Li, *Chinese in Canada,* 90). See also Wayson Choy's memoir *Paper Shadows.*

9 For a discussion of prosopopoeia in terms of an address to the dead, see Paul de Man, "Autobiography as De-Facement," in *The Rhetoric of Romanticism* (New York: Columbia University Press, 1984), 67–81.

10 Wah, *Diamond Grill,* 11.

11 Thien, "Simple Recipes," 9.

12 Wah, *Diamond Grill,* 11.

13 Ibid., 10.

14 Ibid., 65–6.

15 Ibid., 148.

16 Ibid., 174.

17 Ibid., 74.

18 Ibid., 75.

19 Cho, "How Taste Remembers Life," 93.

20 Wah, *Diamond Grill,* 167.

21 Wong, *Chow,* 164.

22 Bates, *Midnight at the Dragon Café,* 112.

23 Ibid., 282.

12

Dishing Dad: "How to Cook a Husband" and Other Metaphorical Recipes

GARY DRAPER

Metaphorical recipes? By that phrase, I mean texts that look like recipes but that, upon examination, prove to be something else again. Invoking the recipe's distinctive, instructional form, they convey a message about the achievement of non-culinary ends, primarily having to do with personal qualities and relationships. In literary terms, the metaphorical recipe is a version of parody. Allow me to illustrate.

About fifty years ago, I – and a lot of other little North American children – sang this song:

> *On top of old Smokey, where nobody goes,*
> *I spied Betty Grable without any clothes.*
> *Along comes Roy Rogers, a clippity-clop,*
> *And looks her all over, from bottom to top.*

What drew us to this ditty? Or, more generally, what draws us to parody existing forms? Fundamentally, only one thing is an absolute necessity: a strong model. Imitation, whatever else it does, pays a compliment to form. The most attractive thing to the imitator – and to the parodist – is a textual form with a distinctive character.

While the recipe has never, for some obvious reasons, achieved high literary status, it is nonetheless a written work with a long history and an admirably clear and effective form. Here's a summary of what's needed, by one who should know, M.F.K. Fisher, the celebrated American food writer: "A good recipe, for modern convenience, should consist of three parts: name, ingredients, method."[1]

This captures perfectly the superstructure, but I would suggest that there are not three elements but four, and that without the fourth – even though it is seldom stated explicitly – the form is hollow. Therefore, we can view the process as one in which (a) under a name, (b) disparate ingredients are (c) taken through transformative steps to (d) create a happy outcome. The happy outcome may be more properly connected to the mood of the piece than to its structure, but no reader of recipes, I suspect, would doubt its presence, at least in the utopian world of the cookbook (which is sometimes a far cry from the dystopic kitchen). What's more, any reader of Jane Austen or Helen Fielding will recognize at once this tripartite schema. It is the traditional form of comedy: the movement from disharmony (or at least disparate elements), through some difficulties, to a happy resolution, often embodied in a marriage or other indicator of social harmony.

Having selected a form (or having been selected by it), the parodist usually follows one of two routes: she makes fun of something inherent in the original, or she expresses in the borrowed form a sentiment that needs articulation and that might otherwise be hard to express.

Let us return momentarily to the top of Old Smokey. The original song, about losing true love "for courting too slow," was ubiquitous in the early fifties in its popular incarnation sung by the American folk group the Weavers. The melody was hauntingly repeatable, and the words were simple.[2] So much for form; what of the message? Emergent, titillating, voyeuristic, little-boy sexuality. I think I can still just barely recall the thrill of uttering that phrase "without any clothes." Did I have the faintest idea who Betty Grable was? Yes, though not in any specific actual sense of the living, breathing human. She was a byword, in those pre-Marilyn days, for the sexually attractive female.

In other words, the parody operated within the limits of convention but subverted, or at least transgressed, those limits by exaggeration and the public expression of private desire.

Back to the kitchen. The community cookbook, as more than a few writers have noticed in the last decade, is a rich form of local expression.[3] Above all, it is a place where women can express themselves in print. As literature, the form may be a modest one. But its social impact can be enormous. And consider this: Is there any equivalent form of publication for the husbands and sons of these women that allows them to see below their compositions the family name in print? I think there is not. In other words, the community cookbook is a forum for women to express themselves in print and, at the same time, to demonstrate their competence in ways that (for better or worse) are part of their socially constructed identity and value.

With these ideas (parody, form, and voice) as welcome mat, let us take a stroll through some community cookbooks published in Canada during the first half of the twentieth century. We find there a rich field of the parodied recipe. The recipe's drawing power as a textual template is apparent in the degree to which even advertisers succumb to its magnetic pull. Recipes may be found for everything from good grooming to a well-maintained car. Some of these commercial recipes are perfunctory, simply playing on the word "recipe." Occasionally, however, the advertiser enters the spirit of the form, as an advertisement for the Canadian Telegraph and Business College in the YWCA *Cook Book*, published in St Thomas, Ontario, in 1908, illustrates:

Recipe (Extraordinary)

Take a good school (Best's is the name), put in a wide awake boy or girl, add one of our expert teachers, mix well for one term and when taken out you will find a WELL DONE GRADUATE, TELEGRAPHY, SHORTHAND, COMMERCIAL.[4]

Not only does this example capture all the essentials – a title, ingredients, process, and outcome – but transformation is at its heart. Interestingly, it is people that are transformed; indeed, the cook and the outcome are more than a little intertwined. This interlacing is even more explicit in "A New Recipe"

A NEW RECIPE

By W. T. Rogers, Principal
Brockville Business College.

Take a little Book-keeping.
Take a little Commercial Arithmetic.
Take a little Rapid Calculation.
Take a little Practical English.
Take a little Spelling.
Take a little Business Penmanship.
Take a little Correspondence.
Take a little of Pitman's Shorthand.
Take a lot of Touch Typewriting.
Mix according to the judgment of The Business College teachers, and you will be equipped to take a position where the wages will enable you to pay for all the ingredients mentioned in all the recipes in this valuable book.

"A New Recipe" (Brockville Business College), in *The Brockville Cook Book*, 1910. Courtesy of Gary Draper.

from the Brockville Business College (*Brockville Cook Book*, 1910). It begins: "Take a little Book-keeping / Take a little Commercial Arithmetic / Take a little Rapid Calculation," and after taking another six subjects and following the instructions "Mix according to the judgment of The Business College teachers," we arrive at this outcome: "and you will be equipped to take a position where the wages will enable you to pay for all the ingredients mentioned in all the recipes in this valuable book."[5] Besides the obvious wit, the recipe raises issues about just what exactly is being cooked and by whom.

Recipes such as this one, aimed at potential customers, are fun, but in many ways those that take their inspiration from sources other than the commercial are of more interest. Certainly they have more to tell us about the readers and the writers of these recipes of 1900 to 1950. Within this category is a broad range of personal outcomes: better citizens, a happy day, a group, a community. Some of these recipes appear often, some only rarely. There are many versions of recipes for happiness, although they do not stray far from the pieties of selflessness and optimism. Here, for example, is one of several versions of a recipe for a "happy life," this one from *Aunt Hannah's War-Time and Peace-Time Recipes*, published in Toronto during World War I: "Take a large quantity of Cheerfulness and let it simmer without stopping. Put with it a brimming basinful of Kindness, then add a full measure of Thought for Other People. Mix into these a piling tablespoonful of Sympathy. Flavor with essence of Charity. Stir well together, and then carefully strain off any grains of Selfishness. Let the whole be served with Love sauce, and Fruit of the Spirit."[6]

Forms may vary, but the main ingredients in happiness (a woman's happiness, that is) are kindness, unselfishness, thoughtfulness, love, usefulness, cheerfulness, sympathy, and charity. Aunt Hanna's admonition to "carefully strain off any grains of Selfishness," for example, effectively captures the tone of self-effacement. Sometimes a smile or a laugh is recommended for topping. In one item – a twelve-line lyric that is a recipe in name only – smiling is pretty much the sole ingredient:

Begin the day with smiling eyes,
Pursue the day with smiling lips
Through clouds perceive the smiling skies,
Up where the smiling sunbeam trips[7]

Moreover, in case the plan is not clear enough in this first verse, the subsequent stanzas reinforce it – attitude is all.

There are other forms of self-transformation. Recipes for "Community," "A Group," and "Better Citizens" point in the same direction of selflessness. They include kindness, tolerance, enthusiasm, friendship, thoughtfulness, tenderness, loyalty, faith, hope, charity, gaiety, sympathy, and good nature. Some are more explicit still. The recipe for "A Sweet Disposition" is a charmer. Its attitudinal ingredients are straightforward: "3 grains of common sense," "1 large heart," and a "bushel [of] contentment." For health, "1 good liver" plus plenty "of fresh air and sunlight." The final ingredient is an interesting one: "1 good husband."[8] The unmarried women who contributed to this cookbook are thus informed, perhaps, that their single status puts a sweet disposition beyond their reach.

The recipe "For Moulding a Kitchen Mechanic" might be expected to concentrate on the more practical aspects of housekeeping, but once again the emphasis is on the cook's selfless attitude, her self-control, consideration, and patience.[9] The extended "Recipe for a Happy Year of Cooking" is likewise about the character of the cook, with predictable words of advice about living for others. The version that most closely emulates the recipe form – title, list, process – is the "Married Woman's Cake," but of course the real product is once again woman herself (a kind of edible woman). What the woman ends up swallowing is her own self-interest. The usual suspect ingredients are here: sympathy, contentment, cheerfulness. A noteworthy variation is "interest in all your husband does."[10] The surprise for me is the amount suggested for this ingredient. One might expect the cook/cake to use a substantial quantity, but in fact she need only add "a sprinkle." It is hard not to see this as a modestly saucy foretaste of the roasting that is to come.

What else were these women being encouraged to cook up in their kitchens? Children, for one thing. Surprisingly, raising children is presented less in terms of the mother's need for self-abnegation than in terms of the environmental requirements. In a typical example, the ingredients are as follows: "6 children, 3 puppies, 1 field, 1 brook, 1 blue sky." The method is similarly simple (and free from domestic pieties), concluding with "Bake in hot sun, and when thoroughly brown set in bathtub to cool."[11] One more literal-minded contributor adds such things as "1/4 cup orange juice," "1 dish whole wheat cereal," "2 slices whole wheat toast," and "1 glass milk."[12]

In looking through several hundred community cookbooks, I have found that some of these recipes are repeated as many as three or four times. Some are unique. One that may be common, but that I have seen only once, is a recipe for "Heavenly Bliss." The recipes I have looked at include (sometimes as an ingredient, sometimes as an outcome) such things as happiness, comfort, and contentment. What does not appear is bliss. When Katherine Mansfield titled a short story "Bliss" (published in 1920, around the time this recipe was published), she was talking about a degree of happiness that was near to ecstasy, and there is a romantic – indeed a sexual – edge to the word.[13] And in the single example I found, how does the housewife whip up a little bliss?

To one piece of piazza, add a little moonlight. Of course, take for granted two persons. Press in two strong hands, one small soft hand. Now sift lightly two ounces of attraction and one of romance; then add a large measure of comfort, followed by a passing mmm ... or two, and one or two whispers. Dissolve half a dozen glances in a well of silence, dust in a small quantity of hesitation, a pinch of yielding; place kisses on a flushed cheek or two red lips. Sift with essence of Ambrosia, and set aside to cool.[14]

The contributor of this bit of romantic frippery is identified as "Dr. Kinneard." The text is, at least in my limited survey, unique. Romantic evenings, by and large, are not what these cookbooks are about.

One further exception to the general rule of sweet domesticity points in a rather different direction:

RECIPE FOR A TERRIBLE DAY!

1 Pint of ILL-HUMOUR
Add: –
1 or more UNFORTUNATE INCIDENTS
Set over a good fire; when boiling point is reached, add a tbsp.
of TEMPER. Baste from time to time with SARCASM. Cook until edges curl. Add handful of naughty words. As mixture curdles, stir FURIOUSLY.
Warning! – Do not cover – may blow top!
Serve while sizzling.[15]

This recipe takes the metaphorical a step further, perhaps, by adding complexity of tone. Although it is presented ironically, however, the substance of this piece is really not so far removed from the recipe for a happy day (a sample of which immediately precedes it in the text). In its use of irony this prescription may prepare us for the cooking of husbands, a process (and a text) presented with a tone that requires a degree of tact and delicacy to unravel.

Most of the recipes I have considered so far appear in only a small number of cookbooks. A recipe that has been frequently reprinted, however, is one generally titled "How to Cook a Husband." While there are some variations from time to time, for the most part the various versions of this recipe resemble one another so closely that it is clear they are the offspring of a common ancestor. Although I have been unable to find a definitive original text, examples of

"How to Cook a Husband" have surfaced in disparate corners of the globe at least as far back as the latter part of the nineteenth century.

My particular sources include twenty-two community cookbooks published in Canada between 1905 and 1951, from Moncton to Vancouver (see the Appendix for this chapter). They include titles as generic as *Cook Book* and as coincidentally apt as *Wise Wives Keep Husbands Happy by Using This Good Guide to Wholesome Cookery*.

Here is a typical, comprehensive version of the recipe, published around 1910:

How to Cook a Husband

A good many husbands are utterly spoiled by mismanagement. Some women keep them constantly in hot water; others let them freeze by their carelessness and indifference. Some keep them in a stew by irritating ways and words; others roast them. Some keep them in a pickle all their lives. It cannot be supposed that any husband will be tender and good managed in this way, but they are really delicious when properly treated. In selecting your husband you should not be guided by the silvery appearance, as in buying mackerel, nor by the golden tint, as if you wanted salmon; be sure to select him yourself, as tastes differ. Do not go to the market for him, as the best are always brought to your door. It is far better to have none unless you will patiently learn how to cook him. A preserving kettle of finest porcelain is best, but if you have nothing but an earthenware pipkin, it will do, with care. See that the linen in which you wrap him is nicely washed and mended, with the required number of buttons and strings nicely sewed on. Tie him in the kettle by a strong silk cord called comfort, as the one called duty is apt to be weak, and they are apt to fly out of the kettle and be burned and crusty on the edges, since, like crabs and lobsters, you have to cook them alive. Make a clear, steady fire out of love, neatness and cheerfulness. Set him as near this as seems to agree with him. If he sputters and fizzles, do not be anxious; some husbands do this until they are quite done. Add a little sugar, in the form of what confectioners call kisses, but no vinegar nor pepper of any account. A little spice

How to Cook a Husband

GOOD MANY HUSBANDS are utterly spoiled by mismanagement. Some women keep them constantly in hot water; others let them freeze by their carelessness and indifference. Some keep them in a stew by irritating ways and words; others roast them. Some keep them in a pickle all their lives. It cannot be supposed that any husband will be tender and good, managed in this way, but they are really delicious when properly treated. In selecting your husband you should not be guided by the silvery appearance, as in buying mackerel, nor by the golden tint, as if you wanted salmon; be sure you select him yourself, as tastes differ. Do not go to the market for him, as the best are always brought to your door. It is far better to have none unless you will patiently learn how to cook him. A preserving kettle of finest porcelain is best, but if you have nothing but an earthenware pipkin, it will do, with care. See that the linen in which you wrap him is nicely washed and mended, with the required number of buttons and strings nicely sewed on. Tie him in the kettle by a strong silk cord called comfort, as the one called duty is apt to be weak, and they are apt to fly out of the kettle and be burned and crusty on the edges, since, like crabs and lobsters, you have to cook them alive. Make a clear, steady fire out of love, neatness and cheerfulness. Set him as near this as seems to agree with him. If he sputters and fizzles, do not be anxious; some husbands do this until they are quite done. Add a little sugar, in the form of what confectioners call kisses, but no vinegar nor pepper of any account. A little spice improves them, but it must be used with judgment. Do not stick any sharp instruments into him to see if he is becoming tender. Stir him gently; watch the while, lest he lie too flat and too close to the kettle, and so become useless. You cannot fail to know when he is done.

If thus treated, you will find him very digestible, agreeing nicely with you and the children, and he will keep as long as you want, unless you become careless and set him in too cold a place.

—4—

"How to Cook a Husband," in *The Maple Leaf Cook Book*, c. 1905. Courtesy of Gary Draper.

improves them, but it must be used with judgment. Do not stick any sharp instruments into him to see if he is becoming tender. Stir him gently; watch the while, lest he lie too flat and too close to the kettle, and so become useless. You cannot fail to know when he is done.

If thus treated, you will find him very digestible, agreeing with you and the children, and he will keep as long as you want, unless you become careless and set him in too cold a place.[16]

In my twenty-two examples, "How to Cook a Husband" is the favourite, most-repeated title by a wide margin. Among the variants, "How to Preserve a Husband" intrigues because of the slight consolation it offers the victim in postponing the ultimate fate of consumption. The hope of preservation is echoed within the recipe by the presence of the preserving kettle and by the assurance in the coda "he will keep as long as you want." Still, there is surely something slightly ominous in that particular phrase "as long as you want." At the very least, it powerfully implies that the cook/wife will decide how long that is. Although it happens infrequently, the preservation theme may also be suggested by the placement of the recipe in a section of the cookbook devoted to jams and other canned goods.

Colleen Cotter, a linguist whose work on the narrative structure inherent in most recipes is invaluable to this study, suggests that after the title and abstract of a recipe come the ingredients list, the orientation clauses, the actions, the evaluations, and, sometimes, the coda. In many older cookbooks, Cotter's ingredients list is embedded within the action/narrative. That is the case here, which seems fitting given that the ingredients are so few: the husband, some sugar, some spice.

Unlike its literal counterparts, this recipe includes many cautionary instructions, not a to-do list, but a to-not-do list. The negatives extend to the ingredients list: no vinegar, no pepper. They are even more liberally scattered throughout the "orientation" clauses, which helps to contextualize the actions. This is significant, I think, because in this recipe – as in some of its metaphorical cousins mentioned earlier – there is a blurring of the line between the actor and the outcome. In other words, "How to Cook a Husband" is in some sense as much a recipe for how to be a good wife as it is a recipe for how to produce a satisfactory husband. In fact, there is an implicit assumption that by being the former, one will inevitably produce the latter – a recipe, it might be argued, for co-dependence. The cook/wife, then, is cautioned against "mismanagement." In the words of the metaphor, she is advised against freezing or roasting her husband, against keeping him in hot water, a stew, or a pickle. For those on whom the metaphor is lost, the authors translate: avoid carelessness, indifference, and irritating ways and words.

A second component of the orientation clauses is the selection process. The husband-as-mackerel image seems to me pure subversive play, without a clear literal counterpart, though the caution against a silvery or golden appearance would seem to imply either that wealth does not ensure a happy outcome or that the *appearance* of wealth may be deceiving. Is it possible that a touch of silver (perhaps around the temples) may indicate that the fish is past its best-before date?

When we reach the actions proper, it begins to look more and more as though "How to Cook a Husband" is a more accurate title than "How to Preserve a Husband," though there is in the former, nevertheless, the promise of a long afterlife as leftovers. In the words of the metaphor, the husband is to be wrapped up, tied into the kettle, cooked near a steady fire, seasoned, stirred, and watched until done. Meaning? The wife is advised to keep his house clean (assuming that every man's home is his kettle); to make him comfortable (which will make him stay); to do his laundry; to be loving, neat, and cheerful; and also to give him some kisses (I'll leave the spice to your imagination) and keep him active (and thus useful).

In "Democracy," Leonard Cohen speaks of "the homicidal bitchin' that goes down in every kitchen to determine who will serve and who will eat." The story the "How to Cook a Husband" recipe tells is a little more complicated. Taking as its base the prevailing notions of gender roles and relations, the recipe empowers by its wit (remember, these cookbooks are written by women, for women). If the wife is constrained to pleasing behaviour and domestic service, the husband is exposed as unpredictable but malleable and both unreliable and ineffective without a woman's intervention and improvement. His behaviour is hopelessly dependent. He may be "utterly spoiled," he may fly the kettle/coop, he may become crusty and sputtering and – finally – useless.

The ultimate declaration of where power lies is in the controlling metaphor, which, stripped of the niceties, is an image of cannibalism. Make no mistake, the husband is, explicitly, to be roasted on a fire. What is more, like a crab or a lobster, he is to be "cooked alive." Is there any question of whether or not he will be eaten? No: when done, he will be both (a) delicious and – more significantly – (b) digestible.

Given the lightness of its tone, I am loath to take the metaphor too seriously. It is, I believe, a playful one despite the deadliness of its ancestry. But I do wish to interrogate it just a bit further. In *Our Cannibals, Ourselves*, Priscilla Walton points out that the earliest reports of flesh-eating incidents were "overtly intertwined with sexuality and sexual power."[17] While the husband-roasting recipes considered here may cloak the sexual in the contemporary terms of socially constructed gender, the fact that they invariably involve the preparation of the male by the female points in the direction of the sexual division.

Lewis Petrinovich, in *The Cannibal Within*, outlines two general categories and five particular types of cannibalism.[18] Following his typology, we might ask if "How to Cook a Husband" exemplifies more clearly exocannibalism (when those eaten are outsiders) or endocannibalism (when those eaten are members of the community). The simplest answer would be that cohabiting husbands and wives are by definition members of the same community. And yet it is here that the taboo is the greatest. I would argue that the degree of otherness ascribed to the husband in these recipes really does inscribe him as an outsider. In terms of Petrinovich's specific types, the consumption of the husband might fall somewhere between survival cannibalism (under the constraints of extreme necessity – in this case, the necessity for a woman of that era to please a husband for the sake of her economic survival) and political cannibalism (essentially the public capturing and killing of one's neighbours as a strategic demonstration of power – in this case, the wittily imaginative exercise of power in what must sometimes have felt like a place of utter powerlessness).

In discourse analysis terms, a recipe may or may not conclude with a coda. This recipe does: the caution to the housewife about losing the husband through coldness. For harmony's sake, this chapter will include one or two codas of its own. I have not attended to the many variations in the reprintings of the basic recipe, but there are two very fine ones that I believe work to validate my belief that the tone of these pieces is, if not revolutionary, at least subversive. The first comes from Rose Valley, Saskatchewan, in 1938, appearing in *Cook Book: Tried and Tested Recipes from the Ladies of the Ponass Lake Municipality*. It offers this novel and judicious opening: "First: Get a husband. Be sure that you experiment with your own. Any other, of course, might result in disaster." While the exhortation points in the direction of strictly moral behaviour, the sly implication that there is another option is in itself transgressive, not least because of the humorous tone with which the caution is offered.

If Exhibit A, then, is sexual transgression, inevitably Exhibit B must be its natural counterpart: violence. And that brings us to the second example of subversion. *The Westminster Church Cookbook,* also from Saskatchewan, makes a subtle adjustment to one of the common cautions: "Do not stick any sharp instruments into him to see if he is tender – use your rolling pin – discreetly – and make sure."

Which brings me back to "On Top of Old Smokey." Just as that parodied song both celebrated and subverted the rules of sexuality, this parodied recipe both celebrates and subverts the gender roles that operate in the kitchen. It may be clear who will serve and who will eat, but husbands have been put in their place and put on notice. In this recipe at least, they and their foibles have been dined out on.

APPENDIX: SOURCES FOR "HOW TO COOK A HUSBAND"

Cook Book. Sunny Brae, NS: Ladies' Aid, United Church: n.d.
Cook Book: Tried and Tested Recipes from the Ladies of the Ponass Lake Municipality. Rose Valley, SK: Ladies Hospital Aid, 1938.
The Cook's Friend. Stony Plain, AB: Stony Plain Women's Institute, 1930.
Food Favorites Cook Book. Belleville, ON: Quintena Rebekah Lodge No. 133, n.d.
Halton Women's Institute Cook Book. Burlington, ON: Halton Women's Institute, 1912.
Hospital Cook Book. Moose Jaw, SK: Daughters of the Empire, 1905.
Jolly Degree Girls Cook Book. London, ON: Rebekah Lodge No. 5.
Jubilee Cook Book. Byron, ON: Byron Women's Institute, 1947.
Jubilee Cook Book. Rossland, BC: Women's Association, St Andrew's United Church, 1947.
The Maple Leaf Cook Book. Kimberly, ON: Kimberly Women's Institute, n.d.
Nourishment: Physical – Spiritual. Marsville, ON: Women's Association, Marsville United Church, 1951.
100 Sugarless Recipes. Yorkton, SK: Fort William Women's Air Force Auxiliary, n.d.
The Pantry Shelf. Revised edition. Brantford, ON: Alexander Graham Bell Chapter, IODE, 1949.
Recipes. Vancouver, BC: Mount Pleasant Methodist Church, 1913.

Saskatoon Souvenir Cook Book. Saskatoon, SK: Philathea Class, First Baptist Church, n.d.

A Selection of Favorite Recipes. Walkerville, ON: Women's Association, Ottawa United Church, n.d.

Tested Tasty Treats. Salford, ON: Junior Bible Class, Salford United Church, n.d.

Three Hundred Dainty Recipes. Vancouver, BC: Willing Workers' Guild, Westminster Presbyterian Church, n.d.

300 Tried and Tested Recipes. Bridgeburg, ON: Central Avenue Methodist Church, 1923.

Westminster Church Cook Book. Saskatoon, SK: Westminster Church, 1929.

Wise Wives Keep Husbands Happy by Using This Good Guide to Wholesome Cookery. St Vital, MB: St Mark's and Regent's Park Churches, n.d.

Y. L. A. Recipes. Moncton, NB: St John's United Church, 1935.

NOTES

1 Fisher, "Anatomy of a Recipe," 23.
2 The song has proven an astonishingly hardy model for parody. "On Top of Spaghetti" is a more recent, more innocent, and likely a more pervasive version than the older version quoted.
3 Two fine examples are Janet Theophano's *Eat My Words* (2002) and *Recipes for Reading* (1997), edited by Anne L. Bower.
4 *Cook Book* (St Thomas, ON).
5 *Brockville Cook Book*, 94.
6 *Aunt Hannah's War-Time and Peace-Time Recipes*, 3.
7 *Evening Auxiliary Cook Book*, 2.
8 *Tested Recipes*, 2.
9 *Our Favourite Recipes*, 2.
10 *Jubilee Cook Book*, 3.
11 *Selected Recipes*, 1.
12 *St. Henry's Jubilee Cook Book*, 1.
13 Katherine Mansfield. *Bliss, and Other Stories*. New York: Alfred A. Knopf, 1920.
14 *Quill Lake Homemakers' Club Cook Book*, 3.
15 *Totem Cook Book*, 5.
16 *Maple Leaf Cook Book*, 4.
17 Walton, *Our Cannibals, Ourselves*, 10.
18 Petrinovich, *Cannibal Within*, 6.

BIBLIOGRAPHY

A.B. of Grimsby. *The frugal housewife's manual*. First edition. Toronto: J.H. Lawrence, 1840.

Abonyi, Sylvia. "Sickness and Symptom: Perspectives on Diabetes among the Mushkegowuk Cree." PhD diss., McMaster University, 2001.

"An Account of a sort of Sugar made of the Juice of the Maple, in Canada." *Philosophical Transactions* 15:988. JSTOR. http://www.jstore.org/stable/1022141. Accessed 2 February 2009.

Adam, Ann. "The Thanksgiving Dinner." *MacLean's Magazine,* 1 November 1928.

Adams, Blaine. "The Construction and Occupation of the Barracks of the King's Bastion." *Fortress of Louisbourg: Report H A 13 – Duquesnel* (1971). http://fortress.uccb.ns.ca/search/ha13_24.htm. Accessed 3 February 2009.

Advertisement for Baker's cocoa. *Canadian Grocer,* 6 March 1891. Thomas Fisher Rare Book Library, University of Toronto, Toronto.

Aitken, Kate. *Kate Aitken's Canadian Cook Book*. Montreal: The Standard, 1945.

Albala, Ken. *Eating Right in the Renaissance*. Berkeley: University of California Press, 2002.

Alcott, William. *The Moral Reformer and Teacher on the Human Constitution* 1 (1835): 351–3.

Alfred, Agnes. *Paddling to Where I Stand*. Edited by Martine J. Reid and translated by Daisy Sewid-Smith. Vancouver: University of British Columbia Press, 2004.

ALHFAM (Association for Living History, Farm and Agricultural Museums). http://www.alhfam.org/index.php. Accessed 24 January 2008.

Allen, John L. "From Cabot to Cartier: The Early Exploration of Eastern North America, 1497–1543." *Annals of the Association of American Geographers* 82, no. 3 (September 1992): 500–21.

Anderson, Benedict. *Imagined Communities: Reflections on the Origin and Spread of Nationalism*. Revised edition. London: Verso, 1991.

Andrews, Jean. "Diffusion of Mesoamerican Food Complex to Southeastern Europe." *Geographical Review* 83 (1993): 194–204.

Apicius. *L'art culinaire*. Paris: Éditions Les belles lettres, 2002.

Appadurai, Arjun. "How to Make a National Cuisine: Cookbooks in Contemporary India." *Comparative Studies in Society and History* 30, no. 1 (1988): 3–24.

Applebaum, Diana K. *Thanksgiving: An American Holiday, an American History*. New York: Facts on File Publications, 1984.

"Armistice Day Linked with Thanksgiving." Canadian War Museum. Government of Canada. http://www.warmuseum.ca/cwm/exhibitions/remember/thanksgiving_e.shtml. Accessed 5 February 2009.

Armstrong, Jeannette C. *We Get Our Living Like Milk from the Land*. Penticton: Theytus, 1994.

Armstrong, Julian. *A Taste of Quebec*. Toronto: Macmillan Canada, 1990.

Assiniwi, Bernard. *Recettes indiennes et survie en forêt*. Montreal: Leméac, 1972.

Atwood, Margaret, ed. *The Canlit Food Book: From Pen to Palate: A Collection of Tasty Literary Fare*. Toronto: Totem, 1987.

Aunt Hannah's War-Time and Peace-Time Recipes. Toronto: Ladies of Ward 2 Patriotic Association, n.d.

Avery, Donald, and Roger Hall, eds. *Coming of Age: Readings in Canadian History since World War II*. Toronto: Harcourt Brace, 1996.

Bacon, Leonard. *The Genesis of the New England Churches*. New York: Harper & Brothers, 1874.

Baird, Elizabeth. *Classic Canadian Cooking: Menus for the Seasons*. Toronto: James Lorimer & Co., 1974.

– *Complete Canadian Living Cookbook*. Toronto: Random House Canada, 2004.

– *Elizabeth Baird's Favourites: 150 Classic Canadian Recipes*. Halifax: James Lorimer & Co., 1984.

Bannerman, Norma, et al. "Canadian Home Economics Association 1939–1989." *Illinois Teacher of Home Economics* 33, no. 1 (September-October, 1989), 2–6.

Bantey, Bill. *Bill Bantey's Expo 67*. Montreal: Gazette Printing Co., 1967.

Barer-Stein, Thelma. *You Eat What You Are: A Study of Ethnic Food Traditions*. Toronto: McClelland & Stewart, 1979.

Barham, Elizabeth. "Translating Terroir: The Global Challenge of French AOC Labeling." *Journal of Rural Studies* 19 (2003): 127–38.

Barss, Beulah. *Oh Canada! A Celebration of Great Canadian Cooking*. Calgary: Deadwood Publishers, 1987.

– *The Pioneer Cook.* Calgary: Detselig Enterprises, 1980.

Barss, Bunny. *Alberta Pictorial Cookbook.* Halifax: Nimbus, 1988.

Barthes, Roland. *Elements of Semiology.* Translated by A. Levers and C. Smith. New York: Hill and Wang, 1967.

– *Mythologies.* New York: Hill and Wang, 1972.

Batcho, Kristine I. "Personal Nostalgia, World View, Memory, and Emotionality." *Perceptual and Motor Skills* 87, no. 2 (1998): 411–32.

Bates, Christina. *Out of Old Ontario Kitchens: A Collection of Traditional Recipes of Ontario and of the People Who Cooked Them.* Toronto: Pagurian Press, 1978.

Bates, J.F. *Midnight at the Dragon Café.* Toronto: McClelland & Stewart, 2004.

Baumeister, Roy F., and Mark R. Leary. "The Need to Belong: Desire for Interpersonal Attachments as a Fundamental Human Motivation." *Psychological Bulletin* 117, no. 3 (1995): 497–529.

Beeson, Patricia. *Macdonald Was Late for Dinner: A Slice of Culinary Life in Early Canada.* Peterborough: Broadview Press, 1993.

Beeton, Isabella. *Household Management.* New York: Oxford University Press, 1861.

Belasco, Warren. *Appetite for Change: How the Counterculture Took on the Food Industry.* New York: Pantheon Books, 1990.

– "Food Matters: Perspectives on an Emerging Field." In *Food Nations: Selling Taste in Consumer Societies.* Edited by Warren Belasco and Philip Scranton, 2–23. New York: Routledge, 2002.

Belegai, Michael M. *Ukrains'ko-angliiskyi kukhar* (Ukrainian-English cook). Edmonton, AB: Ukr. Vydavnychoii Spilky (Ukr. Publishers Co-operation), 1917.

Bell, David, and Gill Valentine. *Consuming Geographies: We Are Where We Eat.* London and New York: Routledge, 1997.

Belon, Pierre. *Petri Bellonii Cenomani De arboribus coniseris, resiniseris, aliisque, nonnullis sempiterna fronde virentibus.* Paris: Gilles Corozet, 1553. http://visualiseur.bnf.fr/Visualiseur?Destination=Gallica&O=NUMM-52155. Accessed 2 February 2009.

Benoît, Jehane. *The Canadiana Cookbook: A Complete Heritage of Canadian Cooking.* Toronto: Pagurian Press, 1970.

– *CBC Take Thirty: Madame Benoit Summer Series.* Canadian Broadcasting Corporation, 1967.

– *La cuisine canadienne.* Montreal: Éditions du Jour, 1979.

– *L'encyclopédie de la cuisine canadienne.* Montreal: Les messageries du Saint-Laurent limitée, 1963.

– *Jehane Benoît dans sa cuisine.* Montreal: Moderne, 1955.

- *Library of Canadian Cooking: Over 6,000 Easy to Prepare Recipes.* 12 vols. Ottawa: Les Messageries du St-Laurent, 1972.
- *Secrets et recettes du cahier de ma grand'mère.* Montreal: Éditions Beauchemin, 1959.

Bentley, William. *The Diary of William Bentley.* Vol. 3. Salem: Essex Institute, 1905.

Berger, John. *Pig Earth.* New York: Pantheon, 1979.

Berton, Pierre, and Janet Berton. *The Centennial Food Guide: A Century of Good Eating.* Toronto: McClelland & Stewart, 1966.

Bertrand, Lise. "Consommations alimentaires." In Institut de la statistique du Québec, *Enquête sociale et de santé auprès des enfants et des adolescents québécois. Volet nutrition.* 2004. http://www.stat.gouv.qc.ca/publications/sante/pdf2004/enq_nutrition04c5.pdf. Accessed 5 February 2009.

Béthune, Guy, and Jacques Rousseau. *Voyage de Pehr Kalm au Canada en 1749: Traduction Annotée du Journal de Route.* Montreal: Pierre Tisseyre, 1977.

Beynon, William. *Potlatch at Gitsegukla: William Beynon's 1945 Field Notes.* Edited by Margaret Anderson and Majorie Halpin. Vancouver: University of British Columbia Press, 2000.

Biggar, H.P., ed. "The Soncino Letters." In *The Precursors of Jacques Cartier 1497–1534: A Collection of Documents relating to the Early History of the Dominion of Canada.* Ottawa: Government Printing Bureau, 1911. http://www.heritage.nf.ca/exploration/soncino.html. Accessed 2 February 2009.

Blackman, Margaret B. *During My Time: Florence Edenshaw Davidson: A Haida Woman.* Seattle: University of Washington Press, 1992.

Bliss, William R. "Thanksgiving: 'The Day We Celebrate.'" *Observer,* 28 November 1872, 1.

Boisvenue, Lorraine. *Le guide de la cuisine traditionnelle québécoise.* Montreal: Éditions Stanké, 1979.

"Bon Appétit: A Celebration of Canadian Cookbooks." *Library and Archives Canada.* Government of Canada. http://www.collectionscanada.gc.ca/cuisine/index-e.html. Accessed 16 February 2009.

Bonnefons, Nicolas de. *Les délices de la campagne: Suitte du "Jardinier françois," où est enseigné à préparer pour l'usage de la vie, tout ce qui croît sur terre et dans les eaux.* Second edition. Amsterdam: chez Raphaël Smith, 1655. http://visualiseur.bnf.fr/Visualiseur?O=NUMM-108861. Accessed 2 February 2009.

Boswell, Randy. "Sorry Americans, First Thanksgiving Was Canadian." *Vancouver Sun,* 10 October 2003, A14.

Bottéro, Jean. *La plus vieille cuisine du monde.* Paris: Éditions Audibert, 2002.

Bouchard, Céline Roland. *Le Pinereau*. Montreal: Leméac, 1971.

Boudreau, Marielle, and Melvin Gallant. *Cuisine traditionnelle en Acadie*. Moncton, NB: Éditions Acadie, 1987.

Bower, Anne. "Cooking Up Stories: Narrative Elements in Community Cookbooks." In *Recipes for Reading: Community Cookbooks, Stories, Histories*. Edited by Anne L. Bower, 29–50. Amherst: University of Massachusetts Press, 1997.

– ed. *Recipes for Reading: Community Cookbooks, Stories, Histories*. Amherst: University of Massachusetts Press, 1997.

Bramham, Daphne. "Tradition Seasons Every Dish at Thanksgiving Table." *Vancouver Sun*, 9 October 2000, B3.

Brant, Beth. "Food and Spirits." In *Food and Spirits*, 67–85. Vancouver: Press Gang, 1991.

Brennan, Teresa. *The Transmission of Affect*. Ithaca: Cornell University Press, 2004.

"Brief Discours." *Archive of Early American Images*. http://www.brown.edu/Facilities/John_Carter_Brown_Library/pages/ea_hmpg.html. Accessed 2 February 2009.

The Brockville Cook Book. Brockville, ON: Recorder Printing, 1910.

Brown, Michael F. "Ethnobotany Blues." In *Who Owns Native Culture*, 95–143. Cambridge, MA: Harvard University Press, 2003.

Bumsted, J.M. *A History of the Canadian Peoples*. Second edition. Toronto: Oxford University Press, 2002.

Byles, Mather. *Mather Byles' Letter Books #4*. New Brunswick, circa 1785. *The Winslow Papers*. http://www.lib.unb.ca/winslow/winslowunb.html. Accessed 2 February 2009.

Campbell, Helen G. "For the Thanksgiving Dinner." *Maclean's Magazine*, 1 October 1936.

– "Picnic Suppers." *MacLean's Magazine*, 1930.

– "The Sunday Dinner." *MacLean's Magazine*, 15 May 1931.

– "Supper Dishes." *MacLean's Magazine*, 1 November 1938.

Campbell, Maria. *Halfbreed*. Toronto: McClelland & Stewart, 1973.

Campbell River Museum and Archives. *The Raincoast Kitchen: Coastal Cuisine with a Dash of History*. Madeira Park, BC: Harbour Publishing, 1996.

Canada. Royal Commission on Aboriginal Peoples. *Report of the Royal Commission on Aboriginal Peoples*. Ottawa: Commission, 1996. http://www.ainc-inac.gc.ca/ap/pubs/sg/sg-eng.asp. Accessed 21 February 2009.

"Canada: Sewage Treatment Lacking in Coastal Communities, Report Finds." Vancouver Aquarium. http://www.vanaqua.org/aquanew/fullnews.php?id=1629. Accessed 28 January 2009.

Canada 2006. Calendar. Vancouver, 2005.

Canadian Home Economics Association. *The Laura Secord Canadian Cook Book*. Toronto and Montreal: McClelland & Stewart, 1966.

Canadian Illustrated News, 3 June 1876.

Cappatti, Alberto, and Massimo Montanari. *La cuisine italienne*. 1971. Paris: Éditions Seuil, 2002.

Caraher, Martin, Paul Dixon, Tim Lang, and Roy Carr-Hill. "The State of Cooking in England: The Relationship of Cooking Skills to Food Choice." *British Food Journal* 101, no. 8 (1999): 590–609.

Cardinal, Harold, and Walter Hildebrand. *Treaty Elders of Saskatchewan: Our Dream Is That Our Peoples Will One Day Be Recognized as Nations*. Calgary: University of Calgary Press, 2000.

"Careers and Marriage Don't Mix." *Saturday Night*, 1 November 1949.

Carême, Antonin. *Le pâtisser royal parisien*. Paris: MM éditeurs, 1841.

Caron, Emmelie. *Directions diverses données par la Rev. Mère Caron pour aider ses soeurs à former de bonnes cuisinières*. Montreal, 1878.

Cartier, Jacques. *Bref récit et succincte narration de la navigation faite en 1535 et 1536 par le capitaine Jacques Cartier aux îles de Canada, Hochelaga, Saguenay et autres*. 1545. Paris: Tross, 1863. http://gallica.bnf.fr/ark:/12148/bpt6k1096855/ f111.chemindefer. Accessed 2 February 2009.

– *Relations*. Edited by Michel Bideaux. Collection Bibliothèque du Nouveau Monde. Montreal: Les Presses de l'Université de Montréal, 1986.

– *The Voyages of Jacques Cartier*. Edited by Ramsay Cook. Toronto: University of Toronto Press, 1993.

Cavell, Richard. "The Cultural Production of Canada's Cold War." Introduction to *Love, Hate, and Fear in Canada's Cold War*. Edited by Richard Cavell, 3–32. Toronto: University of Toronto Press, 2004.

Centre for Indigenous Peoples' Nutrition and Environment (CINE). http://www.mcgill.ca/cine/about/. Accessed 20 February 2009.

"Certificate in Food Security." Ryerson University. www.ryerson.ca/foodsecurity/. Accessed 16 February 2009.

Champlain, Samuel de. *Brief Discours*. In *The Works of Samuel de Champlain*. Vol. 1, pt 1. Translated and edited by H.H. Langton under the series editorship of H.P. Biggar. Toronto: Champlain Society, 1922.

– *Narrative of a Voyage to the West Indiens and Mexico in the years 1599–1602*. Edited by Norton Shaw and translated by Alicia Wilmere. London: printed for the Hakluyt Society, 1859. *Early Canadiana Online*. Scott Library, York University.

http://www.canadiana.org/ECO/PageView/33073/0156?id=0fb85d17d4b1c51e. Accessed 3 February 2009.

– *Des Sauvages*. In *The Works of Samuel de Champlain*. Vol. 1, pt 2. Translated and edited by H.H. Langton under the series editorship of H.P. Biggar. Toronto: Champlain Society, 1922.

– *Les Voyages*. 1613. Book 1, 1604–1607. In *The Works of Samuel de Champlain*. Vol. 1, pt 3. Translated and edited by W.F. Ganong under the series editorship of H.P. Biggar. Toronto: Champlain Society, 1922.

– *Les Voyages*. 1613. Book 2, 1608–1612. In *The Works of Samuel de Champlain*. Vol. 2, pt 1. Edited by H.P. Biggar and translated by John Squair. Toronto: Champlain Society, 1925.

– *The Works of Samuel de Champlain*. Vols 1–2. Under the series editorship of H.P. Biggar. Toronto: Champlain Society, 1922 and 1925.

Chapin, Howard Millar. "New England Vessels in the Expedition against Louisbourg, 1745." *New England Historic Genealogical Register* 77, nos 1 and 2 (1923): 59–71, 95–110. Chignecto Project Electronic Edition. http://fortress.uccb.ns.ca/search/Chapin.html. Accessed 3 February 2009.

Chen, Anne Anling. *The Melancholy of Race: Psychoanalysis, Assimilation, and Hidden Grief*. New York: Oxford University Press, 2001.

Chianello, Joanne. "Turkeytime: The Americans Have It Right, Thanksgiving Is the Real Deal." *Ottawa Citizen*, 9 October 2004, L2.

Child, Lydia M. "The New-England Boys Song About Thanksgiving." In *Flowers for Children*, 2:25–8. Boston: J.H. Francis, 1847.

Cho, Lily. "How Taste Remembers Life: Diasporic Memory and Community in Fred Wah's Poetry." In *Culture, Identity, Commodity: Diasporic Literatures in English*. Edited by Tseen Khoo and Kam Louie, 81–106. Hong Kong: Hong Kong University Press, 2005.

Choice Recipes by Miss Maria Parloa and other noted Teachers, Lecturers and Writers. Dorchester, MA: Walter Baker & Co., 1902.

Chow, Rey. *The Protestant Ethnic and the Spirit of Capitalism*. New York: Columbia University Press, 2002.

Choy, Wayson. *The Jade Peony: A Novel*. Vancouver and Toronto: Douglas & McIntyre, 1995.

– *Paper Shadows: A Chinatown Childhood*. Toronto: Viking Canada, 1999.

Clarke, Anne. "Introductory Observations." In *The Eclipse Cook Book*. 1899. Box 9, Glenbow Museum Library, Calgary.

– *Mrs. Clarke's Cookery Book*. Toronto: Grip, 1883.

Clow, Meribeth, Dorothy Duncan, Glenn J. Lockwood, and Lorraine Lowry, eds. *Consuming Passions: Eating and Drinking Traditions in Ontario.* Willowdale, ON: Ontario Historical Society, 1990.

Clusius, Carolus (de l'Écluse, Charles). *Rariorum plantarum historia.* Antwerp: Plantin, 1601. http://caliban.mpiz-koeln.mpg.de/~stueber/ecluse/index.html. Accessed 2 February 2009.

Clutesi, George. *Potlatch.* Sidney, BC: Gray's, 1969.

Coe, Michael D., and Sophie D. Coe. *The True History of Chocolate.* London: Thames & Hudson, 1996.

Coffin, Charles C. *Old Times in the Colonies.* New York: Harper & Brothers, 1881.

Cohen, Leonard. "Democracy." *The Future.* Don Mills: Sony Music Entertainment, 1992.

Cole, Douglas, and Ira Chaikin. *An Iron Hand upon the People: The Law against the Potlatch on the Northwest Coast.* Vancouver: Douglas & MacIntyre, 1990.

Columbus, Christopher. Letter. http://www.usm.maine.edu/~maps/columbus/translation.html. Accessed 2 February 2009.

The Commercial and Home-Canning Possibilities of Mullets. Report 1, Economic Research. Manitoba: University of Manitoba Departments of Political Economy and Home Economics, in cooperation with the Game and Fisheries Branch, Department of Mines and Natural Resources, 1939.

Cook Book. Regina, SK: B.B. Circle of Westminster Church, [1927].

Cook Book. St Thomas, ON: YWCA, 1908.

Cook Book. Winnipeg: Ladies' Aid of First Lutheran Church, [1929].

Cook Book: Tried and Tested Recipes from the Ladies of the Ponass Lake Municipality. Rose Valley, SK: Ladies Hospital Aid, 1938.

The Cook Book of the Creston and District Women's Institute. Creston, BC: 1930.

Cook Book with Special Apple Recipes. Kentville, NS: Ladies' Auxiliary, Kentville Baptist Church, n.d. [1945–49].

The Cook's Friend. Stony Plain, AB: Stony Plain Women's Institute, 1930.

Co-op Cook Book. Saskatchewan: Outlook Women's Co-operative Guild, 1946.

Cormier, Jeffrey. *The Canadianization Movement: Emergence, Survival, and Success.* Toronto: University of Toronto Press, 2004.

Cornut, Jacques-Phillipe. *Canadensium plantarum ... historia.* 1635. New York: Dover, 1966.

Cotter, Colleen. "Claiming a Piece of the Pie: How the Language of Recipes Defines Community." In *Recipes for Reading.* Edited by Anne L. Bower, 51–71. Amherst: University of Massachusetts Press, 1997.

Coulombe, Caroline. "Entre l'art et la science: La littérature culinaire et la transformation des habitudes alimentaires au Québec." *Revue d'histoire de l'Amérique
française* 58, no. 4 (2005): 507–33.

Crosby, Alfred W. *Ecological Imperialism and the Biological Expansion of Europe,
900–1900.* Cambridge: Cambridge University Press, 1986.

La cuisinière canadienne. First edition. Montreal: Louis Perrault, May 1840.

Culhane, Dara. *The Pleasure of the Crown: Anthropology, Law and First Nations.*
Vancouver: Talonbooks, 1998.

Culinary Chronicles 44 (Spring 2005): 8–10.

"Cultural Treasures: Fur Trade at Your Fingertips: Pemmican." *Rocky Mountain
House National Historic Site of Canada.* http://www.pc.gc.ca/lhnnhs/ab/
rockymountain/natcul/natcul09_e.asp. Accessed 28 January 2009.

D'Alembert, Jean le Rond, and Denis Diderot. *Encyclopedie, ou, Dictionnaire
Raisonné des Sciences, des Arts et des Metiers.* Vol. 3. Edited by D'Alembert. Paris:
Briasson, David, LeBreton, Durand, 1753.

Daly, Richard. *Our Box Was Full: An Ethnography for the Delgamuukw Plaintiffs.*
Vancouver: University of British Columbia Press, 2005.

Darrow, George M. *The Strawberry: History, Breeding and Physiology.* New York:
Holt, Rinehart and Winston, 1966.

Dauenhauer, Nora Marks. *Life Woven with Song.* Tucson: University of Arizona
Press, 2000.

David, Elizabeth. "Mad, Bad, Despised and Dangerous." In *The Wilder Shores
of Gastronomy: Twenty Years of Food Writing from the Journal* Petits Propos
Culinaires. Edited by Alan Davidson, 189–95. Berkeley, CA: Ten Speed Press, 2002.

Davidson, Alan. *The Oxford Companion to Food.* Oxford: Oxford University
Press, 1999.

– *The Penguin Companion to Food.* Harmondsworth, UK: Penguin, 2002.

– ed. *The Wilder Shores of Gastronomy: Twenty Years of Food Writing from the
Journal* Petits Propos Culinaires. Berkeley, CA: Ten Speed Press, 2002.

Day, Chester. Personal communication with Shelley Boyd, 26 October 2007.

Day, Paul. "How Losses Occurred." In Canada, Royal Commission on Aboriginal
People, *Report.* Vol. 2, pt 2, chap. 4: "Lands and Resources," pt A, p. 58.
Ottawa: Commission, 1996. Indian and Northern Affairs Canada.
http://www.ainc-inac.gc.ca/ap/pubs/sg/cg/ch4a-eng.pdf. Accessed
21 February 2009.

Debates of the Senate of the Dominion of Canada, 1893, 3rd Session, 7th Parliament.
Ottawa: Dawson, 1893.

de Scudéry, Madeleine. *La Promenade de Versailles*. Edited by Marie-Gabrielle Lallemand. Paris: Champion, 2002.

Desloges, Yvon, and Marc Lafrance. *A Taste of History: The Origins of Quebec's Gastronomy – Goûter à L'histoire: Les Origines de la gastronomie québecoise*. Ottawa: Service canadien des parcs et Les Éditions de la Chenelière, 1989.

Deur, Douglas, and Nancy J. Turner, eds. *Keeping It Living: Traditions of Plant Use and Cultivation on the Northwest Coast of North America*. Seattle: University of Washington Press, 2005.

Dickenson, Victoria. *Drawn from Life: Science and Art in the Portrayal of the New World*. Toronto: University of Toronto Press, 1998.

Dodoens, Rembert. *Cruijdeboeck* (1554), 506–7. http://leesmaar.nl/cruijdeboeck/lr/00497.jpg. Accessed 2 February 2009.

– *A new herbal or Historie of plants* ... Translated by Henry Lyte. London: Edward Griffen, 1619. http://visualiseur.bnf.fr/CadresFenetre?O=NUMM-98774. Accessed 2 February 2009.

Doran, Lori. "Voices from the Field: The First Nations and Inuit Perspective on Nutrition." In *Encyclopedia on Early Childhood Development*. Edited by R.G. Barr, R.E. Tremblay, and R. de V. Peters, 1–4. Montreal: Centre of Excellence for Early Childhood Development, 2004.

Driver, Elizabeth. *Culinary Landmarks: A Bibliography of Canadian Cookbooks, 1825–1949*. Toronto: University of Toronto Press, 2008.

– "Home Cooks, Book Makers and Community Builders in Canada." In *Food, Culture and Community*. Vol. 6, no. 2, of *Moving Worlds: A Journal of Transcultural Writings*. Leeds, UK: School of English, University of Leeds, 2006.

Dugan, James. "How to Tackle That Turkey." *Maclean's Magazine*, 15 December 1951.

Duncan, Dorothy. *Canadians at Table: Food, Fellowship and Folklore – A Culinary History of Canada*. Toronto: Dundurn, 2006.

DuSablon, Mary Anna. *America's Collectible Cookbooks: The History, the Politics, the Recipes*. Athens, OH: Ohio University Press, 1994.

Elder, Alan C. "Canada in the Sixties: 'It Can Do Almost Anything.'" Introduction to *Made in Canada: Craft and Design in the Sixties*. Edited by Alan C. Elder, 3–14. Toronto: Design Exchange, 2005.

Ellingson, Ter. *The Myth of the Noble Savage*. Berkeley: University of California Press, 1999.

Epp, Marlene. "The Semiotics of Zureback: Feast and Famine in the Narratives of Mennonite Refugee Women." *Sisters or Strangers? Immigrant, Ethnic, and Racialized Women in Canadian History*. Edited by Frances Swyripa, Franca Iacovetta, and Marlene Epp, 314–40. Toronto: University of Toronto Press, 2004.

Estienne, Charles, and Jean Liébault. *L'agriculture, et maison rustique.* Paris: Jacques du Pays, 1578. http://visualiseur.bnf.fr/CadresFenetre?O=NUMM-52718. Accessed 2 February 2009.

The Evening Auxiliary Cook Book. Hensall, ON: Hensall United Church, 1952.

Farmer, Paul. *Infections and Inequalities: The Modern Plagues.* Updated edition. Berkeley: University of California Press, 1999.

"Farm Sanctuary's Adopt-A-Turkey Project." Farm Sanctuary. http://www.adoptaturkey.org. Accessed 10 February 2009.

Favoured Foods. Edited by Fireside Group of the Scandinavian Canadian Club of Toronto. Toronto: n.p., n.d.

Fee, Margery. "Racializing Narratives: Obesity, Diabetes, and the 'Aboriginal' Thrifty Genotype." *Social Science and Medicine* 62 (2006): 2988–97.

Fenton, Alexander, and Trefor Owen, eds. *Food in Perspective: Proceedings of the Third International Conference on Ethnological Food Research.* Edinburgh: John Donald, 1981.

Ferguson, Carol, and Margaret Fraser. *A Century of Canadian Home Cooking: 1900 through the '90s.* Scarborough: Prentice-Hall, 1992.

"The First Thanksgiving Day." *New York Times,* 20 November 1921, 87.

Fischler, Claude. "Gastro-nomie et gastro-anomie: Sagesse du corps et crise bio-culturelle de l'alimentation humaine." *Communications* 31 (1979): 189–210.

Fisher, Matthew. "Bernier, Oda Treat Troops with Whirlwind Thanksgiving Visit." *Vancouver Sun,* 8 October 2007, A4.

Fisher, M.F.K. "The Anatomy of a Recipe." In *With Bold Knife and Fork,* 13–24. London: Chatto & Windus, 1983.

Fitzhenry, Maureen. "Prairie farmers caught in EU/US crossfire at WTO." http://www.cwb.ca/public/en/newsroom/releases/2005/110105.jsp. Accessed 3 February 2009.

Five Roses Cook Book: Bread, Pastry, etc. Montreal: Lake of the Woods Milling Co., 1913.

Flaherty, Martha. "I Fought to Keep My Hair." In *Northern Voices: Inuit Writing in English.* Edited by Penny Petrone, 274–8. Toronto University of Toronto Press, 1988.

Flandrin, Jean-Louis. "Dietary Choices and Culinary Technique, 1500–1800." In *A Culinary History from Antiquity to Present.* Translated by Albert Sonnenfeld and edited by Jean-Louis Flandrin and Massimo Montanari, 403–17. New York: Columbia University Press, 1999.

Flandrin, Jean-Louis, and Massimo Montanari, eds. *Food, A Culinary History from Antiquity to Present.* New York: Columbia University Press, 1999.

Folster, David. *Ganong: A Sweet History of Chocolate.* Fredericton, NB: Goose Lane Editions, 2006.

"For These We Offer Thanks." *Chatelaine,* October 1934.

Foster, Nelson, and Linda S. Cordell, eds. *Chilies to Chocolate: Food the Americas Gave the World.* Tucson: University of Arizona Press, 1992.

Fougère, Ruby. Collections technician, Fortress Louisbourg. Personal communication, August 2005.

Franklin, Sir John. *Thirty Years in the Arctic Regions or the Adventures of Sir John Franklin.* New York: George Cooper, 1859.

Freidberg, Susanne. *French Beans and Food Scares: Culture and Commerce in an Anxious Age.* New York: Oxford University Press, 2004.

French, Alice. "My Name Is Masak." In *Northern Voices: Inuit Writing in English.* Edited by Penny Petrone, 203–9. Toronto: University of Toronto Press, 1988.

Freud, Sigmund. "The Uncanny." In *Art and Literature.* Translated by James Strachey and edited by Albert Dickson, 335–76. Penguin Freud Library, no. 14. London: Penguin Books, 1985.

"From the South-Carolina Gazette, March 31. An Account of the Progress of the First Colony Sent to Georgia." *American Mercury,* 17–24 May 1733.

Fuchs, Leonard. "Den nieuwen Herbarius, dat is dat boeck van den cruyden." Basel, 1543. http://caliban.mpiz-koeln.mpg.de/~stueber/fuchs/herbarius/index.html. Accessed 2 February 2009.

Gabaccia, Donna R. *We Are What We Eat: Ethnic Foods and the Making of Americans.* Cambridge, MA: Harvard University Press, 1998.

Gagné, Mme Charles. *Recettes typiques de la Gaspésie et des Îles-de-la-Madeleine.* Montreal: Leméac, 1973.

Gagnon, François-Marc. "Champlain: Painter?" In *Champlain: The Birth of French America.* Translated by Käthe Roth and edited by Raymonde Litalien and Denis Vaugeois, 302–11. Montreal and Kingston: McGill-Queen's University Press and Septentrion, 2004.

Ganong, W.F. "Identity of Plants and Animals mentioned by the early Voyageurs to Eastern Canada and Newfoundland." In *Transactions of the Royal Society of Canada,* 3rd series, vol. 3 (1909): 197–242.

Gerard, John. Excerpts from *Herball or General Historie of Plantes.* Amended and enlarged edition. Edited by Thomas Johnson. London: Adam Islip, John Norton and Richard Whitakers, 1633. http://www.thousandeggs.com/gerardp1.html. Accessed 2 February 2009.

– *The Herball or Generall Historie of Plantes.* London: John Norton, 1597. http://caliban.mpiz-koeln.mpg.de/~stueber/gerarde/high/IMG_0488.html. Accessed 2 February 2009.

Gillingham, Ethel. "The First Thanksgiving." *Beaver* 72, no. 5 (1992): 48.

Gittelsohn, Joel, Stewart B. Harris, Sara Whitehead, Thomas M.S. Woever, Anthony J.G. Hanley, Annette Barnie, Louisa Kakegamic, Alexander Logan, and Bernard Zinman. "Developing Diabetes Interventions in an Ojibwa-Cree Community in Northern Ontario: Linking Qualitative and Quantitative Data." *Chronic Diseases in Canada* 16, no. 4 (1995). http://www.phac-aspc.gc.ca/publicat/cdic-mcc/16-4/ e_ehtml. Accessed January 2009.

Glasse, Hannah. *The Art of Cookery Made Plain and Easy*. 1805. Bedford, MA: Apple Books, Mass Historical Notes, 1997.

Gotlieb, Sondra. *Cross Canada Cooking: Favorite Recipes of Canadians from Many Lands*. Saanichton, BC: Hancock House Publishers, 1976.

– *Cuisine sans frontières: Recettes préférés de canadiens des quatre coins du monde*. Montreal: Pierre Tisseyre, 1977.

– *The Gourmet's Canada*. Toronto: New Press, 1972.

Gottfred, Angela. "Fur Fort Food – Receipts for the Winter." *Northwest Journal* 2 (1994–2002): 10–14. http://www.northwestjournal.ca/II4.htm. Accessed 2 February 2009.

Gottfred, Angela, and Jeff Gottfred. "A Compendium of Material Culture; or, What We Dug Up." *Northwest Journal* 10 (1994–2002): 8–37. http://www.northwestjournal.ca/X2.htm. Accessed 2 February 2009.

Grand Pre [sic] Cook Book. Grand Pré, NS: Ladies' Aid of Grand Pré United Church, 1939.

Grant, Larry. Musqueam First Nation elder and University of British Columbia adjunct professor. Personal communication with Rhona Richman Kenneally.

Green, Carolyn. "Parsing the Demographics, the Trends, the Flow." *Canadian Grocer* 118, no. 6 (2004): 32–5.

Greenblatt, Stephen. *Possessions: The Wonders of the New World*. Chicago: University of Chicago Press, 1991.

Guerin, Delbert. Personal communication.

Gunew, Sneja. *Haunted Nations: The Colonial Dimensions of Multiculturalisms*. London: Routledge, 2004.

– "Retraining Tongues for Eyes: Food Exchanges in the Asian Diaspora." *Yishu: Journal of Contemporary Chinese Art* 3, no. 3 (2004): 62–7.

Haber, Barbara. *From Hardtacks to Homefries: An Uncommon History of American Cooks and Meals*. New York: Free Press, 2002.

Haber, Barbara, and Arlene Voski Avakian. "Feminist Food Studies: A Brief History." In *From Betty Crocker to Feminist Food Studies*, 1–26 Amherst and Boston: University of Massachusetts Press, 2005.

"The Habitat Restoration and Salmon Enhancement Program, Vancouver and South Island." *Fisheries and Oceans Canada.* http://www-comm.pac.dfo-mpo.gc.ca/pages/release/bckgrnd/1999/bg990602_e.htm. Accessed 16 February 2009.

Hale, Edward E. *New England Boyhood.* New York: Cassell Publishing Company, 1893.

Halifax Gazette, 30 March 1752, sec. 2, 2.

Harmsworth Community Cook Book. Virden, M B: Harmsworth Auxiliary, Virden Hospital, 1924.

Harris, Cole. *Making Native Space: Colonialism, Resistance, and Reserves in British Columbia.* Vancouver: University of British Columbia Press, 2002.

Harris, Douglas C. *Fish, Law and Colonialism: The Legal Capture of Salmon in British Columbia.* Toronto: University of Toronto Press, 2001.

Harris, Misty. "We Don't Eat Together, and Are Paying for It." *National Post*, 15 October 2005, A 2.

Head, Francis Bond. *Indian Treaties and Surrenders from 1680 to 1890.* Ottawa: King's Printer, 1905.

Hedrick, U.P. *A History of Agriculture in the State of New York.* New York: New York State Agriculture Society, 1933.

Heiser, Charles B., Jr. *The Sunflower.* Norman: University of Oklahoma, 1976.

Heldke, Lisa. "But Is It Authentic? Culinary Travel and Search for the 'Genuine Article.'" In *The Taste Culture Reader.* Edited by Carolyn Korsmeyer, 385–94. Oxford, U K: Berg, 2005.

Henry, Sally, Lorraine Swirsky, and Carol Taylor. *The Laura Secord Canadian Cook Book.* 1966. Reprint. Toronto: White Cap, 2001.

Herman, David. "Scripts, Sequences, and Stories: Elements of a Postclassical Narratology." *PMLA* 12 (1997): 1046–59.

Hewitt, Steve. "Spying Goes to College." *Beaver* 84, no. 2 (2002): 15–19.

Hickey, Janice. *Faces of Our Farmers: Producers Grin and 'Bare' It for the Future of Agriculture in Prince Edward County.* Calendar. Picton, ON, 2005.

High River Cook Book. High River, A B: Ladies' Aid of Chalmers Church, 1907.

Hobbes, Thomas. *Leviathan: With Selected Variants from the Latin Edition of 1688.* Edited by Edwin Curley. 1688. Reprint, Cambridge: Hackett, 1994.

Hobsbawm, Eric, and Terence Ranger, eds. *The Invention of Tradition.* New York: Cambridge University Press, 1983.

Hoffman, Frances, and Ryan Taylor, eds. *Much to Be Done: Private Life in Ontario from Victorian Diaries.* Second edition. Toronto: Natural Heritage, 2007.

"Holidays." *Canadian Encyclopedia Online.* http://www.thecanadianencyclopedia.com. Accessed 10 February 2009.

The Home Cook Book. Toronto: Belford Brothers, 1877.

The Home Cook Book. Saint John, NB: Morrow, 1878.

"The Housewife's Business." *Saturday Night,* 7 November 1914.

Hucks, M. Frances. "Supper Dishes." *Maclean's Magazine,* 15 November 1934.

Hulme, Peter. *Colonial Encounters: Europe and the Native Caribbean, 1492–1797.* London: Methuen, 1986.

Iacovetta, Franca. *Such Hardworking People: Italian Immigrants in Postwar Toronto.* Montreal and Kingston: McGill-Queen's University Press, 1993.

Indigenous Peoples Council on Biocolonialism. http://www.ipcb.org. Accessed 16 February 2009.

Inness, Sherrie A. *Cooking Lessons: The Politics of Gender and Food.* Lanham, MD: Rowman & Littlefield, 2001.

– *Dinner Roles: American Women and Culinary Culture.* Iowa City: University of Iowa Press, 2001.

– ed. *Kitchen Culture in America: Popular Representations of Food, Gender, and Race.* Philadelphia: University of Pennsylvania Press, 2001.

– *Secret Ingredients: Race, Gender, and Class at the Dinner Table.* New York: Palgrave Macmillan, 2006.

Innis, Harold. *Staples, Markets and Cultural Change.* Edited by Daniel Drache. Montreal: McGill-Queen's University Press, 1995.

Institut de tourisme et d'hôtellerie du Québec. *Vers une nouvelle cuisine québécoise.* Quebec City: Éditeur officiel du Québec, 1977.

International Cook Book. Arvida, QC: Women's Association of Arvida, First United Church, 1939.

IODE (International Order of Daughters of the Empire), Armistice Chapter, Calgary. *The Modern Cook Book.* Calgary: IODE, Armistice Chapter, Calgary, 1923.

Ireland, Lynne. "The Compiled Cookbook as Foodways Autobiography." In *The Taste of American Place: A Reader on Regional and Ethnic Foods.* Edited by Barbara G. Shortridge and James R. Shortridge, 111–17. Lanham, MD: Rowman and Littlefield, 1998.

Islander. 14 December 1855. *Atlantic Canada Newspaper Survey.* Canadian Heritage Online Reference Library. 871478PS. http://daryl.chin.gc.ca:8000/BASIS/acns/user/www/sf. Accessed 3 February 2009.

James, Allison. "Identity and the Global Stew." In *The Taste Culture Reader.* Edited by Carolyn Korsmeyer, 372–84. Oxford, UK: Berg, 2005.

Janick, Jules, and Harry S. Paris. "Early Evidence for the Culinary Use of Squash Flowers in Italy." http://www.hort.purdue.edu/newcrop/Squash_flowers.pdf. Accessed 2 February 2009.

Journal and Proceedings of the House of Assembly of the Province of Nova Scotia. Halifax, 1839.

Journal of Health 22 (1876): 10.

Jubilee Cook Book. Charlottetown, PEI: Ladies' Aid Society of First Methodist Church, 1897.

Jubilee Cook Book. Rossland, BC: Women's Association, St Andrew's United Church, 1947.

Kaplan, Harvey A. "The Psychopathology of Nostalgia." *Psychoanalytic Review* 74, no. 4 (1987): 465–86.

Karr, Clarence. "Writers and the Market for Non-Fiction." In *History of the Book in Canada, 1918–1980.* Vol. 3. Edited by Carole Gerson and Jacques Michon, 138–42. Toronto: University of Toronto Press, 2007.

Kaufmann, Jean-Claude. *Casseroles, amour et crises: Ce que cuisiner veut dire.* N.p.: Armand Colin, 2005.

Kiefer, Heather Mason. "Empty Seats: Fewer Families Eat Together." *Gallup Poll.* http://www.gallup.com/poll/10336/Empty-Seats-Fewer-Families-Eat-Together.aspx. Accessed 20 February 2009.

King, Caroline H. *When I Lived in Salem, 1822–1866.* Brattleboro, VT: Stephen Day Press, 1937.

Kiple, Kenneth F., and Kriemhild C. Ornelas, eds. *The Cambridge World History of Food.* 2 vols. Cambridge, UK: Cambridge University Press, 2000.

Kittler, Pamela Goyan, and Kathryn Sucher. *Food and Culture in America: A Nutrition Handbook.* New York: Van Nostrand Reinhold, 1989.

Knudsen, E. Eric, and Donald Macdonald, eds. *Sustainable Fisheries Management: Pacific Salmon.* Boca Raton, FL: Lewis, 2000.

Krech, Shepard. *The Ecological Indian: Myth and History.* New York: Norton, 1999.

Kuffert, L.B. *A Great Duty: Canadian Responses to Modern Life and Mass Culture, 1939–1967.* Montreal and Kingston: McGill-Queen's University Press, 2003.

Kuhnlein, Harriet V. "Global Nutrition and the Holistic Environment of Indigenous Peoples." In *The Path to Healing: Report of the National Round Table on Health and Social Issues.* Ottawa: Royal Commission on Aboriginal Peoples, Minister of Supply and Services, 1993.

Kuhnlein, Harriet V., and Nancy J. Turner. *Traditional Plant Foods of Indigenous Peoples: Nutrition, Botany and Use.* Philadelphia: Gordon, 1991.

Kuhnlein, Harriet V., et al. "Arctic Indigenous Peoples Experience the Nutrition Transition with Changing Dietary Patterns and Obesity." *Journal of Nutrition* 134 (2004): 1447–53.

Kwan, Cheuk. "Canada: New Outlook Café; Paper Son; Family and Death." Disc 3 (Three Continents). *Chinese Restaurants*. DVD. Tissa Films, 2005.

Kwong, Kylie. *Recipes and Stories*. Victoria: Penguin, 2003.

Lambert, Carole, ed. *Du manuscrit à la table: Essais sur la cuisine au Moyen âge et Répertoire des manuscrits médiévaux contenant des recettes culinaires* Montreal: Les Presses de l'Université de Montréal, 1992.

Lambert, Michel. *La cuisine familiale au Québec*. Vol. 2. Quebec City: Éditions GID, 2006.

Langdon, John E. *Canadian Silversmiths: 1700–1900*. Toronto: Stinehour Press, 1966.

Large, Michael. "A Flag for Canada." In *Made in Canada: Craft and Design in the Sixties*. Edited by Alan C. Elder, 40–50. Montreal and Kingston: McGill-Queen's University Press, 2005.

Larson, Ronald B. "When Is Dinner?" *Journal of Food Distribution Research* 33, no. 3 (2002): 38–45.

Latour, Bruno. *We Have Never Been Modern*. Translated by Catherine Porter. Cambridge, MA: Harvard University Press, 1993.

Lawson, Mary Jane K. *History of the Townships of Dartmouth, Preston, and Lawrencetown; Halifax Country, N.S.* Edited by Harry Piers. Halifax: Morton and Co., 1893.

LeCroy, Anne. "Cookery Literature – Or Literary Cookery." In *Cooking by the Book*, 7–24. Bowling Green, OH: Bowling Green State University Press, 1989.

Leir, Cliff. Personal communication with author, spring 2005.

Leonardi, Susan J. "Recipes for Reading: Summer Pasta, Lobster à la Riseholme, and Key Lime Pie." *PMLA* 104, no. 3 (1989): 340–7.

Lescarbot, Marc. *History of New France*. Translated by W.L. Grant. Toronto: Champlain Society, 1914.

Levenstein, Harvey. *Paradox of Plenty: A Social History of Eating in Modern America*. New York: Oxford University Press, 1993.

– *Revolution at the Table: The Transformation of the American Diet*. New York: Oxford University Press, 1988.

Lévi-Strauss, Claude. *Le cru et le cuit*. Vol. 1, *Mythologiques*. [Paris]: Plon, 1964.

Leyendecker, J.C. "Pilgrim Stalking Tom Turkey." *Saturday Evening Post*, 23 November 1907, cover.

Li, Peter. *The Chinese in Canada*. Toronto: Oxford University Press, 1988.

Library and Archives Canada. "Revolutions in the Kitchen." In *Bon Appétit: A Celebration of Canadian Cookbooks*. http://collectionscanada.ca/cuisine/002001-5060-e.html. Accessed 5 February 2009.

Litalien, Raymonde, and Denis Vaugeois, eds. *Champlain: The Birth of French America*. Montreal and Kingston: McGill-Queen's University Press and Septentrion, 2004.

Locke, John. *The Second Treatise of Government and A Letter Concerning Toleration*. 1690. Mineola, NY: Dover, 2002.

Love, W. DeLoss, Jr. *The Fast and Thanksgiving Days of New England*. Boston: Houghton, Mifflin and Co., 1895.

Lucas, Fiona. "'The Condition of Turkey will be Seriously Considered by Canadians Today.'" *Food History News* 18 (2006): 5–8.

– *Hearth and Home: Women and the Art of Open-Hearth Cooking*. Toronto: James Lorimer and Co., 2006.

Lux, Maureen. *Medicine That Walks: Disease, Medicine, and Canadian Plains Native People, 1880–1940*. Toronto: University of Toronto Press, 2001.

McAnn, Aida. *The New Brunswick Cook Book*. Sackville, NB: Tribune Printing Co. Ltd, [1938].

McCue, George Allen. "The History and Use of the Tomato: An Annotated Bibliography." *Annals of the Missouri Botanical Garden* 39, no. 4 (November 1952): 289–348.

McDougall, Elizabeth J. "Voices, Stories, and Recipes in Selected Canadian Community Cookbooks." In *Recipes for Reading: Community Cookbooks, Stories, Histories*. Edited by Anne L. Bower, 105–17. Amherst: University of Massachusetts Press, 1997.

McFarlane, Scott Toguri. "Eating in the 'Hot Box' of Biotechnology." *Public* 30 (Winter 2004): 146–62.

McGee, Diane. *Writing the Meal: Dinner in the Fiction of Early Twentieth-Century Women Writers*. Toronto: University of Toronto Press, 2001.

McGee, Harold. *On Food and Cooking: The Science and Lore of the Kitchen*. Revised edition. New York: Scribner, 2004.

McIntosh, Elaine N. *American Food Habits in Historical Perspective*. Westport, CT: Praeger, 1995.

Mack. "The Thanksgiving Turkey." *Saturday Night*, 12 November 1892.

[McMicking, Mrs Robert Burns.] *The King's Daughters Cookery Book*. Victoria, BC, 1904.

Macpherson, Estelle C. "Warm Dinners for Hot Weather Evenings." *MacLean's Magazine*, 15 June 1926.

Maffi, Luisa. *On Biocultural Diversity: Linking Language, Knowledge and the Environment*. Washington, DC: Smithsonian Institution, 2001.

Magee, Paul. "Foreign Cookbooks." *Postcolonial Studies* 8, no. 1 (2005): 3–18.

Mäkelä, Johanna. "Cultural Definitions of the Meal." In *Dimensions of the Meal: The Science, Culture, Business, and Art of Eating*. Edited by Herbert L. Meiselman, 7–18. Gaithersburg, MD: Aspen, 2000.

Manuel de cuisine raisonnée adapté aux élèves des cours élémentaires de l'École normale classico-ménagère de Saint-Pascal. Quebec City: Imprimerie l'action sociale ltée, 1919.

The Maple Leaf Cook Book. Kimberly, ON: Kimberly Women's Institute, n.d.

Maritime Merchant – Maritime Grocer and Commercial Review, 12 January 1893. Nova Scotia Archives and Records Management.

Marks, Jonathan. "A Human Gene Museum?" In *What It Means to be 98% Chimpanzee: Apes, Humans and Their Genes*, 198–218. Berkeley: University of California Press, 2002.

Marks, Susan. *Finding Betty Crocker: The Secret Life of America's First Lady of Food*. Minneapolis: University of Minnesota Press, 2005.

Marling, Karal Ann. "Betty Crocker's Picture Cook Book: The Aesthetics of Food in the 1950s." In *As Seen on T.V.: The Visual Culture of Everyday Life in the 1950s*, 202–41. Cambridge, MA: Harvard University Press, 1996.

Martellotti, Anna. "The Parmesan Pie." *Petit Propos Culinaires* 59 (1998): 7–14.

Martin, Joseph P. *Private Yankee Doodle: Being a Narrative of Some of the Adventures, Dangers, and Sufferings of a Revolutionary Soldier*. Boston: Little, Brown and Co., 1962.

Martin, Paul. "Letter to the General Public." *M&M Meat Shops*. 2005. http://www.mmmeatshops.com/en/aboutmm/mediaroom/pdf/ Prime%20Minister%20Paul%20Martin.pdf. Accessed 30 January 2009.

Martin, Paul-Louis. "Domestication of the Countryside and Provision of Supplies." In *Champlain: The Birth of French America*. Translated by Käthe Roth and edited by Raymonde Litalien and Denis Vaugeois, 205–17. Montreal and Kingston: McGill-Queen's University Press and Septentrion, 2004.

Mason, Laura, and Catherine Brown. *Traditional Food in Britain*. Devon, UK: Prospect Books, 1999.

Mathieu, Jacques, and André Daviault. *Le premier livre de plantes du Canada: Les enfants des bois du Canada au jardin du roi à Paris en 1635*. Quebec City: Les Presses de l'Université Laval, 1998.

Medsger, Oliver Perry. *Edible Wild Plants*. 1939. Reprint, New York: Collier, 1966.

Mennell, Stephen. *All Manners of Food: Eating and Taste in England and France from the Middle Ages to the Present*. Glasgow: Basil Blackwell, 1985.

Menu of La Toundra Restaurant, Canada Pavilion, Expo 67. Fonds Gilberte Christin de Cardaillac. P573/D02. McCord Museum, Montreal.

Meriwether, Louis. "Excerpts from the Journals of Lewis and Clark." *Discovering Lewis and Clark*. http://www.lewis-clark.org/content/content-article.asp?ArticleID=2163. Accessed 2 February 2009.

"A Merry Ode for Thanksgiving." *Norwich Packet*, 1 December 1801, 4.

Miller, Stephen. *Stephen Miller's Letter Books, #1, 1759–1782*. New Brunswick, 1759. In *The Winslow Papers Collection*. http://www.lib.unb.ca/winslow/winslowunb.html. Accessed 3 February 2009.

Milloy, John. *A National Crime: The Canadian Government and the Residential School System, 1879–1986*. Winnipeg: University of Manitoba Press, 1999.

Mills, Antonia. *Eagle Down is Our Law: Witsuwit'en Law, Feasts and Land Claims*. Vancouver: University of British Columbia Press, 1994.

Mintz, Sidney. "Eating American." In *Food in the USA: A Reader*. Edited by Carole M. Counihan, 23–33. New York: Routledge, 2002.

– *Sweetness and Power: The Place of Sugar in Modern History*. New York: Viking, 1986.

"Mission to Grassy Narrows." *Amnesty International*. http://www.amnesty.ca/grassy_narrows. Accessed 28 January 2009.

"MLA in Gastronomy." *Boston University*. http://www.bu.edu/met/adult_college_programs/graduate_school_program/post_graduate_degree/food_science_degree/index.html. Accessed 28 January 2009.

"M&M Meat Shops Hosts National Family Dinner Night." *M&M Meat Shops*. http://www.mmmeatshops.com/en/aboutmm/mediaroom/fall2005_dinner.asp. Accessed 16 February 2009.

The Modern Cook Book for New Brunswick. Saint John, NB: Women's Hospital Aids of the Province of New Brunswick and L'Assomption Society of Moncton, 1920.

Modern Guide to Home Canning. Wallaceburg, ON: National Pressure Cooker Co. (Canada), c. 1947.

Modern Household Cookery Book. Vancouver: Vancouver Gas Co. Ltd, [1909].

Moirs Limited Fonds, 1866–1966, 1-91, 1-71. Nova Scotia Archives and Records Management.

Moisio, Risto, Eric J. Arnould, and Linda L. Price. "Between Mothers and Markets." *Journal of Consumer Culture* 4, no. 3 (2004): 361–84.

Monardes, Nicolás. *Brief traité de la racine mechoacan, venue de l'Espagne nouvelle: Médecine très excellente du corps humain, blasonnée en maintes régions la reubarbe des Indes*. Translated by J.P. Gohory. Rouen: Chex Martin et Honoré Mallard, 1588. http://visualiseur.bnf.fr/CadresFenetre?O=NUMM-53997. Accessed 2 February 2009.

– *Joyfull newes out of the newe founde worlde...* Translated by John Frampton. New York: AMS, 1967.

Moodie, Susanna. *Roughing It in the Bush; or, Life in Canada.* 1852. Reprint, Toronto: McClelland & Stewart, 1989.

Moore Park Big Sister Circle Cook Book. Toronto: Moore Park Circle of the Big Sister Association, 1925.

Moran, Bridget. *Stoney Creek Woman: The Story of Mary John.* 1988. New edition, Vancouver: Arsenal Pulp, 1997.

Morantz, Toby. "Pratiques religieuses des Cris de la Baie de James aux XVIIIe et XIXe siècles (d'après les Europeans)." *Recherches Amerindiennes au Québec* 8, no. 2 (1978): 115–22.

Morton, Desmond, ed. *The Queen vs. Louis Riel.* Toronto: University of Toronto Press, 1974.

Morton, Mark. "Dinner." In *Cupboard Love: A Dictionary of Culinary Curiosities*, 111. Toronto: Insomniac Press, 2004.

Mosco, Vincent. *The Political Economy of Communication.* Thousand Oaks, CA: Sage Publications, 1996.

Mowat, Farley. *The Desperate People.* New York: Bantam-Seal, 1975.

– *People of the Deer.* Boston: Little, Brown, 1952.

Muoio, Anna. "We all go to the same place. Let us go there slowly." *Fast Company Magazine*, 2000.

My Pet Recipes. Quebec City: St Andrew's Church, 1900.

Nabhan, Gary. *Coming Home to Eat: The Pleasures and Politics of Local Foods.* New York: Norton, 2002.

– *The Desert Smells Like Rain: A Naturalist in O'odham country.* Tucson: University of Arizona Press, 1982.

Nandy, Ashis. "The Changing Popular Culture of Indian Food: Preliminary Notes." *South Asia Research* 24, no. 1 (2004): 9–19.

Neering, Rosemary. *The Canadian Housewife: An Affectionate History.* North Vancouver: Whitecap, 2005.

Neeson, J.M. *Commoners: Common Right, Enclosure and Social Change in Common-Field England, 1700–1820.* New York: Cambridge University Press, 1993.

Nettles, Daniel, and Suzanne Romaine. *Vanishing Voices: The Extinction of the World's Languages.* Oxford: Oxford University Press, 2000.

Neuhaus, Jessamyn. *Manly Meals and Mom's Home Cooking: Cookbooks and Gender in Modern America.* Baltimore, London: Johns Hopkins University Press, 2003.

Nightingale, Marie. *Out of Old Nova Scotia Kitchens: A Collection of Traditional Recipes of Nova Scotia and the Story of the People Who Cooked Them.* Toronto: Pagurian Press, 1971; New York: Scribner, 1971.

La Nouvelle Cuisinière Canadienne. First edition. Montreal: Louis Perrault, Rue Ste Thérèse, 1850.

Nylander, Jane C. *Our Own Snug Fireside: Images of the New England Home 1760–1860.* New Haven, CT: Yale University Press, 1994.

Oliver, Margo. *The Good Food Cook Book.* Montreal: Tormont, 1993.

– "Man and His Menu." *Weekend Magazine,* 22 April 1967.

Oliver, Sandra L. *Saltwater Foodways: New Englanders and Their Food at Sea and Ashore, in the 19th Century.* Mystic, CT: Mystic Seaport Museum, 1995.

Ondaatje, Christopher. Preface to *The Canadiana Cookbook: A Complete Heritage of Canadian Cooking.* By Jehane Benoît. Toronto: Pagurian Press, 1970.

Ostry, Aleck Samuel. *Nutrition Policy in Canada, 1870–1939.* Vancouver: University of British Columbia Press, 2006.

Our Best Recipes. Montreal: Montreal Amateur Athletic Association, 1925.

Our Favourite Recipes. Kitchener, ON: St Matthew's Missionary Church, 1940.

"Our most neglected treasure." *Maclean's Magazine,* 29 September 1956.

Owram, Doug. *Born at the Right Time: A History of the Baby-Boom Generation.* Toronto: University of Toronto Press, 1996.

"Oxford Symposium on Food & Cookery." http://www.oxfordsymposium.org.uk/. Accessed 16 February 2009.

Paris, Harry S. "History of the Cultivar-Groups of Cucurbita pepo." *Horticulture Reviews* 25 (2001): 71–170.

Parker, Kaye, ed. *From the Kitchens of Kings Landing.* "Christmas in the Valley" edition. Fredricton, BC: Kings Landing, 1989.

Parkinson, John. *Paradisi in paradisus terrestris.* London: Humfrey Lownes and Robert Young, 1629. http://visualiseur.bnf.fr/CadresFenetre?O=NUMM-97995. Accessed 2 February 2009.

– *Paradisi in Sole. Paradisus Terrestris. Or, a choise garden of all sorts of rarest flowers, with their nature, place of birth, time of flowring, names, and vertues to each plant, useful in physick, or admired for beauty.* London: printed by R.N., sold by Richard Thrale, 1656. http://www.abocamuseum.it/bibliothecaantiqua/ Book_View.asp?Id_Book=458. Accessed Accessed 2 February 2009.

Pattinson, Nellie Lyle. *Canadian Cook Book.* Toronto: Ryerson Press, 1923.

– *Nellie Lyle Pattinson's Canadian Cook Book.* Edited by Helen Wattie and Elinor Donaldson. Toronto: Ryerson Press, 1953.

Penfold, Steve. *The Donut: A Canadian History.* Toronto: University of Toronto Press, 2008.

– "Eddie Shack Was No Tim Horton: Donuts and the Folklore of Mass Culture in Canada." In *Food Nations: Selling Taste in Consumer Societies.* Edited by Warren Belasco and Philip Scranton, 48–66. New York: Routledge, 2002.

Perkins, Simeon. *Diary of Simeon Perkins, 1797–1803*. Edited by Charles Bruce Fergusson. Toronto: Champlain Society, 1967.

Petrini, Carlo. *Slow Food: The Case for Taste*. New York: Columbia University Press, 2003.

Petrinovich, Lewis. *The Cannibal Within*. New York: Aldine de Gruyter, 2000.

Pilcher, Jeffrey M. "Recipes for Patria: Cuisine, Gender, and Nation in Nineteenth-Century Mexico." In *Recipes for Reading: Community Cookbooks, Stories, Histories*. Edited by Anne L. Bower, 200–15. Amherst: University of Massachusetts Press, 1997.

"Pilgrim Pageant." *New York Times*, 27 December 1920, 8.

The P.L.A. Cook Book. St John's, NL: Ladies' Aid Society of St Andrew's Presbyterian Church, 1925.

Pleck, Elizabeth. "The Making of the Domestic Occasion: The History of Thanksgiving in the United States." *Journal of Social History* 32 (1999): 780–1.

Pope, Peter. *Fish into Wine. The Newfoundland Plantations in the 17th Century*. Chapel Hill: University of North Carolina Press, 2004.

Pothier, Bernard. "Le Moyne D'Iberville, Pierre." *Dictionary of Canadian Biography Online* (2000). http://www.biographi.ca/EN/ShowBio.asp?BioId=35062&query=Pierre%20AND%20Le%20AND%20Moyne%20AND%20D'Ibervill. Accessed 3 February 2009.

Poudrier, Jennifer. "Racial Categories and Health Risks: Epidemiological Surveillance Among Canadian First Nations." In *Surveillance as Social Sorting: Privacy, Risk and Digital Discrimination*. Edited by David Lyon, 111–34. London: Routledge, 2003.

Poulain, Jean-Pierre. *Manger aujourd'hui : Attitudes, normes et pratiques*. Paris: Éditions Privat, 2002.

Powers, Jo Marie, ed. *Buon appetito! Italian foodways in Ontario*. Toronto: Ontario Historical Society, 2000.

– *From Cathay to Canada: Chinese Cuisine in Transition*. Toronto: Ontario Historical Society, 1998.

Powers, Jo Marie, and Anita Stewart, eds. *Northern Bounty: A Celebration of Canadian Cuisine*. Toronto: Random House of Canada, 1995.

Pringle, James S. "How 'Canadian' is Cornut's Canadensium Plantarum Historia? A Phytogeographic and Historical Analysis." *Canadian Horticultural History* 1, no. 4 (1988): 190–209.

"Proclamation and Observance of General Thanksgiving Days and Reasons Therefore." Canadian Heritage. Government of Canada. http://www.pch.gc.ca/pgm/ceem/cced/jfa-ha/graces-eng.cfm. Accessed 5 February 2009.

Quill Lake Homemakers' Club Cook Book. Quill Lake, SK: Homemakers' Club, n.d.

Quinepenon. Speech of Chief Quinepenon. 6 September 1806. Library and Archives Canada, RG10, 27. Quoted in Royal Commission on Aboriginal People, *Report*, vol. 2, pt 2, chap. 4: "Lands and Resources," pt A, p. 58. Ottawa: Commission, 1996. Indian and Northern Affairs Canada. http://www.ainc-inac.gc.ca/ap/pubs/sg/cg/ch4c-eng.pdf. Accessed 20 February 2009.

Rabisha, William. *The Whole Body of Cookery Dissected.* 1682. Facsimile edition. Devon: Prospect Books, 2003.

Rappaport, Leon. *How We Eat: Appetite, Culture and the Psychology of Food.* Toronto: ECW Press, 2003.

Rasky, Frank. "The Wondrous Fair: The Tastes." *Gazette* (Montreal), 17 June 1967, 6–9.

Ray, Arthur J. *I Have Lived Here since Time Began: An Illustrated History of Canada's Native People.* Toronto: Lester/Key Porter, 1996.

Rebora, Giovanni. *Culture of the Fork: A Brief History of Food in Europe.* Translated by Albert Sonnenfeld. New York: Columbia University Press, 2001.

Recipes. Toronto: Ladies' Aid Society of Broadway Tabernacle, 1900.

Regan, Nellie. "After-the-Show Suppers." *MacLean's Magazine*, 1 April 1926.

Régnier, Faustine. "Le monde au bout des fourchettes: Le voyage dans l'exotisme culinaire." http://www.lemangeur-ocha.com/uploads/tx_smilecontenusocha/Regnier_Exotisme_culinaire.pdf. Accessed 5 February 2009.

Reid, Ruth D. "Planning the Christmas Dinner." *Chatelaine*, December 1929.

Rempel, Sharon. "Heritage Wheat Project." Old Wheats Home Page. http://members.shaw.ca/oldwheat/oldwheats.html. Accessed 10 April 2003. No longer accessible.

Renouf, Ethel. *The "Black Whale" Cook Book: Fine Old Recipes from the Gaspé Coast Going Back to Pioneer Days.* Montreal: Gnaedinger Printing Co., 1948.

Répertoire des Expo 67 Restaurants Review. Montreal: Apex Press, 1967.

Richards, Henry Ilett, and Elizabeth Richards. *The Canadian Housewife's Manual of Cookery Compiled from the best English, French and American works.* Hamilton, CW: William Gillespie, 1861.

Richardson, Boyce. *Strangers Devour the Land.* Post Mills, VT: Chelsea Green, 1991.

Roberts, Charles G.D. *By the Marshes of Minas.* Toronto: Biggs, 1900.

Robertson, James. *American Myth, American Reality.* New York: Hill and Wang, 1980.

Roberval, Sieur de. "Le voyage de Jean-François de La Rocque, chevalier, seigneur de Roberval, au pays de Canada, Saguenay et Hochelaga … 1542." In *Jacques Cartier, Voyages au Canada, Avec les relations des voyages en Amérique de Gonneville,*

Verrazano et Roberval. Edited by R. Herval, Ch-A. Julien, and Th. Beauchesne. Paris: François Maspero, 1981.

Robinson, Eden. *Monkey Beach.* Toronto: Knopf, 2000.

Roche, Judith, and Meg McHutchison, eds. *First Fish, First People: Salmon Tales of the North Pacific Rim.* Vancouver: University of British Columbia Press, 1998.

Roe, F.G. *The North American Buffalo: A Critical Study of the Species in Its Wild State.* Second edition. Toronto: University of Toronto Press, 1970.

Rousseau, Jacques. "L'annedda et l'arbre de vie." *Revue de l'histoire de l'Amérique française* 8, no. 2 (September 1954): 171–212.

Rousseau, Jean-Jacques. *A Discourse on Inequality.* Translated by Maurice Cranston. London: Penguin, 1984.

Roy, M. l'Abbé E. *Sermon prononcé dans l'eglise de Ste-Marie de la beauce.* Quebec City: Brousseau, 1888.

Royal Gazette and Newfoundland Advertiser, 26 October 1815. Canadian Heritage Online Reference Library. Atlantic Canada Newspaper Survey. 005773. http://daryl.chin.gc.ca:8000/BASIS/acns/user/www/sf. Accessed 2 February 2009.

Royal Victoria Cook Book. Barrie, ON: Woman's Auxiliary to the Royal Victoria Hospital, 1900.

Sainte-Marie-Edith, Soeur. *The Secrets of Good Cooking.* Montreal: Canadian Printing and Lithographing Company, 1928.

St. Henry's Jubilee Cook Book 1908–1938. Melville, SK: Ladies Altar Society, St Henry's Church, 1938.

Salaman, Redcliffe. *The History and Social Influence of the Potato.* 1949. Revised edition. Cambridge: Cambridge University Press, 2000.

– "Why 'Jerusalem' Artichoke?" *Journal of the Royal Horticultural Society* 65 (1940): 338–83.

Sanders, Byrne H. "To the Chatelaines of Canada." *Chatelaine,* December 1929.

Santino, Jack. *All Around the Year: Holidays and Celebration in American Life.* Urbana: University of Illinois Press, 1994.

"Savannah." *New-England Journal,* 22 October 1733.

Schauffler, Robert H., ed. *Thanksgiving; its Origin, Celebration and Significance as Related in Prose and Verse.* New York: Moffat, Yard & Co., 1907.

Scheer, Hermann. "Region Is Reason." In *Slow Food: Collected Thoughts on Taste, Tradition and the Honest Pleasures of Food.* Edited by Carlo Petrini and Ben Watson, 7–11. White River Junction, VT: Slow Food Editor/Chelsea Green Publishing Company, 2001.

Scholes, Robert, and Robert Kellogg. *The Nature of Narrative*. New York: Oxford University Press, 1966.

Scott, David B. *A School History of the United States, from the Discovery of America to the Year 1870*. New York: Harper & Brothers, 1874.

Segers, Yves. "Food Recommendations, Tradition, and Change in a Flemish Cookbook: Ons Kookboek, 1920–2000." *Appetite* 45 (2005): 4–14.

Selected Recipes. London, ON: Women's Association, Metropolitan United Church, 1929.

Shakespeare, William. *The Tempest*. Edited by Stephen Orgel. Oxford Oxford University Press, 1987.

Shapiro, Anna. *A Feast of Words*. New York: W.W. Norton and Co., 1996.

Shapiro, Laura. *Perfection Salad-Women and Cooking at the Turn of the Century*. New York : Farrar, Straus, and Giroux, 1986.

– *Something from the Oven: Reinventing Dinner in 1950s America*. New York: Viking, 2004.

Shkilnyk, Anastasia M. *A Poison Stronger Than Love: The Destruction of an Ojibwa Community*. New Haven, CT: Yale University Press, 1985.

Shun-Wa, Annette, and Greg Aitkin. *Banquet: Ten Courses to Harmony*. Sydney, Australia: Doubleday, 1999.

Simmons, Amélia. *The First American Cookbook*. 1796. Facsimile edition. New York: Oxford University Press, 1958.

Siskind, Janet. "The Invention of Thanksgiving: A Ritual of American Nationality." *Critique of Anthropology* 12 (1992): 182–3, 186.

Skutnabb-Kangas, Tove, Luisa Maffi, and David Harmon. *Sharing a World of Difference: The Earth's Linguistic, Cultural and Biological Diversity*. Paris: UNESCO, 2003.

Sloan, Elizabeth A. "Top 10 Functional Food Trends." *Food Technology* 4 (2006): 22–40.

Smith, Helen E. *Colonial Days and Ways as Gathered from Family Papers*. New York: Century Co., 1900.

Spry, Irene M. "The Tragedy of the Loss of the Commons in Western Canada." In *As Long as the Sun Shines and Water Flows: A Reader in Canadian Native Studies*. Edited by Ian A.L. Getty and Antoine S. Lussier, 203–27. Vancouver: University of British Columbia Press, 1983.

Staebler, Edna. *Food That Really Schmecks: Mennonite Country Cooking*. Commemorative edition. Waterloo, ON: Wilfrid Laurier University Press, 2006.

– *Food That Really Schmecks: Mennonite Country Cooking as Prepared by My Mennonite Friend, Bevvy Martin, My Mother and Other Fine Cooks*. Montreal: McGraw-Hill, 1968.

"The State of Canada's Environment, 1995." Environment Canada. http://www.ec.gc.ca/soer-ree/English/soer/1996Report/Doc/1-6-6-5-5-3-1.cfm. Accessed 28 January 2009.

Stewart, Anita. *Anita Stewart's Canada*. Toronto: HarperCollins, 2008.

– *The Flavours of Canada: A Celebration of the Finest Regional Foods*. Vancouver: Raincoast Books, 2000.

Stewart, Susan. *On Longing: Narratives of the Miniature, the Gigantic, the Souvenir, the Collection*. Durham, NC: Duke University Press, 1993.

Stowe, Harriet B. *Oldtown Folks*. Boston: Houghton, Osgood and Company, 1878.

Suttles, Wayne. "Coast Salish Resource Management: Incipient Agriculture?" In *Keeping It Living: Traditions of Plant Use and Cultivation on the Northwest Coast of North America*. Edited by Douglas Deur and Nancy J. Turner, Coast Salish Resource Management, 181–93. Seattle: University of Washington Press, 2005.

Symko, Stephan. "From a Single Seed: Tracing the Marquis Wheat Success Story in Canada to Its Roots in the Ukraine." Agriculture and Agri-Food Canada (1999). http://www4.agr.gc.ca/AAFC-AA/display-afficer.do?id=1181389481go. Accessed 3 February 2009.

Symons, Michael. "Grandmas to Gourmets: The Revolution of 1963." *Food, Culture and Society* 9, no. 2 (Summer 2006): 179–200.

Taylor, Timothy. *Stanley Park*. Toronto: Vintage Canada, 2001.

Tested Recipes. Edited by St Josaphat's Ladies' Auxiliary. Edmonton: St Josaphat's Ladies' Auxiliary, [1941].

Tested Recipes. Aldershot, ON: East Plains United Church, n.d.

Tester, Frank James, and Peter Kulchyski. *Tammarniit (Mistakes): Inuit Relocation in the Eastern Arctic, 1939–63*. Vancouver: University of British Columbia Press, 1994.

Thacher, James. *History of the Town of Plymouth, from Its First Settlement in 1620, to the Present Time*. Boston: Marsh, Capen & Lyon, 1835.

"Thanksgiving." *Chatelaine*, November 1928.

"Thanksgiving-Day." *Harper's Weekly*, 6 December 1873.

Theophano, Janet. *Eat My Words: Reading Women's Lives through the Cookbooks They Wrote*. New York: Palgrave, 2002.

Thevet, André. *Les singularités de la France Antarctique*. Paris: Maurice de la Porte, 1558. http://visualiseur.bnf.fr/Visualiseur?Destination=Gallica&O=NUMM-109516. Accessed 2 February 2009.

Thiediga, Frank, and Bertil Sylvander. "Welcome to the Club? An Economical Approach to Geographical Indications in the European Union." *Agrarwirtschaft, Frankfurt: Deutscher Fachverlag GmbH* 49 (2000): 444–51.

Thien, Madeleine. "Simple Recipes." In *Simple Recipes*, 1–19. Toronto: McClelland & Stewart, 2001.

Thornton, Lynne. *From the Kitchens of Kings Landing*. Province of New Brunswick: Kings Landing Historical Settlement, 1995.

Tomás, José Pardo, and María Luz López Terrada. *Las primeras noticias sobre plantas americanas en las Relaciones de viajes y crónicas de Indias (1493–1553)*. València: Universitat de València, 1993.

Totem Cook Book. Prince Rupert, BC: Prince Rupert Hospital Auxiliary, 1955.

Toussaint-Samat, Maguelonne. *History of Food*. Translated by Anthea Bell. Oxford: Blackwell, 1992.

Traill, Catharine Parr. *The Canadian Settler's Guide*. 1855. Reprint, Toronto: McClelland & Stewart, 1969.

– *The Female Emigrant's Guide, and Hints on Canadian Housekeeping*. Toronto: Maclear, 1854.

Tried and True Cook Book. Calgary, AB: First Congregational Church, 1910.

Trigger, Bruce G. *Natives and Newcomers: Canada's "Heroic Age" Reconsidered*. Montreal and Kingston: McGill-Queen's University Press, 1985.

Turgeon, Laurier. "French Fishers, Fur Traders, and Amerinidians during the Sixteenth Century: History and Archaeology." *The William and Mary Quarterly*, 3rd ser., 55, no. 4 (October 1998): 585–610.

Turgeon, Laurier, and Denis Dickner. "Contraintes et choix alimentaires d'un groupe d'appartenance: Les marins-pêcheurs français à Terre-neuve au XVIe siècle." In *Du manuscrit à la table. Essais sur la cuisine au Moyen âge et Répertoire des manuscrits médiévaux contenant des recettes culinaires*. Edited by Carole Lambert, 227–42. Montreal: Les presses de l'Université de Montréal, 1992.

Turner, Nancy J. *Food Plants of Coastal First Peoples*. Royal British Columbia Museum handbook. Vancouver: University of British Columbia Press, 1995.

"Two New Beans from America." http://aggie-horticulture.tamu.edu/plantanswers/publications/vegetabletravelers/beans.html. Accessed 2 February 2009.

Ude, Louis Eustache. *The French Cook: Or the Art of Cookery Developed in All Its Branches*. Translated by Louis Eustache Ude. New York: Arco Publishing Company, 1978.

United States Department of Labor and United States Bureau of Labor Statistics. *Women in the Labour Force: A Databook*. By Elaine L Chao and Kathleen P. Utgoff. Report 985. Table 6. Washington, DC: GPO, May 2005. http://www.bls.gov/cps/wlf-databook-2005.pdf. Accessed 2 February 2009.

Vaduva, Ofelia. "The Introduction of Maize into the Food of the Rumanian People and Its Impact." In *Food in Perspective: Proceedings of the Third International Conference on Ethnological Food Research*, Cardiff, Wales, 1977. Edited by Alexander Fenton and Trefor Owen, 333–42. Edinburgh: John Donald, 1981.

La Varenne. *Le cuisinier François*. 1651. Facsimile edition. Houilles: Éditions Manucius, 2002.

Vaugeois, Denis, Raymonde Litalien, and Käthe Roth. *Champlain: The Birth of French America*. Translated by Käthe Roth. Montreal and Kingston: McGill-Queen's University Press, 2004.

Visser, Margaret. *Much Depends on Dinner: The Extraordinary History and Mythology, Allure and Obsessions, Perils and Taboos of an Ordinary Meal*. New York: Grove, 1986.

– *Rituals of Dinner: The Origins, Evolution, Eccentricities, and Meaning of Table Manners*. Toronto: HarperCollins, 1991.

Wa, Gisday, and Delgam Uukw. *The Spirit in the Land: The Opening Statement of the Gitksan and Wet'suwet'en Hereditary Chiefs in the Supreme Court of British Columbia, May 11, 1987*. Gabriola, BC: Reflections, 1989.

Wachowich, Nancy, with Apphia Agalakti Awa, Rhoda Kaukjak Katsak, and Sandra Pikujak Katsak. *Saqiyuq: Stories from the Lives of Three Inuit Women*. Montreal and Kingston: McGill-Queen's University Press, 1999.

Wah, Fred. *Diamond Grill*. Edmonton: NeWest Press, 1996.

Waldram, James B. *As Long as the Rivers Run: Hydroelectric Development and Native Communities in Western Canada*. Winnipeg: University of Manitoba Press, 1988.

Walker, Kathleen. *Ottawa's Repast: 150 Years of Food and Drink*. Ottawa: Ottawa Citizen, 1995.

Walton, Priscilla L. *Our Cannibals, Ourselves*. Chicago: University of Illinois Press, 2004.

Warnock, John W. *Saskatchewan: The Roots of Discontent and Protest*. Montreal: Black Rose Books, 2004.

Wattie, Helen. Personal communication with author.

Wattie, Helen, and Elinor Donaldson. Foreword to *Nellie Lyle Pattinson's Canadian Cook Book*. Edited by Helen Wattie and Elinor Donaldson, n.p. 1953. Reprint, Toronto: Ryerson, 1969.

Wawatay News Online. 7 October 2008. http://www.wawataynews.ca. Accessed 16 February 2009.

Wayland, Bridget. "Let's Talk Turkey." *Harrowsmith Country Life*, October 2007.

Weatherford, Jack. "The Culinary Revolution." In *Indian Givers: How the Indians of the Americas Transformed the World*, 99–115. New York: Fawcett Columbine, 1988.

– "The Food Revolution." In *Indian Givers*, 59–78. New York: Fawcett Columbine, 1988.

– "Indian Agricultural Technology." In *Indian Givers*, 79–97. New York: Fawcett Columbine, 1988.

West, John A. "A Brief History and Botany of Cacao." In *Chilies to Chocolate: Food the Americas Gave the World*. Edited by Nelson Foster and Linda S. Cordell, 105–21. Tucson: University of Arizona Press, 1992.

Westminster Church Cook Book. Saskatoon, SK: Westminster Church, 1929.

"Wheat Boom." *Parks Canada*. http://www.pc.gc.ca/apprendre-learn/prof/sub/ histc-cstore/histc-cstor10_e.asp. Accessed on 3 February 2009.

Wheaton, Barbara Ketcham. *L'office et la bouche*. Paris: Calman-Levy, 1984.

"Why I Am Faddy about Food." *Saturday Night*, 17 January 1914.

Wickwire, Wendy. "Stories from the Margins: Towards a More Inclusive British Columbia Historiography." In *Myth and Memory: Stories of Indigenous-European Contact*. Edited by John Sutton Lutz, 118–39. Vancouver: University of British Columbia Press, 2007.

Williams, Judith. *Clam Gardens: Aboriginal Mariculture on Canada's West Coast*. Vancouver: New Star/Transmontanus, 2006.

Williams, Raymond. *The Country and the City*. New York: Oxford University Press, 1975.

Wilson, Anne Elizabeth. "Do You Decorate for Thanksgiving?" *Chatelaine*, November 1928.

– "A 'Woman's Reason' for Thanksgiving." *Chatelaine*, November 1928.

Winslow, Edward. Letter of 11 December 1621 to a friend. *A Relation or Iournall of the Beginning and Proceeding of the English Plantation Setled at Plimoth in New England*. London: Iohn Bellamie, 1622.

Witt, Doris. "'Look Ma, the Real Aunt Jemima!': Consuming Identities under Capitalism." In *Black Hunger: Soul Food and America*, 21–53. Minneapolis: University of Minnesota Press, 2004.

Wong, Janice. *Chow. From China to Canada: Memories of Food + Family*. Vancouver Whitecap Books, 2005.

Young, Alexander. *Chronicles of the Pilgrim Fathers of the Colony of Plymouth, from 1602–1625*. Boston: C.C. Little and J. Brown, 1841.

Young, Katherine. "'... sauf les périls et fortunes de la mer': Merchant Women in New France and the French Transatlantic Trade, 1713–46." *Canadian Historical Review* 77, no. 3 (1996): 388–407.

CONTRIBUTORS

SHELLEY BOYD is a faculty lecturer in the Department of English, McGill University, Montreal.

NATHALIE COOKE is associate dean of research and graduate studies in the Faculty of Arts, McGill University, Montreal.

VICTORIA DICKENSON is the executive director at the McCord Museum, Montreal.

GARY DRAPER was an associate professor of English at Saint Jerome's University, now retired.

ELIZABETH DRIVER is curator at Campbell House Museum, Toronto.

MARGERY FEE is a professor in the Department of English, University of British Columbia, Vancouver.

SNEJA GUNEW is associate principal at the College for Interdisciplinary Studies and professor of English and Women's Studies at the University of British Columbia, Vancouver.

JEAN-PIERRE LEMASSON is a professor in the Département d'études urbaines et touristiques, École des sciences de la gestion, UQÀM, Montreal.

CATHERINE MACPHERSON is a freelance writer and a contract researcher for McCord Museum, Montreal.

MARIE MARQUIS is associate professor in the Département de nutrition, Université de Montréal, Montreal.

SARAH MUSGRAVE is a food journalist and a graduate student in Media Studies, Concordia University, Montreal.

RHONA RICHMAN KENNEALLY is an associate professor in the Department of Design and Computation Arts, Concordia University, Montreal.

ANDREW SMITH is a professor in the Department of Food Studies, New School, New York; and the editor-in-chief of *The Oxford Encyclopedia of Food and Drink in America*.

INDEX

dried, 60–1; snowberry, 34; strawberry, 37, 41–2; thimbleberry, 69. *See also* blueberries

Berton, Pierre, and Janet Berton, 173, 177, 179–82

bird's nest soup, 253

biscuits: pilot, 69; trade of, 90

bison, 65. *See also* buffalo

black huckleberry (*Vaccinium membranaceum* or *mimayus*), 78n101

The "Black Whale" Cook Book, 206

blueberries, 9, 72, 187, 199, 206; Alaska blueberry, 78n101; oval-leafed blueberry, 78n101. *See also* wines

Boudreau, Marielle, 8

Boyd, Shelley, 135f. *See also* summary of contributions to this volume

bread: as breakfast fare, 88; Red Fife, 154

Brome Lake duckling, 180

Buen Appetito! Italian Foodways in Ontario, 8

buffalo meat: in pemmican, 61; served at La Toundra, 168. *See also* bison

The Buffet (restaurant in Canada Pavilion at Expo 67), 168

Caboto, Giovanni (John Cabot), 24

cacao tree, 80

Calder decision, 60

Campbell, Helen, 133–4

Campbell, Maria, 66, 68

Canada Pavilion: connotations of, 191; restaurants in, 168

Canada's centenary: as galvanizing moment, 14–15; as era of cultural branding, 5–6. *See also* Expo 67

Canadian: distinctive dishes, 180; food culture, 169; native foods, 180; - ness, 191–2; place-specific ingredients, 183; species, 180. *See also* Canadian cuisine; Canadian culinary heritage

The Canadiana Cook Book, 5, 179

Canadian Cook Book, 5; 1923 edition, 207; 1953 edition (by Nellie Lyle Pattinson), 230

Canadian cuisine, concept of: as comprehensive, 181–6; as porous, 168. *See also* Canadian; Canadian culinary heritage; Canadian culinary history; ethnic cuisine; regional cuisine

Canadian culinary heritage, 171–2

Canadian culinary history: affiliation, 4–5; articulation, 5; consolidation, 4; contact and settlement, 4, 10; differentiation, 5–6; introspection, 6–7, 10; summary of, 4–5, 10

Canadian Food Inspection Agency and Red Fife wheat, 155

Canadian Heritage Wheat Project, 151

Canadian Home Economics Association (CHEA), 207–8

The Canadian Housewife's Manual of Cookery, 4

Canadian native foods (e.g., Saskatoon berries, maple syrup, fiddleheads), 180

Canadians at Table, 8. *See also* Duncan, Dorothy

Canadian species (e.g., Malpeque oysters, Winnipeg goldeye, Brome Lake duckling), 180

Canadian Wheat Board (CWB), 155, 159

cancer, 71. *See also* disease

The Canlit Foodbook, 13. *See also* Atwood, Margaret

cannibalism: definitions of, 267–8

caribou, 60

Cartier, Jacques: exploration of the New World, 11, 22–7, 32; his return to the New World, 63

centennial celebrations, 169, 190; as marked by the Canadian Home Economics Association (CHEA), 207–8

Centre for Indigenous Peoples' Nutrition and Environment (CINE), 74

A Century of Canadian Home Cooking, 7. *See also* Ferguson, Carol; Fraser, Margaret

Champlain, Samuel de: exploration of the New World, 24, 27–36; food tastes, 46, 84–5; Thanksgiving traditions of, 124

Chaplin, Charlie, 237

Charlevoix lamb, 161

Chatelaine (magazine), 233

cheese soufflé, 208

Chen, Anne Anling, 252

Chicken à la New Brunswick, 205

diet, 44–5; mashed, 140–1; sweet, 46, 120, 131, 133
potlatch ceremony, 63–4. *See also* feast
Poulain, Jean-Pierre, 213
powdered milk, 67
Powers, Jo Marie, 7, 8
pox (venereal disease), 26
Prem (luncheon meat), 230
La Presse (Montreal), 214, 222, 226
ptarmigan, 64
pumpkin: of the New World, 39; pie, 118; as Thanksgiving fare, 132, 133

qᵒalh'm (first food of spring), 69
Quebec cuisine, 186–9
Quebecers, 12, 15, 99, 189, 213, 220, 224, 226

The Raincoast Kitchen, 209
recipes: definitions of, 258, 266; expressive potential of, 16; for fish, 199; metaphorical, 257, 259–69; similarity in cookbooks of different cities and regions, 198–201
Red Fife Sisterhood, 152
Red Fife wheat: as Canadian-identified product, 147; history, 146, 148–51. *See also* Rempel, Sharon
regional cuisine, 207–9; as foundational to Canadian cuisine, 175–81
Rempel, Sharon, 151–2
residential schools, 66–8, 71
Riel, Louis, 65
Roberval, Sieur de, 25
Rousseau, Jean-Jacques, 57–8
rural life (changing attitudes towards), 157
Rutherford, Agnes, 135

sage dressing, 68, 72, 73
salmon, 61, 66, 73, 74; roe, 60
salt, 42–3
Saskatoon berries, 141, 180
Sawyer, Joseph (Kawahjegezhegwabe), 59
scurvy, 63. *See also* disease
seal, 60
sea lion, 60
Sea Pie (or *cipaye, cipaille, cipare*), 109–10. *See also* tourtière
seaweed, 60

Secord, Laura, 173–4
Seedy Saturday Heritage Seed Exchange, 152
seventies, 189. *See also* sixties
Shapiro, Anna, 13. See also *A Feast of Words*
Shapiro, Laura, 6, 213, 222, 226
sheep (as Thanksgiving fare), 118. *See also* lamb
shellfish, smoked, 60
sixties, 5–6, 189–90. *See also* Expo 67
Slow Food movement, 76n50, 146, 152–4, 162, 209
snowberry, 34
soup, bird's nest, 253
squash, 39
Staebler, Edna, 7
starvation, 65, 68
Stewart, Anita, 7, 197
stories, 57, 60; definition, 55
strawberries, 37, 41–2. *See also* berries; European diet
stuffing (at Thanksgiving), 122
sturgeon, 70, 183
subsidy (of foods), 69
succotash, 120
sugar maple, 27, 60
sugar trade, 62
summary of contributions to this volume: of Boyd and Smith, 12; of Cooke, 5; of Dickenson, 11; of Draper, 13–14, 16; of Driver, 10, 13–15; of Fee, 11; of Gunew, 10, 13–14, 16; of Lemasson, 12; of Macpherson, 12; of Marquis, 10, 13–14, 15–16; of Musgrave, 12–13; of Richman Kenneally, 10, 13–15
supper: definition, 234; dishes served, 235; expressive potential of, 237
Sweetness and Power, 8. *See also* Mintz, Sydney
sweet potato, 38

tea, 62, 66, 79; curative, 26; as late afternoon meal, 235. See also *anneda*; coffee
TEK (traditional ecological knowledge), 56, 72
TERRIBLE DAY, recipe for, 263